LATIN AMERICAN RESEARCH AND PUBLICATIONS AT
THE UNIVERSITY OF TEXAS AT AUSTIN, 1893–1969

# PHISICA, SPECV-
## latio, Æditaper R.

P. F. ALPHONSVM A VERACRVCE, AV-
gustinianæ familiæ Prouintialẽ, artiũ, ̃ sacrẽ Theologiæ Doctorem, atq̃
cathedræ primæ in Academia Mexicana in noua Hispania moderatorẽ

¶ Accessit cõpendium sphęræ Cãpani ad complementũ tractatus de cœlo.
¶ Excudebat Mexici Ioã. Pau. Brisẽ. Anno Dñicę incarnationis. 1557

PHISICA SPECVLATIO

(1557)

*Alfonso de la Veracruz*

*Guides and Bibliographies Series: 3*

# LATIN AMERICAN
# RESEARCH AND PUBLICATIONS
# AT
# THE UNIVERSITY OF TEXAS
# AT AUSTIN

## 1893–1969

INSTITUTE OF LATIN AMERICAN STUDIES
THE UNIVERSITY OF TEXAS AT AUSTIN
AUSTIN · 1971

# INSTITUTE OF LATIN AMERICAN STUDIES

*William P. Glade*, Director    *Karl M. Schmitt*, Associate Director

*$3.75 (paper)*
*$7.50 (cloth)*

PRINTED BY THE UNIVERSITY PRINTING DIVISION OF
THE UNIVERSITY OF TEXAS AT AUSTIN
DESIGN: *Mauricio Charpenel*

MANUFACTURED IN THE UNITED STATES OF AMERICA

*This Publication is being issued
to Commemorate the
30th Anniversary
of the
Establishment of the
Institute of Latin American Studies*

# PRIMERA PARTE DE LOS

# COMMENTARIOS
## REALES,

## QVE TRATAN DEL ORI-
GEN DE LOS YNCAS, REYES QVE FVE-
RON DEL PERV, DE SV IDOLATRIA, LEYES, Y
gouierno en paz y en guerra: de sus vidas y con-
quistas, y de todo lo que fue aquel Imperio y
su Republica, antes que los Españoles passaran a el.

*Escritos por el Ynca Garcilasso de la Vega, natural del Cozco,*
*y Capitan de su Magestad.*

## DIRIGIDOS A LA SERENISSIMA PRIN-
cesa Doña Catalina de Portugal, Duqueza
de Bargança, &c.

*Cou licencia de la Sancta Inquisicion, Ordinario, y Paço.*

## EN LISBOA:
En la officina de Pedro Crasbeeck.
Año de M.DCIX.

---

PRIMERA PARTE DE LOS COMMENTARIOS REALES . . .
(1609)
*El Inca Garcilaso de la Vega*

# Table of Contents

# Foreword

In 1959 the Institute of Latin American Studies of the University of Texas published as No. XVIII in its Latin American Studies Series a booklet entitled *Seventy-Five Years of Latin American Research at the University of Texas.* Although this original printing carried no date of publication, the subtitle indicated that the publication included a listing of Masters Theses and Doctoral Dissertations completed between 1893 and 1958 as well as publications of Latin American interest bearing the University's imprint between 1941 and 1958. Whether from awareness that the original title suggested either Texan expansiveness or simply poor arithmetic or because the record of achievement was impressive and the demand for the publication warranted it, in February 1966 the Institute reissued the booklet with a different cover and the modified title *Latin American Research at the University of Texas, 1893–1958.* The new format included the indication that the "Institute of Latin American Studies plans to update this publication at ten year intervals."

When I arrived in Austin to assume the Directorship of the Institute, the initial ten year period since the original publication was about to come to an end. It was decided to undertake a complete revision and updating of the publication, endeavoring to make it more useful to the reader as well as an accurate guide to the most recent period of productive research and publication related to Latin America at this institution. The result that follows, *Latin American Research and Publications at the University of Texas at Austin, 1893–1969,* not only encompasses a full three-quarters of a century, but one additional year for good measure.

This publication is timely not only in terms of the promised revision every decade, but also because it coincides with two happy events. Late in 1970 the Institute and the Latin American Collection moved to their new facilities in the Sid W. Richardson Hall, and the building was inaugurated in February of 1971, coincident with beginning of the year marking the thirtieth anniversary of the establishment of the Institute, one of the oldest centers devoted to Latin American Studies in the United States.

To increase the utility of this publication it was decided to include a brief summary of each dissertation while retaining the previous format for simply listing the Masters Theses. The large number of dissertations in the field of History include a substantial proportion related to aspects of Mexican and

Texan history. The range and distribution of the subjects are in many instances a reflection of the strengths of the Latin American Collection.

Two significant trends are to be noted when comparing the listing published in 1959 and that included here. First, there has been an enormous increase in the number of studies on Mexican-American subjects, with particular concentration in the language training of Spanish-speaking inhabitants of Texas. This tendency is evident long before the current interest in matters Mexican-American. Second, there has been over the past decade a substantial increase in the number of studies in other disciplines as well as in History, most particularly in Economics, Government and Geology.

The summaries of degrees awarded reveals a substantial increase in the number of MA degrees awarded in Latin American Studies through the Institute, while there has been a relative decrease in the number of doctorates achieved through the interdisciplinary route. The former reflects an increase both of the number of students desiring an area degree in preparation for doing the doctorate in a discipline and of those seeking the MA as a terminal degree. The Institute's doctoral program is not an easy route to the degree since the student meets all of the requirements for the doctorate in his major field in addition to doing thirty hours of work in a second discipline. The doctorate in Latin American Studies remains as a program to meet the special needs of a limited number of students. For their own protection and conservation of time and resources, most students are encouraged to undertake the doctorate in a specific disciplinary program.

The preparation of the material for this guide to Latin American research at the University of Texas was begun by Mrs. Cindy Keever, under grant from the Graduate School of the University of Texas at Austin to the Institute. The task was continued by Dean Dehart and his wife, Evelyn Hu Dehart, under the supervision of my research associate, Miss Heather Fowler, now Dr. Heather Fowler Salamini. Publication has been made possible by the support and encouragement of Chancellor Emeritus Harry Ransom of the University of Texas System, and by the generous assistance of the Edward Larocque Tinker Foundation and its President, Miss Martha T. Muse.

The record of research and publication related to Latin America at the University of Texas is an impressive one constituting persuasive evidence of the strong support which Latin American Studies have received at this institution.

Stanley R. Ross
Provost for Arts and Sciences
The University of Texas at Austin

# Publications of the
# Institute of Latin American Studies

The Institute in recent years has sponsored a variety of publications dealing with Latin America. The original Latin American Studies Series included eighteen works published between 1945 and 1959 which have been reissued by the Greenwood Press. The new Latin American Monograph Series, established in 1964, was started with the intention of making available key historical and social science monographs which would otherwise not be printed. In collaboration with the Bureau of Business Research a number of economic monographs have been brought out also. The Offprint Series reprints articles written by University of Texas faculty members on Latin American topics making them available to a much larger reading public. Finally the Institute has sponsored a Special Publications Series including valuable conference proceedings and other significant teaching and researching aids. Please note that a number of the publications are now out of print (so indicated by an asterisk).

## *Latin American Studies Series*

1  I  Conference on Intellectual Trends in Latin America, University of Texas, 1945. *Intellectual Trends in Latin America*. 1945, 148 pp.

2  II  Conference on Some Economic Aspects of Postwar Inter-American Relations, University of Texas, 1946. *Some Economic Aspects of Postwar Inter-American Relations*. 1946, 117 pp.

3  III  Vernon, Ida (Stevenson) Weldon. *Pedro de Valdivia, Conquistador of Chile*. 1946, 193 pp.

4  IV  Gibson, Charles. *The Inca Concept of Sovereignty and the Spanish Administration in Peru*. 1948, 146 pp.

5  V  Texas. University. Institute of Latin American Studies. *Some Educational and Anthropological Aspects of Latin America*. 1948, 85 pp.

6  VI  Texas. University. Institute of Latin American Studies. *Political, Economic, and Social Problems of the Latin American Nations of Southern South America*. 1949, 107 pp.

7  VII  Cotner, Thomas Ewing. *The Military and Political Career of José Joaquín de Herrera, 1792–1854*. 1949, 336 pp.

8  VIII  Estigarribia, José Felix, Pres. Paraguay. *The Epic of the Chaco:*

*Marshal Estigarribia's Memoirs of the Chaco War, 1932–1935.* Edited and annotated by Pablo Max Ynsfran. 1950, 221 pp.

9   IX   Texas. University. Institute of Latin American Studies. *Basic Industries in Texas and Northern Mexico.* 1950, 193 pp.

10   X   Stanislawski, Dan. *The Anatomy of Eleven Towns in Michoacán.* 1950, 70 pp.

11   XI   Ramos Arizpe, Miguel. *Report that Dr. Miguel Ramos de Arizpe, Priest of Borbon, and Deputy in the Present General and Special Cortes of Spain for the Province of Coahuila, one of the four Eastern Interior Provinces of the Kingdom of Mexico, Presents to the August Congress, on the Natural, Political and Civil Condition of the Provinces of Coahuila, Nuevo León, Nuevo Santander and Texas of the Four Eastern Interior Provinces of the Kingdom of Mexico.* Translation, annotations and introduction by Nettie Lee Benson. 1950, 61 pp.

12   XII   Knapp, Frank Averill. *The Life of Sebastián Lerdo de Tejada, 1823–1889; a Study of Influence and Obscurity.* 1951, 292 pp.

13   XIII   Texas. University. College of Fine Arts. *Proceedings of the Conference on Latin American Fine Arts.* 1952, 132 pp.

14   XIV   Spell, Lota May (Harrigan). *Research Materials for the Study of Latin America at the University of Texas.* 1954, 107 pp.

15   XV   Symposium on the Languages and Literature of Spanish America and Brazil, University of Texas, 1956. *Proceedings.* 1957, 62 pp.

16   XVI   Seminar on the Acquisition of Latin American Library Materials. *Final Report.* 1958, 97 pp.

17   XVII   Sánchez, George Isidore and Howard L. Putnam. *Materials Relating to the Education of Spanish-speaking people in the United States, an Annotated Bibliography.* 1959.

18   XVIII   Texas. University. Institute of Latin American Studies. *Seventy-five Years of Latin American Research at the University of Texas; Masters Theses and Doctoral Dissertations 1893–1958 and Publications of Latin American Interest 1941–1958.* 1959, 67 pp.

## Monograph Series

19   1.   Scobie, James R. *Revolution on the Pampas: A Social History of Argentine Wheat, 1860–1910.* 1964, 206 pp.

20   2.   Kelly, Isabel. *Folk Practices in North Mexico: Birth Customs, Folk Medicine, and Spiritualism in the Laguna Zone.* * 1965, 166 pp.

21   3.   Cooper, Donald B. *Epidemic Disease in Mexico City, 1761–1813: An Administrative, Social, and Medical Study.* 1965, 236 pp.

22    4.    Sommerfield, Raynard M. *Tax Reform and the Alliance for Progress.* 1966, 217 pp.

23    5.    Benson, Nettie Lee (ed.). *Mexico and the Spanish Cortes, 1810–1822; Eight Essays.* 1966, 243 pp.

24    6.    Gardner, Mary A. *The Inter-American Press Association: Its Fight for Freedom of the Press, 1926–1960.* 1967, 217 pp.

25    7.    Cole, William E. *Steel and Economic Growth in Mexico.* 1967, 173 pp.

26    8.    Campos, Roberto de Oliveira. *Reflections on Latin American Development.* 1967, 168 pp.

27    9.    Corwin, Arthur F. *Spain and the Abolition of Slavery in Cuba, 1817–1886.* 1967, 373 pp.

28    10.    Urquidi, Marjory (trans.) *Mexico's Recent Economic Growth: The Mexican View.* 1967, 217 pp.

29    11.    Huddleston, Lee Eldridge. *Origins of the American Indians: European Concepts, 1492–1729.* 1967, 179 pp.

30    12.    Kahl, Joseph A. *The Measurement of Modernism: A Study of Values in Brazil and Mexico.* 1968, 210 pp.

31    13.    Graham, Lawrence S. *Civil Service Reform in Brazil: Principles Versus Practice.* 1968, 233 pp.

32    14.    Cockroft, James D. *Intellectual Precursors of the Mexican Revolution, 1900–1913.* 1968, 376 pp.

33    15.    Dew, Edward. *Politics of the Altiplano. The Dynamics of Change in Rural Peru.* 1969, 216 pp.

34    16.    Singer, Morris. *Growth, Equality and the Mexican Experience.* 1969, 341 pp.

35    17.    Dean, Warren. *The Industrialization of São Paulo, 1880–1945.* 1969, 263 pp.

36    18.    Solberg, Carl. *Immigration and Nationalism: Argentina and Chile, 1890–1914.* 1969, 222 pp.

37    19.    Rout, Leslie B., Jr. *Politics of the Chaco Peace Conference, 1935–1939.* 1970, 268 pp.

38    20.    Liebman, Arthur. *The Politics of Puerto Rican University Students.* 1970, 205 pp.

39    21.    Burnett, Ben G. *Political Groups in Chile: The Dialogue between Order and Change,* 1970, 319 pp.

40    22.    Baker, Richard D. *Judicial Review in Mexico: A Study of the Amparo Suit.* 1971, 304 pp.

41    23.    Agor, Weston H. *The Chilean Senate: Internal Distribution of Influence.* 1971, 218 pp.

[ 3 ]

## Offprint Series

42  1.  Adams, Richard N. *The Community in Latin America: A Changing Myth.**

43  2.  Gardner, Mary A. *The Press of Honduras: A Portrait of Five Dailies.**

44  3.  Ellison, Fred P. *Rubén Darío and Brazil.**

45  4.  Benson, Nettie Lee. *Arturo Taracena Flores Library.**

46  5.  Spell, J. R. *Lizardi in Taxco.**

47  6.  Enguídanos, Miguel. *Introduction to Jorge Luis Borges' Dreamtigers (El Hacedor).**

48  7.  Adams, Richard N. *Politics and Social Anthropology in Spanish America.*

49  8.  Grieder, Terence. *Representation of Space and Form in Maya Painting on Pottery.**

50  9.  Matluck, Joseph H. *La E trabada en la Ciudad de México: estudio experimental.**

51  10.  Harrison, John P. *Learning and Politics in Latin American Universities.**

52  11.  Ellison, Fred P. *The Writer (in Latin America).**

53  12.  Adams, Richard N. *Rural Labor (in Latin America).**

54  13.  Leeds, Anthony. *Brazil and the Myth of Francisco Julião.**

55  14.  Adams, Richard N. *La mestización cultural en Centro-América.**

56  15.  Leeds, Anthony. *Brazilian Careers and Social Structure: An Evolutionary Model and Case History.**

57  16.  Rubel, Arthur J. *The Mexican-American Palomilla and Prognosticative Calendar Systems.**

58  17.  McGann, Thomas F. *The Ambassador and the Dictator.**

59  18.  Iutaka, Sugiyama. *Social Stratification Research in Latin America.**

60  19.  Schaedel, Richard P. *Land Reform Studies.**

61  20.  Adams, Richard N. *The Pattern of Development in Latin America* and *Desarrollo Acelerado.**

62  21.  Gibbs, Beverly J. *"El Tunel: Portrayal of Isolation.**

63  22.  Paredes, Américo. *El cowboy norteamericano en el folklore y la literatura.**

64  23.  Harrison, John P. *Latin American Studies: Library Needs and Problems.**

65  24.  Branco, Raúl. *Brazilian Finances and their Implication for Economic Integration.**

[ 5 ]

89 48. Hereford, Carl F. *La dimensión activo-pasiva en México y los Estados Unidos.*

90 49. Adams, Richard N. *Political Power and Social Structures (in Latin America).*

91 50. Epstein, Jeremiah F. *Terminal Pleistocene Cultures in Texas and Northeast Mexico.*

92 51. Buchler, Ira R. *La organización ceremonial de una aldea mexicana.*

93 52. Schaedel, Richard P. *The Huaca "El Dragón".* *

94 53. Zárate, Alván O. *Fertility in Urban Areas of Mexico: Implications for the Theory of the Demographic Transition.*

95 54. Paredes, Américo. *The Decima on the Texas-Mexican Border.*

96 55. Angelini, Arrigo L., et al. *Problem-Solving Styles in Children: A Cross-National Study.* *

97 56. O'Nell, Carl W. and Selby, Henry A. *Sex Differences in the Incidence of Susto in Two Zapotec Pueblos: an Analysis of the Relationships Between Sex Role Expectations and a Folk Illness.*

98 57. Balán, Elizabeth Jelin de. *Trabajadores por cuenta propia y asalariados: ¿distinción vertical u horizontal?*

99 58. Benson, Nettie Lee. *A Governor's Report on Texas in 1809.*

100 59. Schaedel, Richard P. *Étude comparative des societés paysannes D'Àmèrique Latine.*

101 60. Adams, Richard N. *Nationalization.*

102 61. Spell, Lota M. *The Interplay of Books and Life: J. R. Spell and El Periquillo.*

103 62. Adams, Richard and Rubel, Arthur. *Sickness and Social Relations.*

104 63. Benson, Nettie Lee. *Martín Fierro at the University of Texas.*

105 64. Adams, Nichard N. *El sector agrario inferior de Guatemala.*

106 65. Leeds, Anthony. *Some Problems in the Analysis of Class and the Social Order.* *

107 66. DeCamp, David. *The Field of Creole Language Studies.*

108 67. Balán, Jorge. *Are Farmers' Sons Handicapped in the City?*

109 68. Dean, Warren. *Sources for the Study of Latin American Economic History: The Records of North American Private Enterprises.*

110 69. Roberts, Bryan R. *Protestant Groups and Coping with Urban Life in Guatemala City.*

111 70. Schmitt, Karl M. *Contradictions and Conflicts in U. S. Foreign Policy: The Case of Latin America.*

112 71. Grieder, Terence. *Demons and Discipline in Ancient Peru.*

[ 6 ]

[ 7 ]

*gates to the First Constituent Congress of Mexico, 1822–1823.*

137   96.   Adams, Richard N. *La brecha tecnológica. Algunas de sus consecuencias en el desarrollo de América Latina.*

138   97.   Browning, Harley L. and Waltraut Feindt. *Selectivity of Migrants to a Metropolis in a Developing Country: A Mexican Case Study.*

139   98.   Garcia-Zamor, Jean-Claude. *An Ecological Approach to Administrative Reform: The Brazilian Case.*

140   99.   Grieder, Terence. *Ecología Precolombina.*

141   100.   Gullón, Ricardo. *García Márquez o el olvidado arte de contar.*

## Guides and Bibliographies Series

142   1.   Remmling, Gunter W. (compiler). *South American Sociologists: A Directory.* 1966, 47 pp.

143   2.   Monteiro, Palmyra V. M. *A Catalogue of Latin American Flat Maps, 1926–1964.* 2v, 1967, 1969, 395 pp., 430 pp.

## Special Publications

### Books

144   Bills, Garland D., Bernardo Vallejo and Rudolph C. Troike. *An Introduction to Spoken Bolivian Quechua.* 1969.

145   Brand, Donald D. and others. *Coalcoman and Motines del Oro. An Exdistrict of Michoacán, Mexico.* 1960.

146   ECLA. *Development Problems in Latin America: An Analysis by the United Nations Economic Commission for Latin America.* Foreword by Carlos Quintana, Executive Secretary. 1970.

147   Lewis, Archibald R. and Thomas F. McGann (eds.). *The New World Looks at its History.* Proceedings of the Second International Congress of Historians of the United States and Mexico. 1962.

148   Mecham, J. Lloyd. *The United States and Inter-American Security, 1889–1960.* 1961.

149   Schade, George D. and Miguel González-Gerth (eds.). *Rubén Darío: Centennial Studies.* 1970.

150   Vaughan, Denton R. *Urbanization in Twentieth Century Latin America: A Working Bibliography.* 1970.

### Pamphlets

151   Brothers, Dwight S. *The Financing of Capital Formation in Mexico, 1950–1961.*

152   Buchler, Ira Richard and R. Michael McKinlay. *Decision Processes in Culture: A Linear Programming Analysis.*

[ 8 ]

153 *Latin American Research at the University of Texas, 1893–1958. Masters Theses and Doctoral Dissertations (1893–1958) and Publications of Latin American Interest 1941–1958.* February 1966.
154 Legters, Lyman H. *The National Defense Education Act and Latin American Studies.*
155 Parker, Franklin. *Latin American Education Research: An Annotated Bibliography of 269 United States Doctoral Dissertations.*\* (Reprinted in *Paedagogica Historica,* IV, 2 (1964).
156 Sánchez, Luis Oscar. *Los hijos de Jones.* With English translation. 1963, 1969.

### Hackett Memorial Lecture Series
157 Harrison, John P. *The University Versus National Development in Spanish America.* 1968.
158 Paz, Octavio. *México: La última década.* 1969.

### Translations of Critical Bibliographical Articles of the Latin American Research Review
159 Cline, Howard F. *La Asociación de Estudios Latinoamericanos: Un examen sumario.*
160 Dauster, Frank. *Investigaciones en el teatro hispanoamericano.*
161 Iutaka, Sugiyama. *Pesquisas sôbre estratificão social na América Latina.*
162 Morse, Richard M. *Investigación reciente sobre urbanización latinoamericana: examen selectivo y comentarios.*
163 Oswald, J. Gregory. *Investigaciones contemporáneas soviéticas sobre América Latina.*
164 Pearse, Andrew. *Tendencias de cambio agrario en América Latina.*
165 Schaedel, Richard P. *Estudios sobre reforma agraria.*

### Studies Published in Collaboration with the Seminario de Integración Social Guatemalteca entitled Estudios Centroamericanos.
166 1. Adams, Richard N. *Migraciones internas en Guatemala. Expansión agraria de los indígenas Ketchíes hacia el Petén.* 1965.
167 2. Roberts, Bryan. *El protestantismo en dos barrios marginales de Guatemala.* 1967.
168 3. Zárate, Alván O. *Principales patrones de migración interna en Guatemala,* 1964. 1967.
169 4. Grimes, James Larry. *Cakchiquel-Tzutujil: Estudio sobre su unidad lingüística.* 1968.
170 5. Toness, Odin Alf, Jr. *Relaciones de poder en un barrio marginal de Centroamérica.* 1969.

[ 9 ]

## Studies in Latin American Business

BUREAU OF BUSINESS RESEARCH
IN COOPERATION WITH THE INSTITUTE OF LATIN AMERICAN STUDIES

171   1.   Blair, Calvin Patton. *Fluctuations in United States Imports from Brazil, Colombia, Chile, and Mexico, 1919–1954.* 1959, 225 pp.

172   2.   Krause, Walter. *The United States and Latin America: The Alliance for Progress Program.* 1963, 35 pp.

173   3.   Lower, Milton D., Raymond R. Hannigan, and Rudolf K. Jansen. *Some Aspects of Latin-American Trade Policies: Three Essays.* 1964, 83 pp.

174   4.   Franko, Lawrence G., Michael Dixon, and Carlos Arturo Marulanda R. *Entrepreneurship and Industrialization in Latin America: Three Essays.* 1966, 59 pp.

175   5.   Bullard, Fredda Jean. *Mexico's Natural Gas—The Beginning of an Industry.* 1968, 336 pp.

176   6.   Bennett, Peter D. *Government's Role in Retail Marketing of Food Products in Chile.* 1968, 132 pp.

177   7.   Savage, Allan H. *The Accounting Function in Mexico.* 1968, 126 pp.

178   8.   Mathis, F. John. *Economic Integration in Latin America: The Problems and Progress of LAFTA.* 1969, 111 pp.

# University of Texas Press Latin American Publications

The University of Texas Press has for the past fifty years been publishing works dealing with the Latin American and Mexican-American areas. Recently the volume of publications has increased to include publications commissioned by the Conference on Latin American History and other academic and business organizations or conferences concerned with the area.

## Conference on Latin American History Publications

179  1.  Cline, Howard F. (compiler and editor). *Latin American History: Essays on its Study and Teaching 1898–1965*. 1966, 2 vols.
180  2.  Charno, Steven M. *Latin American Newspapers in United States Libraries: A Union List*. Compiled in the Serial Division, Library of Congress. 1969.
181  3.  Oswald, J. Gregory, (compiler and translator). *Soviet Image of Contemporary Latin America: A Documentary History, 1960–1968*. Introduction by S. Dinerstein, Edited by Robert J. Carlton. 1970.
182  4.  Griffin, Charles (ed.) *Latin America: A Guide to the Historical Literature*. 1970.

## Texas Pan American Series

The Texas Pan American Series is published with the assistance of a revolving publication fund established by the Pan American Sulphur Company and other friends of Latin America in Texas. Publication of the titles in this series was also formerly assisted by grants from foundations made through the Latin American translation program of the Association of American University Presses. Titles include both translations of important Latin American fiction and nonfiction and original contributions.

183  Beteta, Ramón. *Jarano*. Translated by John Upton. 1970.
184  Bobb, Bernard E. *The Viceregency of Antonio María Bucareli in New Spain, 1771–1779*. 1962, 327 pp.
185  Cosío Villegas, Daniel. *American Extremes*. Translated by Américo Paredes. 1964, 227 pp.
186  De la Vega, Garcilaso, El Inca. *Royal Commentaries of the Incas and General History of Peru*. Translated by Harold V. Livermore. 1965, 2 volumes.

187  Guzmán, Martín Luis. *Memoirs of Pancho Villa*. Translated by Virginia H. Taylor. 1965, 512 pp.

188  Maddox, John. *Vasconcelos of Mexico: Philosopher and Prophet.* 1967, 104 pp.

189  Mariátegui, José Carlos. *Seven Interpretative Essays on Peruvian Reality*. Translated by Marjory Urquidi. 1970.

190  O'Leary, Daniel Florencio. *Bolívar and the War of Independence (Memorias del General Daniel Florencio O'Leary: Narración)*. Translated and edited by Robert F. McNerney, Jr. Abridged Version. 1970.

191  Ramos, Samuel. *Profile of Man and Culture in Mexico*. Translated by Peter G. Earle. 1963, 198 pp.

192  Rodrigues, José Honório. *The Brazilians: Their Character and Aspirations*. Translated by Ralph Edward Dimmick. 1967, 186 pp.

193  Schendel, Gordon. *Medicine in Mexico: From Aztec Herbs to Betatrons*. 1968, 330 pp.

194  Sierra, Justo. *The Political Evolution of the Mexican People*. Translated by Charles Ramsdell. 1969, 420 pp.

195  Turner, John Kenneth. *Barbarous Mexico* (second edition). 1969. 356 pp.

196  Varner, John Grier. *El Inca: The Life and Times of Garcilaso de la Vega*. 1968, 414 pp.

### Mexican Literature

197  Arreola, Juan José. *Confabulario and Other Inventions*. Translated by George D. Schade. 1964, 264 pp.

198  Carballido, Emilio. *"The Golden Thread" and Other Plays*. Translated by Margaret Sayers Peden. 1970.

199  Carballido, Emilio. *The Norther*. Translated by Margaret Sayers Peden. 1968, 102 pp.

200  Galindo, Sergio. *The Precipice*. Translated by John and Carolyn Brushwood. 1969.

201  Garro, Elena. *Recollections of Things to Come*. Translated by Ruth L. C. Simms. 1969, 275 pp.

202  Gorostiza, José. *Death without End*. Translated by Laura Villaseñor. 1969, 40 pp.

203  Rulfo, Juan. *The Burning Plain and Other Stories*. Translated by George D. Schade. 1967, 176 pp.

204  Yáñez, Agustín. *The Edge of the Storm*. Translated by Ethel Brinton. 1963, 332 pp.

205   Yáñez, Agustín. *The Lean Lands*. Translated by Ethel Brinton. 1968, 328 pp.

## Argentine Literature

206   Bioy, Adolfo Casares. *The Invention of Morel and Other Stories* (from *La trama celeste*). Translated by Ruth L. C. Simms. 1964, 237 pp.
207   Borges, Jorge Luis. *Dreamtigers*. Translated by Mildred Boyer and Harold Morland. 1964, 95 pp.
208   Borges, Jorge Luis. *Other Inquisitions, 1937–1952*. Translated by Ruth L. C. Simms. 1964, 205 pp.

## Brazilian Literature

209   Adonias Filho. *Memoirs of Lazarus*. Translated with an Introduction by Fred P. Ellison. 1969, 170 pp.
210   Corção, Gustavo. *Who If I Cry Out (Lições de abismo)*. Translated by Clotilde Wilson. 1967, 217 pp.
211   Pereira, Antonio Olavo. *Marcoré*. Translated by Alfred Hower and John Saunders. 1969. 264 pp.
212   Queiroz, Rachel de. *The Three Marias*. Translated by Fred P. Ellison. 1963, 178 pp.
213   Ramos, Graciliano. *Barren Lives*. Translated with an Introduction by Ralph Edward Dimmick. 1965, 131 pp.

## Other Literary Studies

214   Brushwood, John S. *Mexico in its Novel: A Nation's Search for Identity*. 1966. 292 pp.
215   Darío, Rubén. *Selected Poems of Rubén Darío*. Translated by Lysander Kemp. 1965, 130 pp.
216   Díaz Sánchez, Ramón. *Cumboto*. Translated by John Upton. 1969, 130 pp.
217   Nist, John. *The Modernist Movement in Brazil: A Literary Study*. 1966. 223 pp.

## Art

218   Charlot, Jean. *Mexican Art and the Academy of San Carlos, 1785–1915*. 1962, 177 pp.
219   Cordry, Donald and Dorothy. *Mexican Indian Costumes*. 1968. 374 pp.

220 Orozco, José Clemente. *José Clemente Orozco: An Autobiography.* Translated by Robert C. Stephenson. 1962. 171 pp.

221 Toussaint, Manuel. *Colonial Art in Mexico.* Translated and edited by Elizabeth Wilder Weismann. 1967. 498 pp.

## Conferences

222 *Changes in the Economic and Political Situation in the Western Hemisphere and Problems Arising Therefrom, as a Result of the War in Europe.** Proceedings of the Conference held July 2–3, 1940. Includes papers by Russell Fitzgibbon, John H. Frederick, Henry F. Grady, Roscoe R. Hill, John I. B. McGulloch, Dana G. Munro, Roland Hall Sharp, Amos Taylor, and George Wythe. 1940.

223 *Cultural Bases of Hemisphere Understanding.** Proceedings of the Conference held April 14–15, 1942, which includes papers by Justino Fernández, Wendell C. Gordon, Julio Jiménez Rueda, Charles A. Thomson, and Pablo Ynsfran. 1942, 95 pp.

224 *Inter-American Conference on Intellectual Interchange.** Proceedings of the Conference held June 16–17, 1943. Includes papers by Arturo Arnáiz y Freg, Carlos Eduardo Castañeda, Donald Coney, Samuel Guy Inman, Sturgis E. Leavitt, Hugo Leipsiger-Pearce, Ezequiel Ordóñez, Arturo Torres Rioseco, Robert C. Smith, Jefferson Rea Spell, and Manuel Toussaint. 1943.

225 *Mexico's Role in International Intellectual Cooperation.** Proceedings of the Conference held in Albuquerque, February 24–25, 1944, under the joint sponsorship of the University of New Mexico and the University of Texas. Includes papers by Rodolfo Brito Foucher, Alfonso Caso, Pablo Martínez del Río, and Francisco Villagrán Prado issued as *Inter-American Short Papers, VI,* by the University of New Mexico Press. 1944, 60 pp.

226 *Proceedings of the Conference on Latin American Geology, March 29–30, 1954.* Co-sponsored by the Department of Geology and the Institute of Latin American Studies. Edited by Fred M. Bullard. 1955, 99 pp.

## Special Papers and Bibliographies

227 Atkins, W. S. *The Weno and Pawpaw Formations of the Texas Comchean;* and Emil Böse *On a New Ammonite Fauna of the Lower Turonian of Mexico.* Bureau of Economic Geology. 1920. Bulletin No. 1856, 172 pp.

228 Böse, Emil. *The Cretaceous and Tertiary of Southern Texas and Northern Mexico;* and *Cretaceous Ammonities from Texas to Northern Mexico.* 1927. Bulletin No. 2748. Bureau of Economic Geology. 357 pp.

229 Delk, Lois Jo and James Neal Greer. *Spanish Language and Litera-*

[ 14 ]

*ture in the Publications of American Universities. A Bibliography.*\* University of Texas Hispanic Series VI, 1952, 211 pp.

230   Goldstein, Marcus S. *Demographic and Bodily Changes in Descendants of Mexican Immigrants.*\* 1943, 103 pp.

231   Manuel, H. T. *Spanish and English Editions of the Stanford-Binet in Relation to the Abilities of Mexican Children.*\* 1935, 63 pp.

232   Miñano-García, Max H. *Some Educational Problems in Peru.*\* 1945, 70 pp.

233   Patterson, J. T. and G. B. Mainland. *The Drosophilidae of Mexico.*\* Reprint from the University of Texas Publication No. 4445.

234   Schons, Dorothy. *Some Bibliographical Notes on Sor Juana Inés de la Cruz.*\* 1925, 30 pp.

235   Smith, Charles I. *Lower Cretaceous Stratigraphy, Northern Coahuila, Mexico.* Bureau of Economic Geology. Report of Investigations. No. 65. 1970.

236   Timm, Charles A. *The International Boundary Commission, United States, and Mexico.*\* Bulletin No. 4134. Bureau of Research in the Social Sciences. 1941, 99 pp.

237   *A Report on the Health and Nutrition of Mexican Living in Texas.*\* Bulletin No. 1327. Bureau of Research in the Social Sciences, 1931, 99 pp.

238   *Ecology of the Vegetation of Chihuahua, Mexico, North of Parallel Twenty-eight.*\* 1945, 92 pp.

239   *Image of Mexico I & II.* (*Texas Quarterly*, Autumn & Winter, 1969)

240   *Inter-American Education Occasional Papers.* Edited by George I. Sánchez. First Regional Conference on the Education of Spanish-Speaking People in the Southwest (March, 1946); Materials Relating to the Education of Spanish-Speaking People—A Bibliography (February, 1948); Texas Born Spanish-Name Students in Texas Colleges and Universities, 1945–46 (March, 1948); References for Teachers of English as a Foreign Language-A Bibliography (September, 1949); The Spanish-Speaking Population of Texas (December, 1949); Labor Requirements and Labor Resources in the Lower Rio Grande Valley of Texas (December, 1950)\*; Wetbacks in the Lower Rio Grande Valley (July, 1951); Spanish-Name Persons in the Labor Force in Manufacturing Industry in Texas (July, 1951); and Concerning Segregation of Spanish-Speaking Children in the Public Schools (December, 1951)\*.

## Non-Series Latin American Titles

241   Adams, Richard Newbold. *Crucifixion by Power: Essays on Guatemalan National Social Structure*, 1944–1966. 1970.

242   Almaráz, Felix D., Jr., *Tragic Cavalier: Governor Manuel Salcedo of Texas, 1808–1813*. 1971, 216 pp.

243   Bolton, Herbert Eugene. *Texas in the Middle Eighteenth Century: Studies in Spanish Colonial History and Administration*. Reprint, 1970.

244   Byers, Douglas S. (ed.) *The Prehistory of the Tehuacán Valley*. 6 vols. (Vols. 1 and 2, 1968).

245   Callcott, Wilfrid Hardy. *The Western Hemisphere: Its Influence on United States Policies to the End of World War II*. 1968, 506 pp.

246   Cerda, Gilberto, Berta Cabaza and Julieta Farias. *Vocabulario español de Texas.** University of Texas Hispanic Studies V. 1953, 348 pp.

247   Cervantes de Salazar, Francisco. *Life in the Imperial and Loyal City of Mexico in New Spain and the Royal and Pontifical University of Mexico.** A facsimile reproduction of the Juan Pablos edition of 1554 with a translation by Minnie Lee Barrett. 1954, 246 pp.

248   Cotner, Thomas E. and Carlos E. Castañeda (eds.). *Essays in Mexican History.** A memorial volume dedicated to the late Charles Wilson Hackett, with contributions by Nettie Lee Benson, Jack Autrey Dabbs, Guy R. Donnell, Elmer W. Flaccus, Jack A. Haddick, Horace V. Harrison, Fritz Leo Hoffman, Cecil A. Hutchinson, Frank A. Knapp, Jr., Joseph C. McElhannon, Merrill Rippy, Florence Johnson Scott, Charmion C. Shelby, Wilbert H. Timmons, Thomas F. Walker. 1958, 309 pp.

249   Cranfill, Thomas Mabry. *The Muse of Mexico: A Mid-Century Miscellany*. 1959, 117 pp.

250   Cumberland, Charles C. *The Mexican Revolution. Genesis under Madero.** 1952, 288 pp.

251   Davis, Mary L. and Greta Pack. *Mexican Jewelry*. 1963. 262 pp.

252   Dulles, John W. F. *Unrest in Brazil: Political-Military Crises, 1955–1964*. 1970, 449 pp.

253   Dulles, John W. F. *Yesterday in Mexico: A Chronicle of the Revolution, 1910–1936*. 1961, 805 pp.

254   Dulles, John W. F. *Vargas of Brazil: A Political Biography*. 1967, 395 pp.

255   Dunn, William Edard. *Spanish and French Rivalry in the Gulf Region of the United States, 1678–1702.** 1917, 238 pp.

256   Edwards, Emily and Manul Alvarez Bravo. *Painted Walls of Mexico: From Prehistoric Times Until Today*. 1966, 306 pp.

257   Gardiner, Harvey C. *Naval Power in the Conquest of Mexico.** 1956, 253 pp.

258   Gipson, Fred. *"The Cow Killers": With the Aftosa Commission in Mexico.** 1956, 130 pp.

[ 16 ]

259  Haggard, Villasana J., assisted by Malcolm Dallas McLean. *Handbook for Translators of Spanish Historical Documents.** 1941, 198 pp.

260  Jones, Willis Knapp. *Behind Spanish-American Footlights.* 1965, 609 pp.

261  Krieger, Alex D. *Culture Complexes and Chronology in Northern Texas, with Extension of Puebloan Datings to the Mississippi Valley.** 1946, 366 pp.

262  Mann, Graciela. *The Twelve Prophets of Aleijadinho.* Photographs by Hans Mann. 1967, 131 pp.

263  Manuel, H. T. *Education of Mexican and Spanish-Speaking Children in Texas.** 1930, 173 pp.

264  Manuel, Herschel T. *Spanish-Speaking Children of the Southwest: Their Education and the Public Welfare.** 1965, 222 pp.

265  Nance, Joseph Milton, *After San Jacinto: The Texas-Mexican Frontier, 1836–1841.* 1962, 676 pp.

266  Paredes, Américo. *"With His Pistol in His Hand": A Border Ballad and its Hero.* 1958, 300 pp.

267  Pascin, Jules. *Jules Pascin's Caribbean Sketchbook.* 1964, 106 pp.

268  Phipps, Helen. *Some Aspects of the Agrarian Question in Mexico.** 1925, 157 pp.

269  Pichardo, José Antonio. *Pichardo's Treatise on the Limits of Louisiana and Texas.** Edited and annotated by Charles W. Hackett. 4 vols. 1931, 1934, 1941, 1946.

270  Riley, Carroll L., Charles Kelley, Campbell W. Pennington and Robert L. Rands, (eds.). *Man Across the Sea: Problems of Pre-Columbian Contacts.* 1971, 538 pp.

271  Rosenquist, Carl M. and Edwin I. Megargee. *Delinquency in Three Cultures.* 1969, 554 pp.

272  Rubel, Arthur J. *Across the Tracks: Mexican-Americans in a Texas City.* 1966, 266 pp.

273  Spell, Jefferson Rea. *Rousseau in the Spanish World Before 1833: A Study in Franco-Spanish Literary Relations.** 1938, 325 pp.

274  Stephan, Ruth (ed.) *The Singing Mountaineers. Songs and Tales of the Quechua People.** 1957, 203 pp.

275  Tinker, Edward Larocque. *Corridos and Calaveras.* With notes and translations by Américo Paredes. 1961, 60 pp.

276  Tinker, Edward Larocque. *The Horsemen of the Americas and the Literature They Inspired.* Second Edition. 1966, 150 pp.

277  Wauchope, Robert (ed.) *Handbook of Middle American Indians.* 13 vols. 1964–.

278 Waugh, Julia Nott. *The Silver Cradle.* 1955. 160 pp.
279 Weddle, Robert S. *San Juan Bautista: Gateway to Spanish Texas.* 1968, 469 pp.
280 Weddle, Robert S. *The San Saba Mission: Spanish Pivot in Texas.* 1964, 238 pp.
281 Wheelock, Carter. *The Mythmaker: A Study of Motif and Symbol in the Short Stories of Jorge Luis Borges.* 1969, 190 pp.

# Other Publications at the University of Texas

## Books and Journals

282   Bushong, Allen D. *Doctoral Dissertations on Pan American Topics, Accepted by United States and Canadian Colleges and Universities, 1961–1965. Bibliography and Analysis.* Supplement of the *Latin American Research Review.* II:2 (Spring 1967).

283   *Latin American Research Review.* 1965–.

284   Latin American Studies Association. *A Report to the American Academic Community on the Present Argentine University Situation,* 1967.

285   *Revista Interamericana de Psicología.* 1967–.
      *(Interamerican Journal of Psychology)*

## Spanish and Paperback Editions (limited to sale in the U.S.)

286   Arreola, Juan José. *Confabulario and other Inventions.* 1964, 264 pp.

287   Gorostiza, José. *Muerte sin fin.* Bilingual edition. 1969, 40 pp.

288a   Jiménez, Juan Ramón. *Platero y yo.*

288b   Jiménez, Juan Ramón. *Juan Ramón Jiménez: Three Hundred Poems, 1903–1953.* 1962, 297 pp.

289   Yáñez, Agustín. *Al filo del agua.*

## Miscellaneous Articles

290   DeCamp, David. "Diasystem vs. Overall Pattern: The Jamaican Syllabic Nuclei," in E. Bagby Atwood and Archibald A. Hill, eds., *Studies in Language, Literature, and Culture of the Middle Ages and Later.* The University of Texas at Austin, 1969.

291   Dillard, J. L. "Standard Average Foreign in Puerto Rican Spanish," in E. Bagby Atwood and Archibald A. Hill, eds., *Studies in Language, Literature, and Culture of the Middle Ages and Later.* The University of Texas at Austin, 1969.

292   McLemore, Samuel Dale and Harley L. Browning, "The Spanish-Surname Population of Texas," *Comment,* Publication of the Institute of Public Affairs, The University of Texas at Austin, 10 (January 1964).

293   McLemore, Samuel Dale and Harley L. Browning, *A Statistical Profile of the Spanish-Surname Population of Texas.* Population Series No. 1. Bureau of Business Research, The University of Texas at Austin, 1964.

# Language Research Project

The Learning Disabilities Center publishes for the Language Research Project the following paperback books, most of which were doctoral dissertations completed at the University of Texas. They may be obtained by writing to: Learning Disabilities Center, The University of Texas at Austin, 604 West 24 Street, Austin, Texas 78705.

294   Arnold, Richard D. *1965–66 (Year Two) Findings, San Antonio Language Research Project.* 1968.

295   Cornejo, Ricardo Jesús. *Bilingualism: Study of the Lexicon of the Five-Year-Old Spanish-Speaking Children of Texas.* 1969.

296   Fowler, Elaine D. *An Evaluation of Brengleman-Manning Linguistic Capacity Index as a Predictor of Reading Achievement of Spanish-Speaking First Grade Students.* 1969.

297   Horn, Thomas D. *A Study of the Effects of Intensive Oral-Aural English Language Instruction, Oral-Aural English Language Instruction of Reading Readiness in Grade One.* 1966.*

298   Jameson, Gloria Ruth. *The Development of a Phonemic Analysis for an Oral English Proficiency Test for Spanish-Speaking School Beginners.* 1967.

299   Knight, Lester N. *1966–67 (Year Three) Findings: A Comparison of the Effectiveness of Intensive Oral-Aural English Instruction, Intensive Oral-Aural Spanish Instruction, and Non-Oral-Aural Instruction on the Oral Language and Reading Achievement of Spanish—Speaking Second and Third Graders.* 1969.

300   MacMillan, Robert W. *A Study of the Effect of Socioeconomic Factors on the School Achievement of Spanish-Speaking School Beginners.* 1966.

301   McDowell, Neil A. *A Study of the Academic Capabilities and Achievements of Three Ethnic Groups: Anglo, Negro and Spanish Surname, in San Antonio, Texas.* 1966.

302   Ott, Elizabeth H. *A Study of Levels of Fluency and Proficiency in Oral English of Spanish-Speaking School Beginners.* 1967.

303   Pauck, Frederick G. *An Evaluation of the Self-Test as a Predictor of Reading Achievement of Spanish-Speaking First Grade Children.* 1968.

304   Peña, Albar A. *A Comparative Study of Selected Syntactical Structures of the Oral Language Status in Spanish and English of Disadvantaged First Grade Spanish-Speaking Children.* 1967.*

# NOVA
## PLANTARVM, ANIMALIVM
### ET MINERALIVM MEXICANORVM
# HISTORIA
A FRANCISCO HERNANDEZ MEDICO
In Indijs præstantissimo primum compilata,

DEIN A NARDO ANTONIO RECCHO IN VOLVMEN DIGESTA,

A IO. TERENTIO, IO. FABRO, ET FABIO COLVMNA LYNCEIS
Notis, & additionibus longe doctissimis illustrata.

Cui demum accessere

ALIQVOT EX PRINCIPIS FEDERICI CÆSII FRONTISPICIIS
Theatri Naturalis Phytosophicæ Tabulæ

Vna cum quamplurimis Iconibus, ad octingentas, quibus singula
contemplanda graphice exhibentur.

ROMAE · MDCLI.
Sumptibus Blasij Deuersini, & Zanobij Masotti Bibliopolarum,
Typis Vitalis Mascardi. Superiorum permissu.

NOVA PLANTARVM, ANIMALIVM ET MINERALIVM MEXICANORVM
(1651)
*Francisco Hernández*

# Doctoral Dissertations of Latin American Interest, 1893–1969

## 1923

1  Spell, Mrs. Lota May Harrigan. *Musical Education in North America During the Sixteenth and Seventeenth Centuries.* Ph.D. 167 pp. (Education)

The existence of a high level of musical culture among the Aztecs aided the Spanish conquerors in making great progress in the field of music and in using music as a means—via the Catholic Church—to conquer and "civilize" the Indians in the Spanish territories. The Spaniards were the first to introduce European music to North America. The French were also interested in the cultivation of music in North America, but lacked the financial resources of the Spaniard. These early religious musicians and teachers contributed to the later development of American music.

## 1928

2  Holden, William Curry. *Frontier Problems and Movements in West Texas, 1846–1900.* Ph.D. 382 pp. (History)

West Texans developed an intense feeling of sectionalism, handling frontier problems with little aid or support from the rest of the state. Frontier defenses were protection against Indians, conscription evaders and deserters of the Civil War, and lawless whites. The author also describes the main social aspects of this frontier: the railroad construction, the development of agriculture, the mining explorations, droughts and amusement.

## 1929

3  Powell, Anna Irion. *Relations between the United States and Nicaragua, 1898–1925.* Ph.D. 413 pp. (History)

The problems the United States encountered in Central America during its greatest period of imperialism, just after the Spanish-American War of 1898, are exemplified in Nicaragua. After several interventions, the United States government finally established a virtual protectorate over Nicaragua until Wall Street money and American marines finally withdrew in 1925. Afterwards the United States still retained the same vital military, commercial and political interests, continuing its indirect interventionist policies, although it expressed no avowed desire to annex Nicaragua or deprive it of its "political independence."

4    Casey, Clifford B. *The Disposition of Political Proposals by the Various Pan-American Conferences, 1889–1928*. Ph.D. 520 pp. (History)

The author discusses how the disposition of the various proposals affected the movement towards international cooperation for solidarity and mutual benefits in the New World. The major proposals dealt with were: intervention, settlement of international claims and disputes, and the status of the Pan American Union.

5    Knight, James. *A Laboratory Study of the Reading Habits of Spanish-speaking Children*. Ph.D. 179 pp. (Education)

This is an investigation into the reading habits of children whose native speaking language is different from the one in which they receive their first and usually all subsequent reading instruction. The "eye-movement" technique is used to test the reading habits of a group of Spanish-speaking children in Texas public schools. Among other observations, the author was able to show that, despite initial handicaps and retardation in reading, the Spanish-speaking children aften improve in reading maturity with age.

6    Williams, Amelia. *A Critical Study of the Siege of the Alamo and of the Personnel of its Defenders*. Ph.D. 457 pp. (History)

The author intends to shed light on various "dark spots" of the Alamo story. She delves into the historical background of both the American and Mexican sides prior to the Alamo conflict and outlines the major events of the Texan occupation of the Alamo and of Santa Anna's subsequent invasion and siege. Finally, she provides detailed descriptions of the leaders: Travis, Bowie, Crockett and Santa Anna. The emphasis of the work is on certain previously unsolved historical problems primarily involving participants, victims and survivors on both sides.

1932

7    Castañeda, Carlos Eduardo (trans.). *Morfi's History of Texas; A Critical Chronological Account of the Early Exploration, Attempts at Colonization, and the Fnal Occupation of Texas by the Spaniards, by Fr. Juan Agustin Morfi, O.F.M., Missionary, Teacher, and Historian of His Order, 1673–1779*. Tr. into English from the Original Manuscript in the Archives of the Convent of San Francisco el Grande in the National Library of Mexico, with a Biographical Introduction and Annotations. Ph.D. 651 pp. (History)

Morfi's *History of Texas*, discovered by the translator in the National Archives of Mexico, provides the most complete and detailed account known to date (1932) for the entire period of 1673–1779. Morfi included the history of the Spanish settlers and the native tribes of Texas, the French incursions and Spanish explorations of the territory throughout the period of occupation, the establishment of missions, the inspection of Rubi and the attempted reorganization of the Province in 1766–1779.

8   Stenberg, Richard Rollin. *American Imperialism in the Southwest, 1800–1837.* Ph.D. 480 pp. (History)

The United States has been from birth increasingly imperialistic. Stenberg describes chronologically the important diplomatic affairs, the views, motives and actions of those primarily responsible for expansion into Louisiana, the Floridas, Mexico, Cuba and Texas. President John Q. Adams, Sam Houston, Anthony Butler and above all, President Andrew Jackson, were seen as the principal imperialists, while the Texas Revolution was the high point of the Jackson era.

9   Webb, Walter Prescott. *The Great Plains. A Study in Institutions and Environment.* Ph.D. 525 pp. (History)

This work is a new interpretation of the phenomenon that gave western life and institutions in the Great Plains their particular character. Working with a new and precise definition of the Plains, the author shows how the Plains affected the various peoples—Spanish and American—who came to occupy it, and were in turn affected by them. He follows each of the cultural complexes—weapons, tools, law and literature—to see if they were modified in transition to the Plains, and if so, where and how. The Great Plains have bent and molded Anglo-American life by destroying tradition and influencing institutions in a most singular manner.

## 1933

10   Hancock, Walter Edgar. *The Career of General Antonio López de Santa Anna (1794–1833).* Ph.D. 654 pp. (History)

The author covers the two early periods of Santa Anna's long and vigorous life: (1) his early years and activities until he pronounced his opposition to Iturbide in 1822, and (2) the period of struggle and revolution from 1823 to 1833, when he was elected president and literally became the arbiter of Mexico's destiny. Santa Anna's "kaleidoscopic" career during these years characterizes him, successively, as the champion of the empire, of republicanism, of federalism and of centralism. From being a maker of presidents, he finally became president himself.

11    Sprague, William Forrest. *The Life of Vicente Guerrero, Mexican Revolutionary Patriot, 1782–1831.* Ph.D. 104 pp. (History)

Guerrero joined the revolutionary armies in 1810 as a common soldier and advanced to the rank of general of all the rebel forces. From 1821–1831 he served the Republic as general and statesman, including a largely unsuccessful term as president. His tireless efforts for a liberal and democratic government and for sweeping social reforms brought down upon him the enmity of reactionaries who finally murdered him in 1831.

12    Young, Paul Patterson. *Mexican Oil and American Diplomacy.* Ph.D. 219 pp. (History)

North American oil exploitation and exportation in Mexico has been the greatest source of contention between the two governments from the time of Carranza to Calles. Pressured by the oil companies and obliged to uphold the Monroe Doctrine, the American government was forced to deal with the threats of nationalization, high taxation, and government control of the industry by the Mexican government. Each of the nationalistic presidents seemed more "socialist" minded than his predecessors. The conflict was temporarily resolved by the Petroleum Law of 1927, which created a "new working relationship" between the American-owned oil companies and the Mexican government.

1935

13    Caldwell, Edward Maurice. *The War of "La Reforma" in Mexico, 1858–1861.* Ph.D. 364 pp. (History)

This study is the chronicle of the "inevitable" war between the conservative-clerical cause and the victorious, popularly-supported liberal movement, led by the various liberal *caudillos.* The author also details the problems of foreign recognition of Mexico and intervention by the United States, Great Britain, France, Spain and Europe in general.

14    Harris, Mrs. Helen Willits. *The Public Life of Juan Nepomuceno Almonte.* Ph.D. 249 pp. (History)

One of Mexico's ablest statesmen and diplomats, Almonte was damned by the liberals for deserting his early liberal stance for the conservative and monarchical cause of Santa Anna in 1834. On the other hand, the conservatives never appreciated his support. As a diplomat, he served as ambassador to the United States during the trying period when the annexation of Texas was first considered. He was also serving in Europe when Napoleon intervened in Mexico in 1862 and installed Maximilian as emperor. At that time, Almonte was convinced that the monarchy was the only viable form of government for the salvation of Mexico.

15  Hoffman, Fritz Leo (trans.). *Francisco Céliz. Diary of the Alarcón Expedition into Texas, 1718–1719.* Ph.D. 139 pp. (History)

This is a faithful and annotated translation of Fray Francisco Céliz's official diary of the Alarcón expedition. Besides the usual goals of such expeditions, the Alarcón expedition undertook to found missions, to explore certain unknown areas in Texas, to convert and trade with Indians and to make sure the French were not trading in Spanish territories. Despite conflicting reports from other sources, Fray Francisco Céliz concluded that the expedition was carried out successfully by Alarcón.

16  Parker, Ralph Halstead. *Imperialism and the Liberation of Cuba (1868–1898).* Ph.D. 386 pp. (History)

Cuba's movement for independence was tied to two other events of the late 19th century: 1) U.S. imperialist policy, which reached its peak in this period and eventually included Cuba in its sphere of influence; and 2) a movement in Europe aimed at preventing the realization of either the dream of Cuba or of the United States. After the failure of the Revolution of 1868, Cuban liberation leaders under José Martí realized that they needed the aid of the United States to succeed, although they were fully aware of Southern slave interests in Cuba. The author also discusses the Philippine Islands as part of the "large policy" by which all the nations interested in the Cuban question were trying to solve the problem of imperialist expansion.

17  Shelby, Charmion Clair. *International Rivalry in Northeastern New Spain, 1700–1725.* Ph.D. 275 pp. (History)

The French in the Louisiana territory were interested in expanding their influence and trade with the Spanish settlers in northeastern New Spain, while the Spanish authorities in Pensacola were anxious to control French encroachment on their land. Spain was forced to tolerate the usurpation of her territory in the New World because she was dependent on her French ally in European politics. Under the impetus of the French threat, Texas was decisively occupied by the Spaniards and plans made for its effective colonization. Despite persistent French efforts to trade, they were largely unsuccessful and never really expanded beyond the Louisiana territory.

18    Gregory, Gladys Grace. *"El Chamizal": A Boundary Problem between the United States and Mexico.* Ph.D. 399 pp. (Government)

Two attempts failed to settle the dispute over the tract of land known as El Chamizal lying partially within the city of El Paso. This case is unique in the history of international boundary disputes because it has persisted over a long period of time (50 years at the time of writing of this dissertation) and because the United States refused to accept the arbitration award of 1911 which amounted to a compromise. The author is not optimistic about the prospects of settlement of the dispute, which has evoked disproportionate emotional reactions in Mexico. She proposes settlement through the trade or transfer of land, through monetary payment by the United States, or through a combination of the two.

19    Strickland, Rex Wallace. *Anglo-American Activities in Northeastern Texas, 1803–1845.* Ph.D. 404 pp. (History)

After the Louisiana Purchase in 1802, President Jefferson commissioned the first American exploration to describe the region, previously explored by the Spanish and French. By 1820 the first American settlements were established in Miller County, noted subsequently for its shifting boundaries and uncertain legal status. Some major preoccupations of the settlers were: conflict of jurisdiction between the American government and the Mexican empresarios; frontier problems; participation in the Texas revolution and the Republic of Texas; and the usual struggles against Indians and nature.

20    Johnson, Richard Abraham. *The Mexican Revolution of Ayutla, 1854–1855.* Ph.D. 236 pp. (History)

The revolution of Ayutla of 1854 signaled the second revolutionary period of Mexican history, which saw the final struggle between the old federalist-liberal and centralist parties. The war concluded with a clear cut triumph for federalism and liberalism, enunciated in the Constitution of 1857, the destruction of the political power of the clergy, and the rise of the "mestizo"—men as Benito Juárez—to top political offices. Despite its failures and the resultant economic instability, the revolution left a residuum of constructive reforms, intellectual freedom and advanced social consciousness.

21    LeSueur, Hardeman David. *The Ecology and Vegetation of Chihuahua, Mexico, North of Parallel Twenty-Eight.* Ph.D. 118 pp. (Botany)

Although collectors have gathered specimens of plant life in the northern region of the state of Chihuahua, no extensive work had been done on the structure, limits and distribution of the plant formations of this region, and their co-action and responses to their environment. This work is divided into three parts: geology and description of the terrain; the climate; and plant formations and their ecological relationships.

22   Murphy, Henrietta. *Spanish Presidial Administration as Exemplified by the Inspection of Pedro de Rivera, 1724–1728*. Ph.D. 442 pp. (History)

The *presidios* or military posts in northern New Spain contributed substantially to the institutional life of the frontiers and to the problems of the governing officials in both Madrid and Mexico City. Pedro de Rivera's reforms produced only temporary benefits to New Spain, largely because they were not enforced after the first five years. The keynote of these reforms was retrenchment, which was followed by a period of declining Spanish influence in North America. Settlers, missionaries and soldiers tended to attribute the loss of this territory primarily to Rivera and his zeal for economy, not all together a fair judgement. The author is inclined to believe that the causes for the collapse of Spanish colonialism in this region was the inevitable result of the confrontation between a weakened Spain and a strong England.

## 1939

23   Eckert, Jacqueline Clara. *International Law in United States-Mexican Boundary Relations*. Ph.D. 391 pp. (Government)

With two exceptions, the author concludes, the accepted principles, rules, and practices of international law have been applied to the solution of Mexican-American boundary disputes. The Chamizal tract and the various water allocation problems were specifically analyzed in terms of difficulties posed by accretion, erosion and avulsion.

24   Johnston, Marjorie Cecil. *Cognate Relationships between English and Spanish Vocabularies as a Basis for Instruction*. Ph.D. 224 pp. (Education)

The author sees a need for a standard basic vocabulary list in the teaching of first year Spanish and English as a foreign language. She compiles a list of some 4,000 basic words on the assumption that cognate relationships between the two languages is a means of affecting more economical vocabulary learning. Three basic questions arise in this task: (1) What words should be considered basic? (2) How can the cognates within these vocabularies be determined? (3) What are the advantages of this cognate list in teaching Spanish or English as a foreign language?

25   Morton, Ohland. *The Life of General Don Manuel de Mier y Terán as it Affected Texas-Mexican Relations, 1821–1832.* Ph.D. 439 pp. (History)

The activities of Mexican patriot General Mier y Terán were divided between national politics in Mexico and his many commissions to Texas, then a part of independent Mexico. Mier y Terán played a prominent role in Mexico's war for independence as well as an illustrious political career in the Republic of Mexico. He went to Texas to settle boundary problems with the United States; later he became Commissioner of Colonization and cooperated with Stephen Austin in the affairs of Texas until 1832, when he unexpectedly committed suicide in despair over the state of affairs in Mexico.

26   Price, Grady Daniel. *The United States and West Florida, 1803–1812.* Ph.D. 437 pp. (History)

This period was critical in the dispute between the United States and Spain over West Florida, which the United States claimed was part of the Louisiana Territory. Although treaty provisions and geographical factors gave the United States legal and strategic advantages over Spain, it had to resort to force to incorporate Florida into American territory. Eventually West Florida was divided and annexed to the United States as parts of the states of Louisiana and Mississippi.

1940

27   Bridges, Clarence Allan. *Southward Expansion Projects, 1848–1861.* Ph.D. 319 pp. (History)

This synthesis based on the existing information describes southward expansion projects of this period. The American expansionists were primarily interested in Cuba, Mexico and parts of Central America. Most of these expeditions, uncoordinated and unconnected in purpose, ended in fiascos. Failure was due precisely to the lack of a common plan of action among prominent southerners interested in the expansion for economic reasons. At the same time, the dominant North voiced strong opposition to the increase of slave territory.

28   Shearer, Ernest Charles. *Border Diplomatic Relations between the United States and Mexico, 1848–1860.* Ph.D. 333 pp. (History)

This period from the Mexican War to the Civil War was full of border conflicts arising from raids, depredations, and filibustering activities into Mexican territory. The subsequent diplomatic relations between the United States and Mexico were insincere and deceptive, with threats and exaggerated reports from both sides. The North American government was pressured by the "manifest destiny" advocates to act; its diplomats were generally unsympathetic to Mexico; and Mexicans in turn made the North Americans pay dearly for what they coveted. The Civil War, which diverted the attention of adventurers and government, finally brought an end to a very strained period of United States-Mexican relations.

29 Whitwell, Charles Garland. *Spanish Educational Policy in the Philippine Islands*. Ph.D. 258 pp. (History)
Education for the masses was not a Spanish policy in the eighteenth and nineteenth centuries. The Catholic Church was solely responsible for education in the Philippines until 1863 and did surprisingly well in raising literacy levels in the Islands, especially when compared with other European colonies. The author evaluated the 330 years of Spanish educational policy in terms of the language problem the Spanish educators faced, the various levels of educational facilities they instituted, the books, printing facilities, and writers of the period.

1941

30 Blair, Evelyn. *Education Movements in Mexico: 1821 to 1836*. Ph.D. 348 pp. (Education)
This study traces the attempt to develop a public education system in Mexico, with special emphasis on the states of Coahuila and Texas. The author discusses the roles played by the federal, state and municipal governments; private individuals and organizations; the Lancasterian system of education and other foreign influences; trade and professional schools. Not much was actually realized, despite the great enthusiasm and the many plans proposed. In conclusion, the author suggests that Mexico's failure to establish a public educational system during this period was related to the failure to establish a democratic government.

31 Morton, Ward McKinnon. *Government Regulation of Labor in Mexico Under the Constitution of 1917*. Ph.D. 354 pp. (Government)
The formulation of labor legislation was part of Mexico's struggle to better social conditions. The study deals specifically with the provisions and failures of Article 123 of the 1917 Constitution and the Labor Law of 1931. The author is inclined to think that tradition and history point to some form of paternalistic collectivism, directed by the government, as the inevitable course towards solution of Mexico's labor and other social problems. However, despite its basic mistrust of the United States, Mexico's

economy is greatly dependent upon the United States, and hence its labor legislation and other social legislation is dependent upon the attitudes of the United States.

1942

32    Broom, Perry Morris. *An Interpretative Analysis of the Economic and Educational Status of Latin Americans in Texas, with Emphasis upon the Basic Factors Underlying an Approach to an Improved Program of Occupational Guidance, Training and Adjustments for Secondary Schools.* Ed.D. 500 pp. (Education)

The author studied the contemporary social and economic status of Latin Americans (Mexicans) in Texas and the nature and scope of the available, but highly inadequate, program of vocational training, guidance and placement for this minority group. He discovered racial discrimination against them in both occupational opportunities and remuneration. A new improved program of vocational guidance and adjustment should not only be educational, psychological and economic, but also sociological and even philosophical, in character.

33    Callicutt, Laurie Timmons. *The Construction and Evaluation of Parallel Tests of Reading in English and Spanish.* Ph.D. 442 pp. (Education)

The author believes that suitable tests can appraise the language ability of bilingual Spanish-speaking children. However, as such tests do not exist, the author devised her own set of vocabulary tests for comprehension in reading. These tests are designed to examine both Spanish and English language abilities. Included in this dissertation are samples of both the original and the revised second edition of the tests.

34    Estep, Raymond. *The Life of Lorenzo de Zavala.* Ph.D. 421 pp. (History)

Lorenzo de Zavala's often complicated and misunderstood motives for leaving Mexico after its independence earned him the reputation of the Benedict Arnold of Mexico. As the greatest Mexican liberal who advocated all forms of social changes for the masses, he turned against the Mexican Republic which he helped create when it became an instrument of oppression under the centralist government of Santa Anna. He went to Texas and played another important revolutionary role in the independence of Texas from Mexico.

35    Etheridge, Truman Harrison. *Education in the Republic of Texas.* Ph.D. 522 pp. (Education)

Education in the Republic of Texas was the progenitor of education in the State of Texas. This historical investigation discusses: educational backgrounds of the Anglo-Americans and the Spanish-Americans in Texas; educational views of Texas leaders; government proposals and efforts towards a public school system; extra-governmental efforts; and the characteristics of the existing schools of the period.

36   Haggard, Juan Villasana. *The Neutral Ground between Louisiana and Texas, 1806–1821.* Ph.D. 244 pp. (History)

The Texas-Louisiana boundary had been a source of contention between Spain and the United States. The organizing of the "neutral ground" was an attempt at settlement, but dispute continued until the piece of land was awarded to the United States in 1821. The history of the "neutral ground" was marked by the establishment and eradication of frontier colonies, by a flourishing trade between the two territories, by filibustering activities, and by its role as a bridge to Texas for fugitive slaves.

37   Hogan, William Ransom. *A Social and Economic History of the Republic of Texas.* Ph.D. 587 pp. (History)

This study spans the spectrum of "social and economic" problems of early Texas: immigration and agriculture; speculation and industry; the necessities of life; transportation, communication and navigation; amusement; education; culture and science; health and medicine; religion; judicial and legal system; law enforcement; and the characteristics of the "rampant individualism" present on the Texas frontier.

## 1944

38   Herr, Selma Ernestine. *The Effect of Pre-first Grade Training upon Reading Readiness and Reading Achievement among Spanish American Children in the First Grade.* Ed.D. 323 pp. (Education)

The author discusses the factors influencing lower scholastic achievement among Spanish American children, the use of standardized tests for bilingual children, and physiological aspects in the process of reading. She designed a testing program, including a detailed daily preparation of material and directions for teachers, and applied it to a control and experimental group of pre-first grade Spanish American children. The results indicate overwhelmingly that pre-first grade training improves reading achievement with the children, who show more cooperativeness and emotional stability upon entering first grade.

39   Rodríguez-Bou, Ismael. *A Study of the Parallelism of English and Spanish Vocabularies.* Ph.D. 294 pp. (Education)

The author helped devise and test a series of parallel Spanish and English tests (the Inter-American Tests) for Puerto Rican children, who speak Spanish at home and learn English at school. This work is an evaluation of the intermediate and advanced vocabulary tests of the series. The validity of such tests as instruments for comparing ability in English and Spanish hinges upon the soundness of the concept of parallelism and the degree to which this ideal has been attained. The author hopes that his results will have application in the teaching of a second language.

1945

40   Apstein, Theodore. *The Contemporary Argentine Theatre.* Ph.D. 305 pp. (Latin American Studies: Romance Languages)
Apstein presents a "severe criticism" of the Argentine theatre since 1920, including a complete resumé and analysis of the works of Samuel Eichelbaum, the leading Argentine playwright of the era. He discusses also in detail other aspects of theatre: direction, design, acting, as well as the various forms of theatre expression. Although Argentine theatre is developing, it still lacks scope and universality. Above all, the "literary" playwrights must overcome the domination of the public by the "commercial" playwrights.

41   Callahan, Sister M. Generosa. *The Literature of Travel in Texas, 1803–1846: An Analysis of Ideas and Attitudes.* Ph.D. 355 pp. (English)
Through the travel literature of the period, the author studied the attitudes and opinions of five cultural groups—Spanish-American, Anglo-American, English, French and German—who came to Texas for predominantly economic reasons. The travelers' logs provide discussions on religious conditions, political ideas and cultural differences, as well as fictional writing.

42   Nelson, Eastin. *The Development of Economic Policy in the Republic of Panama.* Ph.D. 306 pp. (Economics)
The author sees the basis of administrative law of Latin America rooted in Mediterranean antiquity and the Iberian past. He denounces the injection of the tenets of Anglo-American classical liberalism into a discussion of twentieth century Latin American economic policy and its administration. Latin America is evolving into its own kind of welfare liberalism, which often means state intervention in economic matters. The detailed case study of the history and development of the economic policy of Panama from its foundation in 1904 to 1940 supports the author's theoretical framework.

43   Vernon, Mrs. Ida Stevenson Weldon. *Pedro de Valdivia, Conquistador of Chile.* Ph.D. 443 pp. (History)

Pedro de Valdivia was a typical Spanish conquistador. Despite his lack of money as well as the "evil reputation" of Chile left by his unsuccessful predecessors, he set out from Peru for Chile in 1539. He saw the agricultural rather than the mining possibilities in Chile, and his vision was to colonize it. Valdivia spent fourteen years there until his death in 1553. As governor, he faced the usual problems of Indians and colonization.

1947

44   Cotner, Thomas Ewing. *The Military and Political Career of José Joaquín de Herrera, 1792–1854.* Ph.D. 623 pp. (History)

As a military officer, Herrera fought with Iturbide for Mexico's independence. Later, in the political sphere, he worked for moderate liberalism and a federalist republic, opposing the dictatorships of Iturbide and Santa Anna. During his two terms as president of the Republic, he grappled with political, economic, racial, diplomatic, religious, educational and military reform problems, while Mexico enjoyed an era of relative internal stability and economic and constitutional progress.

45   Maxwell, Mrs. Vera Rogers. *The "Diario Histórico" of Carlos María Bustamante for 1824; Edited, with Notes, Annotations and a Complete Life of the Author.* Ph.D. 817 pp. (Latin American Studies: History)

This is a faithful reproduction (in the original Spanish) of the 1824 excerpt from Bustamante's *Diario histórico de México,* which covered the years 1823–1841. Notes and annotations help clarify the events and persons mentioned. The author also provides a historical background of Bustamante's time (1774–1848) as well as a detailed biography. The year 1824 was chosen because the federal constitution was adopted and a new government was established at that time. Bustamante himself was a member of the Constituent Congress which drew up the constitution.

1948

46   Hutchinson, Cecil Alan. *Valentín Gómez Farías: A Biographical Study.* Ph.D. 864 pp. (History)

This biography of Gómez Farías, patriarch of liberal reform in Mexico, relates his life to the period of constant civil and foreign strife of 1820–

1857. He twice served as president during periods of great controversy. As other liberals of his era, he had to contend with, and fell victim to, the the schemes of General Santa Anna. He lived through the first reform government of General Álvarez of 1854 and died shortly after he signed the liberal Constitution of 1857.

47   Peevy, Lucien Elliot. *The First Two years of Texas Statehood, 1846–1847.* Ph.D. 855 pp. (History)

This historical survey of the first two years of Texas statehood covers many diverse subjects. The author provides a background of Texas statehood as well as information on the political organization and proceedings of the first legislature, on economic welfare, social conditions, education, religion, and Indian affairs. He also discusses the role of Texas in the Mexican War of 1846–1848.

## 1949

48   Benson, Nettie Lee. *The Provincial Deputation in Mexico: Precursor of the Mexican Federal State.* Ph.D. 365 pp. (Latin American Studies: History)

The various provincial deputations, established in 1812–1814, are characterized as the precursor to the Mexican federal system of government adopted in 1823–1824. The author discusses the history and development of the various provincial deputations, the friction between the provinces and the Spanish-controlled central government, the strong popular support for federalism, and finally, the establishment of states and state legislatures as well as the election of members to the constituent assembly from the various states.

49   Cumberland, Charles Curtis. *Francisco I. Madero, Revolutionary.* Ph.D. 734 pp. (History)

Madero's government of 1910–1913 failed largely because neither the psychology of the Mexican people nor the actual political conditions of the country were ready for reform or conducive to the efficient working of the government. Apart from weaknesses in his character, Madero failed to attract or to hold the vital cooperation of the American ambassador, the military, the intellectuals and the press. Victoriano Huerta's coup brought a return to the Díaz philosophy, and an end to Madero's reformist policies for the time being.

50   Manfredini, James Manfred. *The Political Role of the Count of Revillagigedo, Viceroy of New Spain, 1789–1794.* Ph.D. 318 pp. (Latin American Studies: History)

Acclaimed as the greatest viceroy of the eighteenth century in New Spain, Revillagigedo acted successfully as governor, captain-general and vice patron of New Spain, as well as the economic and financial administrator and superintendent of the *real hacienda,* despite the continued efforts of his enemies at court to discredit him. The author sees him as a precursor to the revolution of independence in New Spain in his reforms, his egalitarian and liberal philosophy, his understanding of the frontier, and his foresight in the handling of colonial problems.

51   Timmons, Wilbert Helde. *The Life of José María Morelos: the Founder of the Mexican Nation.* Ph.D. 553 pp. (History)

The mestizo priest, Morelos, described here as the "founder of the Mexican nation and the soul of the people," succeeded Father Hidalgo to the leadership of Mexico's independent movement. He served in his last years (1811–1815) as military commander, statesman, spokesman for social, economic and political reforms, and the inspirer of Mexico's new constitution. While head of the insurgent troops, he was captured, tried, and executed by the royalist forces of Iturbide.

1950

52   Dabbs, Jack Autrey. *The Political and Military Administration of Marshall Francois-Achille Bazaine in Mexico (1862–1867).* Ph.D. 539 pp. (Latin American Studies: History)

This study evaluates Bazaine's attempts to prepare Mexico to accept Maximilian of Austria as its emperor. Marshall Bazaine largely succeeded in his efforts to destroy the Mexican Republican Army, to organize an imperial army to replace it, to hold elections to support the candidacy of Maximilian, to secure Maximilian's position under unofficial French domination with an administrative organization on the French pattern, and, finally, to withdraw nearly all French troops from Mexico.

53   English, William Embry. *Fray Alonso de la Veracruz in Mexican Colonial Education.* Ph.D. 159 pp. (Latin American Studies: History)

Fray Alonso (Gutiérrez) exercised an influential role in colonial American education. The philosophical and institutional harbingers of the Mexican system are reviewed. Apart from teaching, preaching, profusive writing and publishing, Fray Alonso founded many institutions of higher learning. He was instrumental in fomenting legislation that protected the Indians from abuses of the "white man."

54  Florstedt, Robert Frederick. *The Liberal Role of José María Luis Mora in the Early History of Independent Mexico.* Ph.D. 569 pp. (Latin American Studies: History)

This study of the life and career of Dr. Mora devotes particular attention to his liberal and reformist principles and achievements. He was active in the vanguard of the liberal movement which promoted educational and fiscal reforms, "states rights" in the centralist-federalists split and anti-clerical reforms. The Constitution of 1857 was in great part reflective of his principles.

55  Knapp, Frank Averill. *The Life of Sebastián Lerdo de Tejada, 1823–1889: A Study of Influence and Obscurity.* Ph.D. 534 pp. (History)

This study reconstructs the extended political career of Lerdo, which has been obscured by the shadow cast by Benito Juárez, analyzes his influence on the events and trends of the time, and recaptures his life and personality. Among other things, Lerdo was the principal minister and advisor to Juárez during exile, became prime minister when Juárez reassumed the presidency, and finally became president himself, only to be ousted after re-election by Porfirio Díaz.

56  Rippy, Merrill. *Oil and the Mexican Revolution.* Ph.D. 630 pp. (History).

The hypothesis presented here maintains that the Mexican Revolution of 1910 was in many ways influenced by the relationship existing between the oil industry and Mexican society. The oil industry, which had been dominated by foreign interests, attacked the "Revolution" in Mexico through foreign and domestic intervention prior to and during expropriation. By surviving the economic "attacks," internal insurrection, and foreign diplomatic pressure, the Revolution realized, insofar as mineral wealth was concerned, its goal.

1951

57  Bernstein, Marvin David. *The History and Economic Organization of the Mexican Mining Industry, 1890–1940.* Ph.D. 1,341 pp. (Latin American Studies: Economics)

The economic, historical and political setting of the mining industry and the technological organization of metal production in Mexico is discussed exhaustively, with the inclusion of a survey of the field of mineral economics. If one assumes that the mining industry is essential to the industrialization of Mexico, then (1) Mexicans themselves must become more interested in this highly risky enterprise, traditionally dominated by foreign entrepreneurs, and (2) the government must make certain sacrifices towards a nationalized mineral industry.

58   Davis, Joe Edward. *The Development of Justo Sierra's Educational Thought.* Ph.D. 413 pp. (Latin American Studies: Education)

Justo Sierra Méndez (1848–1912) was a prolific writer on topics ranging from politics to literature. His educational thought was derived primarily from the positivism of Auguste Comte and the principles of non-specialization held by Gabino Barreda. He introduced theoretical and practical innovations in the fields of compulsory education, teacher training, and higher education.

59   Donnell, Guy Renfro. *United States Intervention in Mexico, 1914.* Ph.D. 350 pp. (Latin American Studies: History)

The social and historical roots of the political and economic disturbances which contributed to the demise of the *Porfiriato* and later unrest resulting in the intervention of the United States are analyzed. Special attention is given to the rationale for, and the mechanics of, the invasion and occupation.

60   Flaccus, Elmer William. *Guadalupe Victoria: Mexican Revolutionary Patriot and First President, 1786–1843.* Ph.D. 748 pp. (History)

Guadalupe Victoria, first president of Mexico, played a crucial role in the military campaigns of José María Morelos and in the ascendency and later the downfall of Iturbide. Elected president in 1824, he was an effective administrator in the first two years. The latter part of his administration was characterized by oscillation and indecision. Finally, he was reduced to a figurehead by the Victorious Yorkino rebels who made shambles of his constitutional government.

61   Friend, Llerena Beaufort. *The Great Designer—Sam Houston in the American Political Scene.* Ph.D. 731 pp. (History)

Sam Houston, as president of the Republic of Texas, worked vigorously and deviously to accomplish annexation. As senator from Texas (1846–1859),he effectively defended Texas' interests until 1855, when he incurred the condemnation of the Texas legislature for having supported the Kansas-Nebraska bill. His pronounced Union stand helped him win the governorship of Texas in 1859 and returned him to political favor. Houston's project to establish a protectorate over Mexico, designed to give him renewed recognition to win the presidency, did not materialize. When Texas seceded from the Union, Houston was forced from the governorship because he refused to take the oath of office to the Confederate States of America.

62   Harrison, Horace Virgil. *Juan Pablo Anaya, Champion of Mexican Federalism.* Ph.D., 553 pp. (Latin American Studies: History)

This biographical study analyses Anaya's public career from 1810–1850. It interprets the significant historical incidents and movements in which Anaya played an important role: the Republican conspiracy against Emperor Iturbide, the controversy between Mexico and Guatemala over the border district of Soconusco, and the diplomatic relationships between the Mexican Federalists and the Republic of Texas.

63   Kahle, Louis George. *Deviations from the "de facto" Principle in the Latin American Recognition Policy of the United States.* Ph.D. 417 pp. (Latin American Studies: Government)

When Thomas Jefferson applied the "de facto" recognition principle to the French republican government in 1792, it became the practice of the United States to recognize governments of revolutionary origin. The first departure and application of the "de jure" principle occurred when President Wilson refused to recognize the Huerta government in Mexico. Another important deviation was President Harding's attempt to use conditional recognition against the Obregón government of Mexico. By 1930, the "de jure" deviation was recognized as an ineffective instrument of policy. Mere non-recognition, unsupported by economic and military sanctions, was shown to be inadequate in preventing Latin American revolutions.

64   Lynn, Vela Leatrice. *Political Career of Teodosio Lares, 1848–1867.* Ph.D. 406 pp. (History)

The legacy of Spanish sovereignty after independence caused a three-way conflict between Church, State and "the will of the people," resulting in a power vacuum which fostered chaos and revolution. A creole conservative, Lares' formula for harmony was sovereignty of the State, including a compromise with the Church and a policy to conserve the Spanish heritage. Lares supported the installation of Maximilian, hoping that stability would be secured. After the Empire, when the liberals returned to power, Lares had to flee the country.

65   McElhannon, Joseph Carl. *Foreign Relations of Imperial Mexico, 1821–1823.* Ph.D. 452 pp. (History)

The author studies the efforts of the Imperial Mexican government under Agustín Iturbide to assume its place in the world affairs following its declaration of independence from Spain. He presents a comprehensive account of Mexican annexation of Central America and diplomatic relations with the United States.

66   McLean, Malcolm Dallas. *The Life and Works of Guillermo Prieto (1818–1897)*. Ph.D. 305 pp. (History)

Guillermo Prieto was a Mexican political and literary figure of the nineteenth century. He served nineteen times as deputy in the National Congress. As Postmaster General, he established the system of pre-paid postage. As Minister of Finance he issued the famous Decree of February 5, 1861 which provided for the secularization of church property. He wrote political economies, history, travel books, popular poetry and was recognized as the first native to write *costumbrista* sketches.

67   Martin-Vegue, George Boyd. *The Silversmiths in Mexico—A Study in Colonial Trade Guilds*. Ph.D. 217 pp. (History)

The guild system was a transplanted institution in Mexico, having a history in Europe dating back many centuries. Although restricted almost entirely to the colonial period, the silversmith guild was the strongest and most representative of that era. The highly perfected artistry of the Old World and the indigenous motifs unsurpassed in other parts of the New World were fused into a distinctive style that has found its expression in the silver works of present-day Mexico. Although the guild was largely self-governed, the Spanish Crown retained control by the appointment of key officials and the right to issue confirming ordinances of the trade organization.

68   Parrish, Leonard Durvin. *The Life and Works of Nicolás Bravo, Mexican Patriot (1786–1854)*. Ph.D. 368 pp. (History)

Bravo began his career fighting under José María Morelos for independence from Spain. Motivated by the principle of "convenience," he was vaguely centralist in his beliefs before 1824. He was Grand Master of the Scottish Rites Masons and believed they should have ruled Mexico until the masses became politically educated. After the Decree of Expulsion, Bravo joined the Plan de Montaño, devised to support the Federalist Constitution of 1824, to correct the abuses of the present constitution and to reform the administration. The Plan was put down by "Yorkino" Grand Master Vicente Guerrero and Bravo was forced into exile.

69    Patterson, Ernest Finney. *The Finances of the National Government of Argentina.* Ph.D. 406 pp. (Economics)

Argentina's drive for industrialization has extended state control into new fields and has brought about innovations in the system of public finances. Enormous and continuous increase in gross expenditures and spending under the Five Year Plan as well as multiplication in number and importance of "so called Independent Agencies" are the most salient results.

The evolution of the tax structure based solely on customs duties to the institution of income, sales, excise and excess profits taxes is another innovation. The system of financing public debt has changed from exclusive dependence on foreign sources with high interest rates to the development of an internal loan market charging lower interest rates.

70    Vigness, David Martell. *The Republic of the Rio Grande: An Example of Separatism in Northern Mexico.* Ph.D. 269 pp. (History)

Four factors led the separatist movement of 1824–1840 in Northern Mexico: geographical isolation from the seat of Mexican government; the fierce nomadic and intractable spirit of the Indians of that region; the method of settlement of the area; and the turbulence of Mexican politics during the first quarter century of independence. Seceding in 1838, the secessionists achieved several military victories, with Texas furnishing volunteers and supplies, although it maintained strict "official neutrality." When the United States government declared itself against separatism in the area, the movement died.

71    Walker, Thomas Fonso. *Pre-revolutionary Pamphleteering in Mexico, 1808–1810.* Ph.D. 326 pp. (Latin American Studies: History)

The role of Mexican pamphleteering and its importance are examined growing out of its European antecedents. In 1808 Ferdinand was helped by "folletos" of patriotic poetry which recorded widespread declarations of allegiance to the imprisoned Spanish king. During the fateful year of 1810, "conservative" and "liberal" pamphlets poured from the presses. Liberal publications called for a constitutional monarchy with a free press and a system of public instruction. Conservatives appealed to Mexicans to forget political differences and to support the mother country that was fighting for her national existence.

1952

72    Ewing, Floyd Ford, Jr. *Carranza's Foreign Relations: An Experiment in Nationalism.* Ph.D. 384 pp. (Latin American Studies: History)

The purpose of this study is to examine Carranza's contributions to the success of the Mexican Revolution. Carranza attempted to eliminate the restrictive effects of foreign political and economic domination. His intransigence, gained "de facto" and later "de jure" recognition of his government. He took advantage of the "new idealism" propounded at Versailles by Wilson.

1953

73   Alisky, Marvin Howard. *Educational Aspects of Broadcasting in Mexico.* Ph.D. 309 pp. (Latin American Studies: Education)

Broadcasting, a handy tool for communications officials and educators in attacking isolation and ignorance, has been at least a minor weapon in Mexico's social reform since the 1920's. This study discusses all aspects of broadcasting in Mexico: the history, education and official government programs, official foreign programs (Voice of America, BBC), U.S.-Spanish language programs along the borderland, rural and urban broadcasting systems, and finally, Mexico's nascent television media. In thirty years, Mexico's broadcasting system has grown to be the biggest complex in Latin America.

74   Anttila, Earl. *United States Educational Policies in the Caribbean.* Ph.D. 329 pp. (Education)

Cuba, Haiti, Santo Domingo, the American Virgin Islands and Puerto Rico are treated in separate studies. In general, educational policies have been formulated by American officials, sometimes assisted by local authorities. However, American pride in the achievements of its own public education system sometimes defeats the purpose of education when dealing with foreign peoples. All too often, the cultural content of the Caribbean civilizations was ignored in the endeavor to hasten the creation of educational institutions. In many cases, a short history of the past would have illustrated the unadaptability of an imported educational system.

75   Breswick, William Neale. *Texas' Stake in Foreign Trade.* Ph.D. 101 pp. (Business Administration)

To ascertain the importance of foreign trade in Texas in its overall economic activity and economic expansion, the author presents a derivation of concrete measurements of the extent and significance of Texas' foreign trade, and relates these measurements to corresponding ones for the United States. His findings indicate that Texas' foreign trade is higher than expected and growing faster than the United States' in general. It has stimu-

[ 43 ]

lated the State's economic expansion and contributed to the stability of its overall economic activity.

76  Cramer, Martin John. *Causes, Symptoms, and Specialized Reading Difficulties and a Series of Biographical Stories Constructed for Use in Remedial Reading Classes.* Ph.D. 215 pp. (Latin American Studies: Education)

This dissertation consists of a review of literature on reading handicaps and a series of biographies of the following personages: Thomas Jefferson, Francisco de Miranda, José de San Martín, Bernardo O'Higgins, Benito Juárez, Mariana Grajales, and Dom Pedro II. The purposes of the dissertation were (1) to provide interesting reading material to be used on an instructional level in remedial reading classes and (2) to provide reading material that will be of interest to normal readers on an independent reading level.

77  Crow, George Davis, Jr. *"Los Colloquios Satíricos, con un Colloquio Pastoril, por Antonio de Torquemada," A Critical Edition.* Ph.D. 330 pp. (Romance Languages)

This dissertation presents a critical edition of Antonio de Torquemada's *Colloquios satíricos,* based on an original folio edition published at Mondoñedo in 1553. Torquemada shows considerable knowledge of the classics and exemplifies the spirit of inquiry and constructive criticism representative of the best dialogue literature of the Spanish Renaissance. He presents an excellent portrayal of many customs of his day.

78  Kerr, Homer Lee. *Migration into Texas 1865–1880.* Ph.D. 579 pp. (History)

The quantity and quality of immigration to Texas between 1865 and 1880 is measured in its many facets. Nativity figures are compared with other migration data to analyze the sources and rates of immigration. To determine the age of settlement in a particular area, the author studied the percentage of Texas-born in relation to the aggregate population in the country. Cotton production figures for 1859 and 1879 are compared by counties to show changes in cotton centers, and to indicate the rate of immigration into certain areas of the state.

79  White, Theodore Lawrence. *The Marqués de Rubí's Inspection of the Eastern Presidios on the Northern Frontier of New Spain.* Ph.D. 249 pp. (History)

The inspection by the Marqués de Rubí in 1765 constituted the last futile effort of Spain to stem the onrushing tide of inevitable events which eventually resulted in the loss of all her possessions in North America. Since almost thirty-five years had lapsed since the last inspection and the viceroys of New Spain had repeatedly failed to carry out royal orders to examine the area, the Marqués was commissioned directly by the King. Deplorable conditions and threats of Indian and foreign aggression were remedied by comprehensive reforms and reorganization of the local governments.

80    Wilson, Joe Harvey. *Secondary School Drop-outs, with Special Reference to Spanish-Speaking Youth in Texas.* Ph.D. 244 pp. (Education)

This study found that 82% of the Spanish-speaking boys and girls under consideration have left school before high school graduation. Values and attitudes in the family emphasizing the importance of formal education are lacking. The drop-outs are not accepted by their peer group in school. Classroom teaching is irrelevant in the case of the drop-outs. The study recommends a new, enforceable compulsory school law, legislation to protect potential drop-outs from illegal child labor, work-study programs, guidance services, and teachers trained in Spanish-speaking peoples' culture.

1954

81    Brookshire, Mrs. Marjorie Shepherd. *The Industrial Pattern of Mexican-American Employment in Nueces County, Texas.* Ph.D. 306 pp. (Economics)

The author surveys the industrial employment picture of Mexican-Americans in Nueces County as a whole, as well as several specific non-agricultural industries, to determine the pattern of industrial employment of Mexican-Americans. Most Mexican-Americans were found to be unskilled workers with low occupational status and often receiving lower wages. But there is no evidence of a group characteristic that keeps them from seeking and obtaining advancement and joining unions. The pattern suggests a gradual integration of Mexican-Americans into the whole industrial labor force is taking place through equal employment opportunities with more efficient utilization of manpower in an industrializing community.

82    Carter, James David. *Freemasonry in Texas: Background, History and Influence to 1846.* Ph.D. 613 pp. (History)

The author claims that Freemasonry as a powerful, intellectual force in the formation of American and Texan history to 1846 has been neglected by historians. He relates the Masons and their liberal philosophy to the Anglo-American colonization of Texas, to the Texas Revolution, and to their prominent role in the Republic of Texas. He contends that the political philosophy and the organization of the Texan Revolution and the Texan Republic can be directly traced to Masonic philosophy.

83   Haddick, Jack Allen. *The Administration of Viceroy José de Iturrigaray.* Ph.D. 337 pp. (History)
The author not only examines the salient events just before the Independence movement in Mexico, but also studies the vast and generally successful projects of the viceregal administration, such as the innoculation campaign against smallpox and the construction of a direct road between Veracruz and Mexico City. Of all the events that occurred under Iturrigaray, the forceful execution of the 1804 Decree concerning the pious funds provoked the most bitter reactions against the Spanish government. The author concludes that the forces for independence were so strong that neither Iturrigary nor any other viceroy would have been able to turn aside the revolution.

84   Johnson, Cecil Earl. *The Case of the Pious Fund of the Californias: First Hague Tribunal Settlement.* Ph.D. 364 pp. (Latin American Studies: History)
The Pious Fund of the Californias was a trust estate created by gifts from private individuals for the Christianizing and civilizing of Indians in the area. When Mexico obtained independence it became the new trustee. On October 24, 1842, Santa Anna incorporated the fund into the National Treasury of Mexico, but he reneged on his promise to pay 6% interest per annum of its capitalized value. In 1869 the U.S. prelate of Northern California demanded payment of the interest accrued over the twenty-one year period. The case was appealed until it was finally submitted to the Hague for arbitration. Every contention of the prelates was upheld except for the form of payment.

85   Leifeste, Sam Andrew Dietrich. *Characteristics of the Texas Latin American Market.* Ph.D. 250 pp. (Business Administration)
Texas' nearly two million Latin Americans constitute a fast growing, rapidly developing market, which has been largely ignored. Since Spanish is universally preferred by Latin Americans, many marketeers are rendering a special service to the group by using Spanish in their radio programs and by employing competent Spanish-speaking personnel in stores to serve them. Above all, Latins expect business transactions to be informal and personal. "Word of mouth advertising" assumes an unusual significance. Since a large portion of the market can read English or Spanish only with

difficulty, pictorial trade marks featuring familiar culture items are of great importance.

86  Sánchez, Mrs. Luisa G. G. *The "Latin American" of the Southwest: Backgrounds and Curricular Implications.* Ph.D. 257 pp. (Education)

This study traces the racial and cultural development of the "Latin American" from his earliest known antecedents to his modern relatives. Included is a critical review of the significance of the Latin American's racial and cultural background to current educational programs in the Southwest. Examples of sound educational practices in some school settings in the Southwest conclude the investigation.

## 1955

87  Bacarisse, Charles Albert. *The Baron de Bastrop: Life and Times of Philip Hendrick Nering Bogel, 1759–1827.* Ph.D. 398 pp. (Latin American Studies: History)

The Baron de Bastrop was instrumental in the opening up of Texas for colonization by Anglo-Americans beginning 1805. Bacarisse traces his life history, from his first attempts at colonization and trading to his prominent role as citizen, politician and legislator of the early Republic of Texas, with special emphasis on his collaboration with the Austin family. In all these endeavors, the Baron realized the need of governmental cooperation, be it Spanish, Mexican or American, in the settlement of Texas.

88  Daniel, James Manly. *The Advance of the Spanish Frontier and the Despoblado.* Ph.D. 318 pp. (History)

The Despoblado was the unpopulated area of eastern Chihuahua and western Coahuila, an area avoided in the northward advance of the Spanish frontier because it was thought unfit for Spanish settlement. It was thus left wide open for use as a staging ground by certain nomadic and fierce Indian tribes to strike settlements far south of the Rio Grande. The exposure of the Spanish settlements of Nueva Vizcaya and Coahuila to the constant danger of Indian attacks greatly retarded their growth, until the Spanish military forced the Indians to peaceful settlement in the Despoblado. The Despoblado serves, then, as a stage on which the interaction of three forces may be studied in detail: the Wild Land, the Indian, and the Spaniard.

89  Glade, William Patton, Jr. *The Role of Government Enterprise in the Economic Development of Underdeveloped Regions: Mexico, a Case Study.* Ph.D. 620 pp. (Economics)

The underdeveloped countries have rejected the classical, "market mechanism" theory of economic development. For practical, rather than any new theoretical reasons, the governments of these countries are playing an increasingly active and positive role in their respective national economic development. As a case study, the author studies in great detail the various government enterprises of Mexico: banking, petroleum, electricity, transportation, commerce, etc. From the specific conclusions he reached on Mexico, the author also makes some general propositions concerning the role of government enterprise and intervention in underdeveloped countries in general.

90   Hadley, Bedford Keith. *The Enigmatic Padre Mier.* Ph.D. 341 pp. (History)

This "unbroken, critical, chronological, and narrative" account of the life of Padre Servando Teresa de Mier stresses the three most important aspects of his life: as a member of the Catholic Church, as a writer, and as a political figure in the independent and republican eras. Special attention is given to his second visit to the United States in 1821–1822. The impression Padre Mier leaves is that of a complex, dramatic, megalomaniacal, and above all contradictory, personage.

91   Helms, James Ervin. *Origins and Growth of Protestantism in Mexico to 1920.* Ph.D. 575 pp. (History)

Protestant missionary work in Mexico began with the British and American bible societies, just after the liberal Constitution of 1857 permitted religious freedom. In fact, every president from Juárez to Carranza at least tolerated, if not actively welcomed, the Protestant movement. This study traces the various kinds of work engaged in by the Protestant denominations, from the early Baptists to the 20th century evangelical groups. Although Protestantism has played a minor part in the history of Mexico, it has definitely had a "liberal" influence on the country and on the Catholic Church, especially in terms of education.

92   Lewis, Frank Marshall. *The Political Effects of a Multi-Party System upon the Presidential Form of Government in Chile.* Ph.D. 455 pp. (Government)

The Chilean Constitution of 1925 permitted an unusual combination of the presidential form of government with a multiparty system. The author traces the major political events and party maneuvers of the four presidential administrations from 1932 to 1952 to indicate the steady reshaping of government institutions as a result of strong party pressure upon the presidency.

The government tends towards a type of "parliamentarism." The author also sees an evolution towards a "collegial executive" in which the president would provide continuity and serve as focal point and manager for party policies infused through the Ministry.

93   Maisel, Jay Max. *The Origin and Development of Mexican Antipathy Toward the South, 1821–1867*. Ph.D. 391 pp. (Latin American Studies: History)

The anti-American feeling still prevalent in Mexico today can be traced back to the period 1821–1867. From the Mexican point of view, the failure of her foreign policy and the loss of much of her national territory were due directly to the activities of Southern expansionists and slavocrats. The author discusses in detail several major events between the two countries that led to Mexico's growing resentment: the Texas and California acquisitions, the Mexican War, and the major Confederate activities in Mexico.

94   Neighbours, Kenneth Franklin. *Robert S. Neighbors in Texas, 1836–1859: A Quarter Century of Frontier Problems*. Ph.D. 738 pp. (History)

Robert S. Neighbors was most active in Texas in the period between the Texas Revolution and the Civil War. He was an explorer, a colonizer, and most of all a friend of the Indians. His greatest contribution to Texas was in the capacity of Superintendent of Indian Affairs, when he eased the frontier situation for both white settlers and Indians. After his tragic death at the hands of assassins, the situation of the northern Texas frontier immediately deteriorated.

95   Robertson, Frank Delbert. *The Military and Political Career of Mariano Paredes y Arrillaga, 1797–1849*. Ph.D. 325 pp. (History)

General Paredes was a liberal turned conservative-centralist, who became more and more convinced of the virtues of constitutional monarchy for Mexico. He had great concern for the masses and especially for his troops, whose destitute condition led him to revolt against the government on more than one occasion. Beginning in 1841, he led a series of revolts that toppled each successive government until he himself ascended to the presidency on the eve of war with the United States. After the great loss of territory to the United States, Paredes made one last, but abortive, attempt to rally the nation to a monarchy. Although a great patriot, Paredes lived during the wrong time in history and for this reason, history has neglected him.

96   Teichert, Pedro Carlos Máximo. *Industrial Development Policy in Uruguay*. Ph.D. 307 pp. (Latin American Studies: Economics)

Uruguay has persisted in following the "revolutionary" economic policies of President José Batlle y Ordóñez who advocated, at the turn of the century, private industrial development through government action. This paper emphasizes the post World War II evolution of state and private enterprises, the foreign trade pattern, the rapid growth rate of private industries and the various state monopolies which became the backbone of Uruguay's industrialization drive. Batlle's policies on Uruguay's rate of economic growth had a long-term impact and also influenced general economic theories of development for Latin America.

97   Tunnell, William Kerr. *Bernardo O'Higgins, Chilean Patriot*. Ph.D. 246 pp. (Latin American Studies: History)

The *caudillo* Bernardo O'Higgins was the hero of Chile's war of independence. At the same time that he was fighting in southern Chile to rid the country of the Royalist forces entrenched there, he was also trying to create a navy and organize an expeditionary force to liberate Peru. However, O'Higgins was less successful with the internal administrative problems while serving as president from 1817–1823. Growing dissatisfaction of the people with his failure to improve the economic conditions of the country forced him to resign and go into exile. This paper also includes a detailed study of the Constitution of 1822.

98   Vaughan, Ernest Heath, Jr. *A Study of the Development of National Steel Plants in Selected Latin American Countries*. Ph.D. 264 pp. (Latin American Studies: International Trade)

The basic problem of this study is: Can Latin American nations produce steel and do so profitably? The author studies the national steel plants of Brazil, Chile, Colombia, Mexico and Venezuela in terms of formation, location, physical facilities, production and financing. The investigation continues with how the establishment of national steel plants affects foreign trade and how, in turn, changes in the foreign trade position affect the whole economy. His conclusion is that "national steel plants can provide steel; can do so profitably; and thereby, can benefit the nations which erect and operate them."

99   Whiteside, William J. *Educational Implications of Population Changes in Texas*. Ph.D. 269 pp. (Education)

The author studies the immediate impact upon the framework of public education of the following demographic features: growth and distribution, age structure, and the fertility ratio of the Texas population. The three most potent factors affecting public education in Texas are: the density and ethnic composition of the population, and the production of oil, which affects the socioeconomic conditions behind the support for public education. He provides solutions for some of the problems raised, such as the effects of population trends on educational planning with the development of a more flexible plan for allocation of funds.

## 1956

100   Ashby, Joe Charles. *The Role of the Mexican Labor Movement in the National Economic Policy of the Cárdenas Administration.* Ph.D. 734 pp. (Latin American Studies: Economics)

The author describes how the vital cooperation of the Mexican labor movement, under the leadership of Vicente Lombardo Toledano and the Confederación de Trabajadores Mexicanos, in the 1934–1940 period made possible the realization of President Cárdenas' nationalistic economic policy to free Mexico from economic dependence. The three most important events discussed in great detail are: (1) the nationalization of the national railways: (2) the expropriation and redistribution of cotton *latifundios* in the Laguna district; and (3) the expropriation and nationalization of the foreign-owned petroleum industry.

101   Korth, Eugene Henry. *The Jesuits and the Struggle for Social Justice in Chile, 1535–1674.* Ph.D. 512 pp. (History)

Out of greed and ambition, the Spanish overlords of 16th century Chile treated the Araucanian Indians in such a harsh and abusive way that it provoked a long conflict between the two groups. The Indians were unwilling to surrender their much-prided liberty to foreign rule. At the heart of this conflict was the Indian slave question. Imbued with a sense of social justice, the Jesuits helped the Indians mount an organized campaign against slave labor, with the long-range goal of eliminating all social abuses of the Indian. The Jesuits continued their work with the Indians until "the peaceful conquest" of the Araucanians.

102   Middleton, Russell, Jr. *The Agrarian Programs of Mexico, Yugoslavia, and Israel: A Study in the Social Planning.* Ph.D. 760 pp. (Sociology)

The lack of a theoretical guidepost has led to general aimlessness in much social planning, as well as popular mistrust and confusion about its nature. This study covers in great detail the agrarian planning programs of Mexico, Yugoslavia and Israel. In the case of Mexico, agrarian programs mean primarily the individual and collective ejidos. The purpose is to find any implications in these various programs for future social planning theory, and to investigate the specific conditions that are responsible for the success or failure of these planning ventures.

103   Morton, Luis Meza. *The Close of an Era: Act One of the Mexican Tragedy.* Ph.D. 509 pp. (Latin American Studies: History)

A realistic version of the first phase of the Revolution of 1910 portrays the end of the *Porfiriato,* the dramatic rise and fall of Madero, and the seizing of power by Huerta, who was to lose it again to Carranza. The author also intends to ascertain the more distant and immediate causes of the Revolution and the cross-currents that have confused previous writers on the subject. Madero is presented here as a "well-meaning utopian visionary" rather than as the "redeemer" or the "great genius of democracy." The Revolution itself is presented as a sociological phenomenon arising from discontentment due to institutional abuses. Finally Carranza supplanted Huerta in the name of "constitutionalism" and re-channeled the Revolution towards its true course of social reform.

104   Paredes, Américo. *El Corrido de Gregorio Cortez, A Ballad of Border Conflict.* Ph.D. 454 pp. (English)

El Corrido de Gregorio Cortez is the prototype of the ballad of border conflict between Texas and Mexicans along the lower Rio Grande. This was mostly a cultural conflict between the old, Spanish-speaking inhabitants and the English-speaking newcomers. This dissertation is a critical study of the ballad, from both the historical and the literary points of view. The author hopes to contribute to the comparative study of the folk ballad. He includes in this work a study of the *milieu* that produced the ballad; the development of the ballad of border conflict in general; a transcript of two tunes of the ballad; an English translation by the author of the ballad; and also a discussion of Gregorio Cortez, man and legend.

105   Pike, Frederick Braun. *The Cabildo in Spanish American Colonial Administration.* Ph. D. 830 pp. (Latin American Studies: History)

To study how the average city functioned in the Spanish colonies from 1492–1701 as part of the Hapsburg colonial administration, the author examined the following aspects of the city governments or *cabildos*: the acquisition of office by local officials and the nature of their duties; the acquisition and disbursement by the city of its income; the administration of justice; the conscientiousness and success of local administrators seeking to achieve the "common good" of the citizens; and finally, its relation with other government agencies. Although the *cabildo* was controlled more and more by an oligarchic clique of property owners, it was generally successful in handling litigations, exercising police duties, and contributing to the public welfare.

106  Putnam, Howard L. *The Relation of College Programs of Community Service to the Needs of the Spanish-speaking People.* Ph.D. 317 pp. (Education)

This study is based on the working assumption that colleges can be important instruments in meeting needs of minority groups for acculturation, and that colleges should devote part of their efforts to the social needs of the community. Basing his research in Texas, the author (1) defines the needs of the Spanish-speaking minority in the local community; (2) analyzes the so-called community service programs of various community colleges; and (3) interprets the relationship between the two factors.

107  Rexroat, Ruth. *"Diario de México," First Daily of New Spain: Its Literature.* Ph.D. 309. (Latin American Studies: Romance Languages)

This study portrays the literary activities of Mexico of the early 19th century as shown in the *"Diario de México"* of 1805–1812, whose editors, Juan Wenceslao Barquera and Carlos María Bustamente, were prominent men of letters of the period. The emphasis is on the following subjects: Mexican social types and customs, drama, political discussion of events leading to the War of Independence, books read by the Mexican intellectuals, and, especially, poetry. The *"Diario"* was the springboard for several literary figures of the 19th century, such as the poet Fray Manuel Navarrete.

108  Stauffer, David Hall. *The Origin and Establishment of Brazil's Indian Service: 1889–1910.* Ph.D. 353 pp. (History)

The Serviço de Proteção aos Indios was founded in 1910 to protect the Brazilian Indians against extinction, due to the work of a few far-sighted liberal statesmen. Stiff opposition arose among federalists, businessmen who exploited the Indians, and the Catholic Church, previously responsible for Indian affairs. The author studies in depth (1) the deep penetration and widespread invasion of Indian territory since the founding of the Brazilian Republic in 1889; (2) the debate over whether to exterminate or pacify the hostile Indians who obstructed industrial and national expansion into their territory; and (3) steps by which the national government assumed responsibility for the Indians' welfare.

1957

109  Blair, Calvin Patton. *Fluctuations in United States Imports from Brazil, Colombia, Chile, and Mexico, 1919–1954.* Ph.D. 291 pp. (Economics)

In this empirical study of the impact of United States business cycles on imports from Brazil, Colombia, Chile and Mexico, the author presents in detail a record of fluctuations of imports of these countries and applies a Keynesian analysis to these fluctuations. Although the study cannot satisfactorily explain the international transmission of United States business cycles, it does shed some light on the relation of domestic economic activity to import trade in the United States.

110   Cheavens, Sam Frank. *Vernacular Languages and Education.* Ph.D. 540 pp. (Education)

The study, which encompasses the whole world, includes a section on Latin America, in which the author reports on the use of the vernacular languages in education among the Indians in the various Latin American countries. The research was based mainly on UNESCO programs and reports.

111   Clinkscales, Orline. *Bécquer in Mexico, Central America, and the Caribbean Countries.* Ph.D. 253 pp. (Latin American Studies: Romance Languages)

The author analyses Gustavo Adolfo Bécquer in terms of his poetic qualities, his popularity and his work. He traces the influence of Bécquer on the major poets of Cuba and the Antilles, the Dominican Republic, Puerto Rico and Mexico, where he left his deepest mark, and on the poet Rubén Darío. From Bécquer these American poets learned to draw on their Spanish heritage and have prolonged in Spanish-American poetry a strain of "pure lyricism."

112   Neal, Joe West. *State and Local Government in Northeastern Mexico: Nuevo León, Coahuila and Tamaulipas.* Ph.D. 404 pp. (Latin American Studies: Government)

The greatest difficulty encountered in the evaluation of the Mexican political system is the discrepancy between the constitutional (theoretical) and the actual (operational) governments. The author discusses the heritage of state and local governments from colonial times; the history of the formation of states in Mexico; the political parties and elections; the municipal organization and administration; and the three branches of state government. The national administration and political parties must permit local improvement and reforms, for there is growing local resentment against subjugation of local interests in national policies.

113   Renner, Richard Roy. *Some Characteristics of Spanish-Name Texans and Foreign Latin Americans in Texas Higher Education.* Ph.D. 427 pp. (Education)

This is the study of the adaptability of two cultural minorities—the

Texas-Mexican and the foreign Latin American—to Texas higher education. At the University of Texas, the author investigated the differences between these two cultural groups, especially in terms of socio-economic backgrounds, as well as their differences with the majority Texas Anglo group. Cultural attitudes seem to be the greatest hindrance to adjustment for both groups to American and Anglo dominated schools. This study hopes to help both the Texas-Mexican and the Latin American student take better advantage of Texas higher education.

114   Wheat, Raymond Curtis. *Francisco Zarco, the Liberal Spokesman of La Reforma.* Ph.D. 453 pp. (Latin American Studies: History)

As editor of the leading liberal newspaper of Mexico City—*El Siglo Diez y Nueve*—from 1849 to his death in 1869, Francisco Zarco led the movement for political reform in the years after the war with the United States. He led the rally of liberal forces after the defeat of Santa Anna and exerted a powerful influence on the ideology of La Reforma and the Constitution of 1857. He also served his country as member of the cabinet and member of congress. This study is confined to his work in political journalism, mainly developed in the editorials he wrote for his newspaper.

1958

115   Bushnell, Clyde Gilbert. *The Military and Political Career of Juan Álvarez, 1790–1867.* Ph.D. 361 pp. (Latin American Studies: History)

The controversial Mexican *caudillo*, Don Juan Álvarez, was a liberal who alienated both the Church and the Military. The author brings him out of oblivion by tracing his political and military career, his fight alongside Vicente Guerrero against the Spanish, his victory over Santa Anna at Ayutla, his term as president, and finally his role in the War of Reform and the Wars of Intervention, when he helped drive the French out of Mexico.

116   Frazier, Charles Edward, Jr. *The Dawn of Nationalism and its Consequences in Nicaragua.* Ph.D. 614 pp. (History)

The interventionist and "imperialist" role of the United States in Nicaragua since 1909 led to the nationalist movement of the late twenties led by Augusto Calderón (César) Sandino, pursued and persecuted by both the United States government and the two political parties of Nicaragua as a bandit and a "communist." Finally, in 1936, the self-proclaimed assassin of Sandino, General Somoza, rose to power with the support of the *Guardia Nacional,* an organization imposed upon the Nicaraguans by the United States. Throughout this period of Nicaraguan history, the United

States government vacillated betwen a "hands off" and an interventionist policy.

117   McNeely, John Hamilton. *The Politics and Development of the Mexican Land Program*. Ph.D. 753 pp. (History)

The author studies the Mexican land problem and its intimate relations to political trends and the personalities of the various leaders of the movement, particularly that of Villa. He discusses the background of the land situation, the Indians and their land problem, the colonization laws and the *latifundios*. Then he traces the rise of the agrarian movement from colonial days to its revolutionary apex, and to its recession upon the defeat of the Villa-Zapata alliance at the "Sovereign Convention" of 1915. Mining, petroleum and the railroads are related to the land program because the principle of expropriation of private property rights was applied to these cases. The study brings the picture of the agrarian programs up to date.

118   Niemeyer, Eberhardt Victor, Jr. *The Public Career of General Bernardo Reyes*. Ph.D. 379pp. (Latin American Studies: History)

This study intends to clear up the confusion concerning the tragic blunders and mistakes Bernardo Reyes made during the last four years of his life. Acclaimed popularly as the natural successor to Díaz, he was branded a coward when he refused out of personal loyalty to challenge his former superior. Subsequently he was branded a traitor for his two abortive revolts against Madero, in 1911 and in 1913, in which he died heroically. As the most successful governor of the *Porfiriato,* he created an industrial and commercial center in Nuevo León under his "benevolent dictatorship." He was a true product of, and contributor to, the authoritarian porfirian régime, and could not adapt to the new liberalism of Madero.

119   Ronan, Charles Edward. *Francisco Javier Mariano Clavigero: A Study in Mexican Historiography*. Ph.D. 201 pp. (History)

Clavigero, along with Sahagún and Torquemada, is a prominent figure in the literature on ethnography of Middle America. His main contribution lies in making known to Europe the existence of ancient Mexico at a time when the Enlightenment was stirring up debate over the relative virtues of the Old and New World. The author analyzes his main work, the *Historia antigua,* in terms of the history of its publication, the work itself, and its sources.

120   Walper, Jack Louis. *Geology of the Coban-Purulha Area, Alta Verapaz, Guatemala*. Ph.D. 113 pp. (Geology)

The Coban-Purulha area in Central Guatemala lies in the folded and faulted ranges of the Central Mountain System which extends eastward from Chiapas, Mexico, across Guatemala and into the Caribbean Sea. The author studies the stratigraphy, structural geology, beomorphology, geologic history and the economic geology of the area.

## 1959

121   Broussard, Ray Francis. *Ignacio Comonfort: His Contributions to the Mexican Reform, 1855–57*. Ph.D. 288 pp. (History)

Ignacio Comonfort emerges in this study as a figure of strength and tolerance who attempted to end the violent cycle of revolution and counter-revolution in nineteenth century Mexico. Succeeding Álvarez as president from 1855–1857 he worked diligently to hold back his more radical liberal companions as well as the reactionaries, in order to put his ideas of unity and slow moderate reform into effect. Broussard concludes that although Comonfort's efforts to establish a nonpartisan government failed, some of his economic and educational changes still remain in force.

122   Donald, Carr Lowe. *The Brazilian Municipio: The Myth of Local Self-Government*. Ph.D. 344 pp. (Government)

An examination of the theoretical and practical relationships between governmental authorities by examining historical and contemporary institutions points up the lack of self-government and the unpopularity of localism in Brazil. Comparing Brazilian local government with its American counterpart, Donald emphasizes the detrimental effect of centralism in Brazil as it has molded popular attitudes, encouraged the multi-party system, and reduced the status of *municipios* to dependent administrative entities.

123   Gibson, Delbert Lee. *Protestantism in Latin American Acculturation*. Ph.D. 298 pp. (Sociology)

This study deals with the problem of testing the major hypothesis that Protestant churches are significant cultural mechanisms through which Latin Americans acquire basic American values. Statistical data were gathered primarily from a case study of Latin Americans in Austin, Texas, in which a control group of Catholic families and an experimental group of Protestant families were interviewed. Gibson concludes that Protestant church affiliation is both a cause for and an evidence of acculturation, just as in the basic institutional changes of the family, economics and religion.

124   Holmes, Jack David Lazarus. *Gallant Emissary: The Political Career*

*of Manuel Gayoso de Lemos in the Mississippi Valley, 1789–1799.* Ph.D. 215 pp. (Latin American Studies: History)

The political career of Manuel Gayoso de Lemos illustrates the problems of Spanish colonial administration in the Mississippi Valley. As governor of the Natchez District, 1789–97, and as governor-general of Louisiana and West Florida, 1797–99, he was to attract Americans to Louisiana and to maintain Spanish rights in the Mississippi Valley without provoking war. Simultaneously he built an alliance with the southern Indian nations and strengthened the defenses, in order to restrain American expansion into Mexico.

125  Lewis, George King. *An Analysis of the Institutional Status and Role of the Petroleum Industry in Mexico's Evolving System of Political Economy.* Ph.D. 403 pp. (Latin American Studies: Economics)

A cross-reference of the historical experience and organizational development of the Mexican petroleum industry with the institutional structure and development of the Mexican political economy contributes to this quantitative analysis of the economic performance of Petróleos Mexicanos in the postwar period. Lewis considers Mexico's efforts (1) to nationalize the subsoil, 1918–38; (2) to integrate Pemex within the national institutional structure, 1938–47; and (3) to reorient the economic and technological operations of Pemex to satisfy domestic demand, 1947–58.

126  Meador, Bruce Staffel. *Minority Groups and Their Education in Hays County, Texas.* Ph.D. 373 pp. (Education)

Attempts to explain personality as a function of "racial" inheritance are not tenable in the light of modern research. The school and community environment in Hays County, Texas, could inhibit personality development among many Latin American and Negro inhabitants. Teacher opinion interviews, a detailed description of school attendance, chronological ages of students, and information on scholastic achievement test results are included.

127  Sáenz, Gerardo. *El "Viejecito": vida del poeta Luis G. Urbina.* (Spanish Text). Ph.D. 391 pp. (Romance Languages—Literature)

Sáenz emphasizes the autobiographical aspects of the works of the Mexican poet, Luis G. Urbina (1864–1934). Urbina's poetic and prose work, including protests against social ills, literary criticism and commentaries on contemporary theater, is also discussed and a comprehensive bibliography lists in chronological order all his writings published in newspapers and magazines. By establishing his date of birth as earlier than previously believed, it becomes clear that he was not a real pupil of Manuel Gutiérrez Nájera, for he was too young to have been so decidedly influenced.

128   Troike, Rudolph Charles, Jr. *A Descriptive Phonology and Morphology of Coahuilteco.* Ph.D. 139 pp. (Romance Languages—Linguistics)

Coahuilteco, an extinct Indian language formerly spoken in southern Texas and northeastern Mexico, was pivotal in the development of Sapir's hypothesis regarding the Hokan-(Coahuiltecan)-Siouan languages super stock. This first descriptive linguistic analysis of Coahuilteco is based on the Spanish-Coahuilteco text of a confession written in 1760 by Bartholomé García.

129   White, Byron. *Cuba and Puerto Rico: A Case Study in Comparative Economic Development Policy.* Ph.D. 443 pp. (Economics)

This comparison of economic development policies suggests that Cuba with its wider unused resource base is likely to surpass Puerto Rico's growth rate during the next planning period. White presents background information on the principal sources of aggregate income and the cane sugar industry in both countries, and then discusses the industrialization and developmental programs which both began around 1950.

1960

130   Brubaker, George Allen. *Santa Fé de Bogotá: A Study of Municipal Development in Eighteenth-Century Spanish America.* Ph.D. 187 pp. (History)

The cultural, educational, religious, economic, financial and political development of the municipality provides an insight into the environment in which the eighteenth-century governing institution, the *Cabildo,* operated. The Spanish American *cabildo* touched almost every aspect of day-to-day activity in Santa Fé de Bogotá and was intricately involved in all economic, social, and religious matters. The *cabildo* was not democratic or representative, but it was an important force among the people, and provided, however haphazardly, for the material needs, law enforcement, and even entertainment of the community.

131   Bryant, Bill Bernice. *Certification Requirements for Elementary-School Principles in the United States and Puerto Rico.* Ed.D. 277 pp. (Education)

This analysis of minimum certification requirements in general education, undergraduate professional education, and graduate professional education compared data obtained from each state department of education with a list of criteria drawn from a survey of professional literature. The comparison showed the minimum requirements for general and professional education to be deficient, especially in graduate professional preparation.

132 Jeffery, Sylvia Viera. *An Examination of the Cultural Materials in the State-Adopted Textbooks Currently in Use for the Teaching of Spanish in the Secondary Schools of Texas.* Ph.D. 197 pp. (Education—Curriculum and Instruction)

The purpose of this study is to determine the extent to which textbooks for the teaching of Spanish currently in use in the public schools in Texas help to achieve the objective of cultural understanding between North America and Spanish America. The author emphasized the objective of cultural understanding as one of the basic tenets of foreign-language instruction. The author hopes for a more functional and valid use of cultural and linguistic materials in the teaching of Spanish to students with English-speaking backgrounds. Such a task necessarily places a huge burden on the teachers of the foreign language.

133 Mudie, John Howard. *The Role of the Government Development Bank in Puerto Rico's Economic Program.* Ph.D. 204 pp. (Latin American Studies: Economics)

Mudie contends that the Government Development Bank for Puerto Rico, an autonomous public agency of the Commonwealth, has contributed to that country's rapid economic progress. As examples of Bank leadership, he points to the mobilization of private capital for developmental lending and the Bank's role as a fiscal agency for the government channeling investment funds into public projects to support the growing industrial community. The Bank also provides leadership and initiative in Puerto Rico's financial development, gives technical assistance to other governmental agencies, and serves as a clearing house for checks.

134 Oberdoerffer, Marianne. *Contemporary Mexican Theater 1923–1959.* Ph.D. 244 pp. (Romance Languages—Literature)

An appraisal of the Mexican theater from 1923–1959 shows how both drama and comedy reflect the ideas, attitudes and tendencies of certain periods. The chapters are divided into threee chronological groups emphasizing the thematic development of the theater and its gradual change from the treatment of problems peculiar to the Mexican scene to topics of universal interest and significance. Although the decade from 1940–1950 was a period of transition, the 1950's ushered in a new phase, reflecting a diversity of trends and topics.

135   Graham, Thomas Richard. *The British Impact on Brazil, 1850–1918.* Ph.D. 439 pp. (History)

One of the chief aspects of the British impact was the exportation to Brazil of goods, capital, and technology, but there was also a significant transfer of middle-class ideology to an aristocratic society. The economic and social transformations within Brazil were reflected in its changing relationship with Great Britain.

Historians studying the eclectic Brazilian society must consider the British influence as a key factor in that country's development. Before 1850 Brazil knew little of Britain's economy or ideology, while by the time of World War I other countries were becoming increasingly important. The period from 1850 to 1918 can be called the age of British impact.

136   Powell, James Daniel. *Stratigraphy of Cenomanian-Turonian (Cretaceous) Strata, Northeastern Chihuahua and Adjacent Texas.* Ph.D. 112 pp. (Geology)

The Ojinaga Formation in the Chihuahua-Texas border region includes the least interrupted sequence of strata of the latter part of early Cenomanian through early Turonian age in North America and has yielded the best known collections of late early Cenomanian ammonites. The scarcity of late Cenomanian fossils in the seemingly conformable shale section of the formation is attributed to lack of preservation in the 800 to 1,000 feet of shale between the middle Cenomanian matelliceratine beds and the Salmurian.

137   Smith, Margaret Harrison. *The Lower Río Grande Region in Tamaulipas, Mexico.* Ph.D. 448 pp. (Geography)

The historical, physical, and economic geography of the Mexican portion of the Rio Grande flood plain and delta is described, based on five periods of field study from 1952–1957. It was not until the nineteenth-century that the opening of the port of Matamoros, the pacification of the region, and more recently the construction of large-scale irrigation and drainage works that the region has started developing. The lower Rio Grande region in Tamaulipas has become the leading cotton, natural gas, and oil producing area in Mexico; and is becoming one of that country's most important agricultural and future industrial districts.

138   Travis, David Edward. *The Life and Works of Carlos González-Peña.* Ph.D. 203 pp. (Romance Languages—Literature)

This analysis of the life and work of Carlos González-Peña (1885–1955) assigns him an important place in Mexican literature. His naturalistic novels, textbooks on Spanish and Mexican literature, travel books, ten volumes of selected essays, chronicles, newspaper articles, and literary and music critiques, illustrate his versatility as a writer and his thoroughness as a scholar. The accompanying bibliography is as complete as the author could make.

## 1962

139   Bridges, Luther Wadsworth, II. *Geology of Mina Plomosas Area, Chihuahua, Mexico.* Ph.D. 272 pp. (Geology)

Three previously unrecognized outcrops of pre-Carboniferous rocks in the Mina Plomosas-Placer de Guadalupe area have a total area of slightly less than four square miles. The 2,000 feet pre-Permian section is predominantly limestone. The 2,000 feet to 3,000 feet Permian section is predominantly siltstone and conglomerate, and the 3,000 feet Late Jurassic rock is shale, sandstone, and limestone. Lead, zinc and gold mineralization is thought to be Tertiary in age.

140   Daugherty, Franklin Wallace. *Geology of the Pico Etereo Area, Municipio de Acuña, Coahuila, Mexico.* Ph.D. 170 pp. (Geology)

The area covered lies within one of the most important fluorspar districts in Mexico, between the Serranía del Burro and the Sierra del Carmen arches. Approximately 3,200 feet of Cretaceous sedimentary rock, predominantly limestone, rest on a base of pre-Mesozoic schist. The Tertiary Sytem consists almost entirely of sodic intrusive igneous rocks. The area bears great promise for the discovery of new ore bodies and the extension of known ore bodies.

141   Dunn, Brother Fabius. *The Administration of Don Antonio Cordero, Governor of Texas, 1805–1808.* Ph.D. 498 pp. (History)

Don Antonio Cordero became acting governor of the Spanish province of Texas in 1805, where there were only three settlements with a total population of about 4,000 persons after over 100 years of Spanish occupation. The account of Cordero's efforts on behalf of the security and development of the province reveals the faults of overcentralzation and bureaucracy in the existing system of military government and speculates on the alternative courses Spain might have adopted to save Texas.

142   Goldwert, Marvin. *The Argentine Revolution of 1930: The Rise of Modern Militarism and Ultra-Nationalism in Argentina.* Ph.D. 259 pp. (History)

A historical background of the rise of militarism in Argentina shows the changing role of the army from 1825 to 1916. The economic depression, collapse of the political system, the discontentment of the secret military society, and the emergence of new power factors set the stage for the Argentine Revolution of 1930, the army's first overt intervention in politics. The study concludes with the emergence of General Augustín P. Justo in the struggle for power with General José F. Uriburu.

143   Gonzalez, Alfonso. *Land Utilization of Southwestern Coastal Mexico: Colima and Michoacán.* Ph.D. 885 pp. (Geography)

Agriculture has been the dominant economic endeavor of the region of Colima and Coastal Michoacán from Pre-Cortesian times. However, crop production and land use have changed considerably, reflecting shifts in market conditions and the development of regional and commodity competition. The staple commodities of subsistence agriculture and the dietary habits of the inhabitants have changed very little since the colonial period. The region was for many years out of the mainstream of development and was a fringe area of settlement and economic exploitation. Since the agrarian reforms of the 1930's, however, the government has encouraged development and exploitation of the coastal region and expanded and intensified the land under cultivation.

144   Hoskin, Charles Morris. *Recent Carbonate Sedimentation on Alacran Reef, Yucatan, Mexico.* Ph.D. 270 pp. (Geology)

Hoskin analyzes recent surface sediments on the Alacran Reef, a living coral continental shelf atoll in the Gulf of Mexico. The proportion of each size grade in sediment reflects the depositional environment of the three major areas: the windward reef, the leeward reef, and the lagoon. Hard parts from marine organisms composed of aragonite and calcite, and a trace of siliceous particles form the sands, silts and gravels of the deposits.

145   Porter, Kenneth Raymond. *Evolutionary Relationship of the* BUFO VALLICEPS *Group in Mexico.* Ph.D. 157 pp. (Zoology)

A study of the evolutionary relationships of the *Bufo valliceps* group in Mexico was made through consideration of the species distribution, morphological comparisons, mating call comparisons, and chromotographic comparisons of the parotoid gland secretions. Because of morphological similarities, the following species were included: *Bufo canaliferus* Cope, *B. cristatus* Wiegmann, *B. cavifrons* Firschein, *B. coccifer* Cope, *B. gemmifer* Taylor, *B. mazatlanensis* Taylor, and *B. valliceps* Wiegman.

146   Sáez, Mercedes de los Angeles. *Puerto Rican-English Phonotactics.* Ph.D. 157 pp. (English)

The order characteristics of phonemes and the recurrences of certain arrangements of phonemes in English are compared with Puerto Rican Spanish based on the spoken language. Data gathered from questionnaires administered to twenty-two informants reveal some of the problems in teaching and learning English in Puerto Rico and point to possible procedures for avoiding difficulties.

147   Van Patton, James Jeffers. *Education in the United Mexican States.* Ph.D. 449 pp. (Education)

This analysis of the Mexican school system of Mexico discusses its philosophical base, organization, and administration from pre-Conquest period to the present, in view of its geographical and cultural heritage and historical background. It surveys the various levels of Mexican education and the legal base for each level of education. The government places great emphasis on education, devoting approximately 20% of its budget as a prime means to raise the standard of living of the country.

148   Wilkins, Billy Hughel. *Effects on the Economy of Venezuela of Actions by the International Petroleum Industry and United States Regulating Agencies.* Ph.D. 263 pp. (Economics)

Wilkins examines the fluctuations of the world petroleum market, dominated by the United States, and examines the consequences on the oil industry in Venezuela. Since the overall development of Venezuela and many other small countries depends heavily on the petroleum industry, Wilkins suggests that the United States take the lead in proposing certain revisions in current regulations which could yield greater market flexibility while maintaining a high U.S. production potential and giving the exporting nations an assured minimum market.

## 1963

149   Bennett, Robert Lee. *Financial Intermediaries in Mexican Economic Development, 1944–1960.* Ph.D. 480 pp. (Economics)

An analysis of the role of financial intermediaries in the Mexican capital funds market during the "take-off" period uses linear least square regression equations to study four sectors and subsectors of real flow of funds. Using a theory which emphasizes the allocation function of financial intermediaries rather than their role as repositories of the public's liquid savings, Bennett concludes that planned financial intermediary flows of funds may play a significant permissive role during the early stages of industrial development.

150   Cooper, Donald Bolon. *Epidemic Disease in Mexico City: 1761–1813.* Ph.D. 280 pp. (History)

This social and medical history of the five severe epidemics, chiefly small-pox and typhus, in Mexico City between 1761 and 1813 is based almost entirely on unpublished manuscript materials from the National Archives of Mexico and the Municipal Archives of Mexico City. It suggests that the epidemics, which claimed over 50,000 lives, were the single most potent threat to human life and well-being during the closing years of the colonial period.

151   Cowart, Billy Frank. *The Educational Philosophy of Jaime Torres Bodet and its Implications for Mexican and World Education.* Ph.D. 284 pp. (Education)

The educational philosophy of Jaime Torres Bodet and its practcial application in both Mexican and world education is examined. Cowart presents a historical analysis of the problems confronting Mexican education prior to Bodet's first term as Secretary of Public Education. An annotated chronology describes the major events of his life. A detailed analysis of the major postulates of his philosophy presents a discussion of his conception of the Real, the cosmos as it is today, and the Ideal, as it "ought to be." As Secretary of Education and of UNESCO, Bodet has stressed the elimination of illiteracy and the primary school problem, as well as the enhancement of the love for books.

152   Gabbert, Jack Benton. *The Evolution of the Mexican Presidency.* Ph.D. 461 pp. (Government)

An examination of the Mexican presidency in its legal, historical, and political setting as it evolved from a highly personalized to an institutionalized agency of government since 1824 indicates that the office itself has become more significant than the personal characteristics of its incumbent. While this trend has lessened the likelihood of a military dictatorship occurring, it has not necessarily detracted from the presidential power. Gabbert concludes that the modern Mexican presidency is a reasonably responsible instrument of government because it must respond to a series of complex political and economic pressures.

153   Key, E. Mary Ritchie. *Comparative Phonology of the Tacanan Languages.* Ph.D. 131 pp. (Romance Languages—Linguistics)

The several Tacanan languages of northern Bolivia comprise a family in an area which is notable for its many "unclassified" or "independent" languages. The relationship of these languages has long been recognized, but this is the first study which gives in detail the correspondences and the conditioning of the reflexes. Three languges, Cavineña, Tacana, and Chama, make up the main material. Additional data are given from Reyesano and Huarayo, showing the reflexes from the proto-language, which can be established.

154   Key, Harold Hayden. *Morphology of Cayuvava.* Ph.D. 98 pp. (Romance Languages—Linguistics)

Based on data obtained from two of the last six known fluent speakers of the Cayuvava language of the Bolivian jungles, Key has found that 50% of the words occurring in general utterances are of verbal semantic value, 25% are nouns, and the other three classes comprise the remaining 25%. This emphasis on the verb illustrates the nucleus-satellite relation of the components of the language.

155   Lemus, George. *Francisco Bulnes: Su Vida y Sus Obras.* (Spanish Text) Ph.D. 263 pp. (Latin American Studies: Literature)

Lemus presents the life of Francisco Bulnes, one of the most controversial and outspoken deputies of the Mexican Congress of Porfirio Díaz. As a political and intellectual leader of the positivist school of thought, he contributed to its European-oriented, "elite" group theory of politics. His sociological and historical writings, although not always accepted as real scholarship, were in their time seen as positivist criticism of the social conditions in Mexico, whose solution could only come through heavy immigration to change the predominantly Indian and mestizo population of the Republic.

156   Waits, Caron Richard. *Financial and Real Growth in Venezuela: A Study of the Relationship between Financial and Real Variables.* Ph.D 205 pp. (Economics)

This study of Venezuela, as typical of financial development in an expanding economy, concludes that the pattern of financial institution development reflects a change in the attitudes of savers and a willingness to hold indirect as well as direct securities. Policy should also be guided by the potential these institutions have for achieving real growth through more efficient fund allocations and greater opportunities to increase the propensities to save and invest.

157   Walker, Elna LaVerne. *Teaching English as a Second Language to Spanish-Speaking Adults.* Ph.D. 184 pp. (Education)

Walker describes certain principles and facts about the English language which have been discovered by modern linguistic science and selects those which can be used in the teaching of American English pronunciation to Spanish-speaking adults. The second objective was to construct a manual of pronunciation drills based upon the application of these selected linguistic data which would aid teachers without linguistic backgrounds and for Spanish-speaking adults with low level scholastic achievement.

## 1964

158 Aponte, Barbara Ann Bockus. *The Spanish Friendships of Alfonso Reyes*. Ph.D. 656 pp. (Romantic Languages—Literature)

The lifelong friendship and correspondence of Mexican author Alfonso Reyes with seven Spanish writers, Azorín, Ramón Gómez de la Serna, Ramón Menéndez Pidal, Juan Ramón Jiménez, Ramón del Valle-Inclán, José Ortega y Gasset, and Enrique Díez-Canedo, is discussed. Aponte concludes that the influence of the Spanish atmosphere on Reyes' literary career and, conversely, the effect of the Mexican writer on the cultural life of Madrid, formed one of the first significant links between the Spanish and Latin American writers.

159 Bourgeois, Louis Clarence. *Augusto d'Halmar, Chilean Novelist and Storyteller*. Ph.D. 399 pp. (Romance Languages—Literature)

The primary importance of the legendary Chilean writer Augusto d'Halmar (Augusto Goemine Thompson, 1882–1950) was a mentor and inspiration for his own and succeeding generations as he channeled new European literary ideas to South America. His works did affect two changes in Chilean prose by introducing an element of fantasy or imagination and by serving as models for a more elegant style.

160 Brown, Lyle Clarence. *General Lázaro Cárdenas and Mexican Presidential Politics, 1933–1940: A Study in the Acquisition and Manipulation of Political Power*. Ph.D. 344 pp. (Government)

In acquiring and manipulating political power, Cárdenas combined talents of personal leadership with organizational skill and political acumen. He achieved his objectives with a minimum use of force and under conditions, which, if handled differently, might well have plunged Mexico back into chaos such as had happened in earlier years with damaging results. Through his agrarian, education, and labor reforms, conciliatory policy towards the church, oil expropriation, and institutionalization of the political party, he was able to guide Mexico through a transitional period from an epoch of revolt into an extended period of political stability and socio-economic progress.

161 Cárdenas, Leonard, Jr. *Municipal Administration in Mexican Border States*. Ph.D. 195 pp. (Latin American Studies: Government)

This Study seeks to explain how municipal administration in the Mexican states of Chihuahua, Coahuila, Nuevo León, and Tamaulipas meets urban problems; to determine the influence of the United States on the municipality; and to analyze the status of the border municipality within the state and in the nation. Structural rigidity and lack of independent city government, similar to the United States' institution, has prevented municipal administrations from meeting urban and border problems.

162   Coons, Dix Scott. *Horacio Quiroga—The Master Storyteller:A Study of the Creative Processes.* Ph.D. 319 pp. (Romance Languages—Literature)

Coons says that Quiroga's fictional narratives on man and his search for meaning in life are valuable examples of the processes through which a writer's experiences become literature and through which the reader enters the poetic world and shares in its experiences. Bibliographic and chronological information on Quiroga's literary production is included.

163   Lozano, Anthony Girard. *A Study of Spoken Styles in Colombian Spanish.* Ph.D. 181 pp. (Romance Languages—Linguistics)

Lozano examines each of eight recorded samples representing different social contexts on phonological, morphological, syntactic, and other pertinent levels. For example, consideration is given to formal relationships between sentences. Within the overall pattern of language, he strives for a more thorough definition of style in terms of a set of linguistic features.

164   McClendon, Juliette Jane Canfield. *Spanish-Speaking Children of Big Spring — Educational Challenge.* Ph.D. 177 pp. (Latin American Studies: Education)

This is a sociological, psychological and linguistic analysis of the clash of two cultures in the lives of Spanish-speaking primary age school children enrolled in the public schools of Big Spring, Texas. Personal contact with children and interviews with their parents and with adults in the community have provided the research data. The child from an ethnic minority group has contacts which are limited by indefinable barriers in the larger societal structure.

165   McFarland, Floyd Brant. *An Analysis of Relationships between Foreign Economic Policy and Economic Development in Mexico.* Ph.D. 269 pp. (Economics)

The lack of adequate capital formation, the inefficiency and smallness of the scale of domestic enterprises, and the continuing practice of exporting primarily agricultural crops and raw materials has made it difficult for

Mexico to secure the necessary quantities of foreign exchange for purchases of machinery and materials essential for development in the postwar protected economy. McFarland contends that good economic planning, including reform of the public revenue system and large-scale standardization of manufacturing for export, could increase government earnings to finance better social services and to buy up some of the present foreign holdings.

166 Oei, Hong Lan. *Petroleum Resources and Economic Development: A Comparative Study of Mexico and Indonesia.* Ph.D. 314 pp. (Economics)

With the framework of institutional change caused by the social revolution in both countries, this analysis attempts to show whether petroleum resources have been utilized efficiently and economically for the achievement of development goals which evolved during the revolution in both countries. Petroleos Mexicanos, the state monopoly of petroleum in Mexico since 1938, has indeed paved the way for industrialization by inducing domestic consumption of energy. The Indonesian industry, which is dominated by major integrated international companies, is still basically export-oriented.

167 Parigi, Sam Frank. *A Case Study of Latin American Unionization in Austin, Texas.* Ph.D. 407 pp. (Economics)

This case study traces the stages of organization from the workers' initial inquiries about unionism, through secret meetings and organization campaigns, to the problems of servicing and maintaining a union once it has been recognized. In a twelve-point "Blueprint for Organizing Minority Groups," Parigi concludes that semi-skilled workers belonging to minority groups in the South and Southwest, despite hindering economic and non-economic human factors, are ready for unionization, but that unions must take a fresh, vigorous approach to organization in order to capitalize on this opportunity.

168 Scaperlanda, Anthony Edward, Jr. *The Contribution of the Latin American Free Trade Association to Latin American Welfare: A Preliminary Survey Applying the Theory of Economic Integration.* Ph.D. 377 pp. (Economics)

This integrated, preliminary survey analysis of the Latin American Free Trade Associations' impact on industrial production supplements the traditional theory of economic integration with a "dynamic institutional aspect of the theory." This approach provides the possibility of institutional mutation in both LAFTA's public and private sectors to permit the application of advanced technology and the creation of intrazonal financial arrangements and external economics. Influence of the Church and of market size is used also to evaluate and LAFTA impact. Scaperlanda says that if LAFTA is to achieve its potential, internal transportation facilities must be improved.

## 1965

169   Bennett, Peter Dunne. *The Role of the Government in the Promotion of Efficiency in the Retail Marketing of Food Products in Greater Santiago, Chile.* Ph.D. 183 pp. (Business Administration)

Both national and municipal governments in Chile participate actively in the food marketing process. Their roles include regulator of prices, provider of the infrastructure and market information, collector of taxes, regulator of market participation, and as entrepreneur. Acting as entrepreneur— entering the market as a competitor—the government has been the most successful in promoting efficiency, while in its regulator capacity, it has tended to have the opposite effect.

170   Carter, Thomas Pelham. *An Analysis of Some Aspects of Culture and the School in Peru.* Ph.D. 355 pp. (Education)

This comparative educational analysis of the school in relation to Peruvian society surveys the nation's history and its present changing culture. The school in operation, including curriculum, goals, and philosophy, are described. Carter concludes that the present teaching of absolute and unrealistic values and academic abstractions must be modified if Peruvian education is to significantly aid in the formation of a democratic twentieth-century nation.

171   Cole, William Edward. *The Mexican Steel Industry and its Impact on the Mexican Economy.* Ph.D. 280 pp. (Economics)

This historical survey of the growth of the Mexican steel and iron industry considers its impact on other sectors of the economy and the role of government in financing and protecting the industry. Cole says that the continuing growth of the steel industry has promoted growth of those industries which supply steel's inputs such as domestic coal and iron ore mining, as well as having an impact upon both unit cost and foreign exchange savings per unit of output.

172   Cornehls, James Vernon. *Mexico's Rural Road to Progress: An Analysis of Agrarian Reform and Agricultural Development.* Ph.D. 253 pp. (Economics)

President Lázaro Cárdenas (1934–1940) was the man most responsible for turning agrarian promises into reality after the 1910 Revolution. Social reforms and institutional adjustments involving land redistribution into ejidos, reorganization of privately owned lands, have both promoted greater growth and efficiency. Cornehls says that in spite of barriers erected by opponents, the land reform program has served as a catalyst in a complex chain of socio-economic adjustments which have sped the development of agriculture and hastened the arrival of the Mexican economy to the level of sustained growth.

173   Jaén, Didier Tisdel. *Hispanoamérica como Problema a través de la generación romántica en Argentina y Chile.* Ph. D. 237 pp. (Romance Languages—Literature)

Jaén says that in spite of many efforts and attempts, Spanish America has not attained a degree of human felicity and development that satisfies the hopes and expectations that have been centered around it by the Spanish Americans themselves. He then examines the manifestations of this preoccupation as a result of the impact of Romantic thought and sentiment in Argentina and Chile in the first part of the nineteenth-century. The Romantics rightfully saw that states must know the peoples that are to be governed and laws should emerge from the life and history of the people; but this democratic view was ignored due to economic problems.

174   Jones, Lamar Babbington. *Mexican-American Labor Problems in Texas.* Ph.D. 244 pp. (Economics)

This examination of manpower policy as it pertains to agricultural labor and immigration reveals that domestic workers have had employment opportunities usurped by alien contract farm workers resulting in forced seasonal migration for Mexican-American workers. Jones calls for the development of broader and more stable employment opportunities for Mexican-Americans in Texas through revisions of immigration procedures and existing worker retraining programs.

175   Lancaster, Michael Odell. *Pedrarias Dávila.* Ph.D. 270 pp. (Latin American Studies: History)

At the age of 74, Pedrarias Dávila (1440?–1531) went to America as the first royal Spanish governor of Panamá and Nicaragua. He pitted his experience and cunning against the ambition and intrigue of numerous young adventurers. He resorted to all measures to eliminating opposition to him, as well as robbing and killing thousands of the Indian inhabitants.

[ 71 ]

His influence in the conquest of America continued after his death in the exploits of his famous lieutenants: De Soto, Pizarro, Almagro and Belalcázar.

176   Landolt, Robert Garland. *The Mexican-American Workers of San Antonio, Texas.* Ph.D. 396 pp. (Economics)

The nature of the utilization of Mexican-American workers in Texas cities and the probable causes of ethnic imbalances in employment and incomes are considered in this study. The programs designed to accelerate assimilation of the economically disadvantaged are evaluated. Inadequate education and training, compounded by English language deficiency and *de facto* segregation in schools, are cited as the greatest barriers to economic advancement of Mexican-Americans.

177   Macaulay, Neill Webster, Jr. *Sandino and the Marines: Guerrilla Warfare in Nicaragua, 1927–1933.* Ph.D. 337 pp. (History)

The guerrilla campaign in Nicaragua led by General Augusto C. Sandino from 1927–1932 adopted the hit-and-run tactic in response to a "new kind of intervention" involving American military occupation of the country and maintenance of order while political power remained nominally in the hands of the native government. Macaulay credits this U.S. policy with turning Sandino, a former friend of the Americans, into the idol of the Latin American opponents of "Yankee imperialism."

178   Myers, Ralph Lawrence, II. *Biostratigraphy of the Cardenas Formation (Upper Cretaceous), San Luis Potosí, Mexico.* Ph.D. 186 PP. (Geology)

The Cardenas Formation is a very fossiliferous 1050 meter thick unit of finely clastic sedimentary rock that crops out in an asymmetric syncline in the folded Sierra Madre Oriental. Of the eleven measured sections, two were structurally uncomplicated and complete enough to establish the sequence of stratigraphic units.

179   Schooler, Robert Dale. *An Inquiry into Product Bias and Predilection within the Central American Common Market.* Ph.D. 104 pp. (Economics)

One hundred respondents in this study evaluated each of two products four times as coming from four different countries. Actually, the products were from the same country. The results reveal that: (1) a similar pattern of "inter-country" differences exist for each of the two test products. (2) For three of the four countries there is an absence of "inter-country" difference. (3) Attitude toward the people of the nation is related to existing preconceptions regarding the products of that nation.

180   Wyatt, James Larkin. *An Automated Portuguese to English Transformational Grammar.* Ph.D. 959 pp. (Romance Languages—Linguistics)

This transformational Portuguese to English grammar also includes a computer program, automating the grammar, and a sample of randomly generated kernel sentences in Portuguese and English to which one and two-string transformations have been applied. The purpose of the computer program and the execution output is to establish the degree of the bilingual grammar's validity.

181   Zimdars, Benjamin Frank. *A Study of Seventeenth-Century Peruvian Historiography: The Monastic Chronicles of Antonio de la Calancha, Diego de Córdova Salinas, and the* COMPENDIO Y DESCRIPCIÓN *of Antonio Vásquez de Espinosa.* Ph.D. 600 pp. (History)

Although the chronicles of the Augustinian Antonio de la Calancha and the Franciscan Diego de Córdova Salinas are predominantly monastic histories, both men also present evidence from other available sources in accordance with their Biblical interpretations of history. The Spanish Carmelite Antonio Vásquez de Espinosa gathered all types of information for royal administrators, drawing not only on written sources but also from personal knowledge and eye-witness accounts.

## 1966

182   Aponte-Hernández, Rafael. *The University of Puerto Rico: Foundations of the 1942 Reform.* Ph.D. 267 pp. (Education)

This historic-educational investigation of the foundations and principles underlying the 1942 reform of the University of Puerto Rico gives particular attention to the principles of academic freedom and university autonomy. These principles were embodied in the University theory of Chancellor Jaime Benítez and explicitly set forth in the organic statutes. The reforms dealt with internal reorganization of the University. the transformation of programs of study based on the general education movement, and the reorientation of the functions of the University to act as an agent of peaceful social and economic reform.

183   Bishop, Bobby Arnold. *Stratigraphy and Carbonate Petrography of the Sierra de Picachos and Vicinity, Nuevo León, Mexico.* Ph.D. 515 pp. (Geology)

The stratigraphic section in the Sierra de Picachos is approximately 4,900 feet thick, is divisible into seven formations, and ranges in age from Neocomian and Campanian and possibly Maestrichtian (Early and Late Cretaceous). Bishop identifies a new formation within the group, the Sobreretillo. The formations are from oldest to youngest: Cupido, La Peña, Tamaulipas, Sombreretillo, Cuesta del Cura, San Felipe, and Méndez.

184   Brien, Richard Herman. *Petroleum Refining in Costa Rica: A Study in Industrial Development.* Ph.D. 156 pp. (Economics)
Brien considers possible economic repercussions stemming from the establishment of a relatively heavy industrial facility in a small agrarian economy lacking a refinery. The impact of the plant on the vertical integration linkages of the oil companies and on Costa Rica's balance of payments, employment, fiscal revenue, and potential growth is analyzed. Consideration is given also to the role and importance of the refinery within the young Central American Common Market.

185   Clemons, Russell Edward. *Geology of the Chiquimula Quadrangle, Guatemala, Central America.* Ph.D. 156 pp. (Geology)
Clemons presents the first detailed study of the Chiquimula quadrangle, an area of about 500 square kilometers in southeastern Guatemala. The oldest rocks exposed comprise the Santa Rosa group of probable middle to late Paleozoic age. The predominant east-northeasterly structural trends parallel major structural and physiographic lineaments of Nuclear Central America. Late Tertiary and Quaternary faulting appears to have been controlled by recurring movements on older fractures.

186   Doan, William Franklin. *The Effect of Response Meaningfulness on Verbal Paired–Associate Learning in Anglo-American and Mexican-American Fifth-Grade Children.* Ph.D. 64 pp. (Romance Languages—Linguistics)
A comparison of the paired-associate performance of 32 Anglo-Ameriman, middle-class fifth-grade children with that of 32 lower-class, Mexican-American children indicated that both groups were comparably facilitated by increased meaningfulness. These results were obtained despite the supposition that individuals from a culturally deprived environment would not possess the verbal linguistic habits essential to the facilitation of learning performance on high meaningfulness material.

187   Haenggi, Walter Tiffany. *Geology of El Cuervo Area, Northeastern Chihuahua, Mexico.* Ph.D. 477 pp. (Geology)
Stratigraphic units in the El Cuervo area range from Jurassic to Recent.

Outcropping strata are principally Cretaceous in mountainous areas and Cenozoic in bolson areas. Subsequent to vulcanism, the region was uplifted thousands of feet from sea level, and Late Tertiary block-faulting was superimposed on Laramide structure in the eastern part.

188    Kilgo, Reese Danley. *The Development of Education in El Salvador.* Ph.D. 125 pp. (Education)

Education at all levels has been recognized in El Salvador as essential in the economic and social development of Central America's smallest but most densely populated country. According to Kilgo, primary education has priority but Salvadorans have also recognized their great need for technical and vocational education at the middle level. The University over the past decade has been reformed from a traditional-classical professional system to a modernized institution.

189    McDowell, Neil Allen. *A Status Study of the Academic Capabilities and Achievement of Three Ethnic Groups: Anglo, Negro, and Spanish Surname in San Antonio, Texas.* Ph.D. 186 pp. (Education)

This comparison of intelligence, general ability, and reading achievement of children from Anglo, Negro, and Spanish surname groups showed significant differences favoring Anglo children in intelligence and general ability. Spanish surname children scored higher than Negro children in intelligence. When reading achievement was measured while holding age, intelligence, and pretest scores constant, interaction occurred among groups which prohibited further analysis. When pretest and post-test reading scores were analyzed, the children from upper class families excelled.

190    MacMillan, Robert Wilson. *The Study of the Effect of Socioeconomic Factors on the School Achievement of Spanish-Speaking School Beginners.* Ph.D. 272 pp. (Education)

This analysis using multiple linear regression techniques shows that the independent variables of parent's occupation, the child's school attendance, preschool experience, IQ, and pretest scores were found to be significant predictors of achievement for this population. Ethnic group membership and socioeconomic status with the Anglo and Mexican-American groups were analyzed among 305 first-grade Mexican-Americans in the San Antonio school district. Weather conditions rather than any of the above independent variables proved to be important as a predictor of attendance.

191    Meyer, Walter. *An Analysis of Factors Affecting the Development of Education in Peru from the Inca Period to the Republic.* Ph.D. 213 pp. (Education)

Meyer examines the Inca period, the Colonial period, and the period of the Republic of Peru as to how each phase was organized politically, socially, economically, and culturally. He contends that the entire character of the country can be altered by cultural reforms, i.e. total educational changes and reform.

192    Mulhollan, Paige Elliott. *Philander C. Knox and Dollar Diplomacy, 1909–1913.* Ph.D. 283 pp. (History)

Philander Knox served as President Taft's Secretary of State from 1909–1913, during which he developed the foreign policy known as "dollar diplomacy." Taft and Knox relied heavily upon American investments to secure the chief foreign policy goals of the United States: peace and stability. The United States played an active peacemaking role in boundary disputes between Peru and Bolivia; between Peru and Ecuador; and between Costa Rica and Panama. Knox also intervened in the disputes between Haiti and the Dominican Republic. He believed that the State Department's firm action during the Mena Revolt in Nicaragua prevented a general Central American conflict. Knox and Taft were also active in "peacemaking" efforts in Europe and the Far East.

193    Svec, William Rudolph. *A Study of the Socio-economic Development of the Modern Argentine Estancia, 1852–1914.* Ph.D. 273 pp. (Latin American Studies: History)

Motivated by the expansion of European industry in the 19th century, the Argentine government promoted the socio-economic development of the estancia by encouraging settlement of the wilderness by independent farmers and by maintaining peace to assure growth. The transformation of ranching in the pampa was largely the result of high standards imposed by trans-Atlantic trade with the introduction of scientific innovations first in sheep and then in cattle breeding. The estancia shaped the nation's life style, and its modernization with the introduction of railroads, technology and European labor inadvertently propelling Argentina into its position of leadership among Latin nations.

194    Toward, Agnes Elizabeth. *Some Aspects of the Federal Education Council in the Brazilian Education System.* Ph.D. 157 pp. (Latin American Studies: Education)

This examination of the Federal Education Council's interpretation and implementation of the Law of Directives and Bases during the period 1962–1964 compares education theory as expressed in the Law with education practices and policies since its promulgation in 1961. According to Toward, the newly created Council has performed conscientiously in the areas of curriculum, finances and planning, but has functioned at less than optimum efficiency because of administrative conflicts and technical problems.

195   Wilson, Jacques Marcel Patrick. *The Development of Education in Ecuador.* Ph.D. 245 pp. (Latin American Studies: Education)

The history of education in Ecuador traces its institutional development from the colonial period of Catholic domination and control, through its secularization after 1895, and to the reforms attempted after the Military Junta took power in 1963. The Junta has improved the quality of higher education, expanded and improved secondary and primary level, and shifted some emphasis to vocational skills. Wilson says that although the policies and programs of the Junta are laudable, political stability and continuity are needed to insure their successful implementation.

196   Wolleben, James Anthony. *Biostratigraphy of the Ojinaga and San Carlos Formations of West Texas and Northeastern Chihuahua.* Ph.D. 81 pp. (Geology)

Correlation coefficients of twenty-six stratigraphically unrelated samples are statistically compared with an established *Placenticeras* evolutionary sequence, and time correlations are made at the 90% probability level. Results of the biostratigraphic analysis suggest that the Senonian strandline in Presidio and Jeff Davis counties in Texas and northeastern Chihuahua moved in a southeasterly direction during an extensive marine regression.

1967

197   Anderson, William Woodrow. *The Nature of the Mexican Revolution as Viewed from the United States, 1910–1917.* Ph.D. 280 pp. (Latin American Studies: History)

Opinions in the United States of the Mexican Revolution were sharply divergent. Those Americans with liberal tendencies viewed the Mexican conflict as akin to the great French Revolution; those of a more conservative outlook saw nothing but a disruption of the *status quo*, a situation which would lead only to chaos and turmoil. This schizophrenic reaction is illustrated by the ineffective Mexican policies of William Howard Taft and Woodrow Wilson.

198   Baena-Zapata, Luis Angel. *The Phonology of the Spanish of Antioquia (Colombia).* (Spanish Text) Ph.D. 117 pp. (Romance Languages—Linguistics)

The phonological description of Spanish proposed by Alarcos Llorach in

"Fonología española" is accepted as the basis for the conclusion that Antioquian Spanish can be characterized as the best code for Spanish speaking persons in general. The syllable is the smallest unit one can use to observe and describe the phonotactical components of the segments of the system and before applying it to Antioquian Spanish, it is necessary to describe the syllabic structure of the best code.

199   Berry, Charles Redmon. *The Reform in the Central District of Oaxaca, 1856–1867: A Case Study*. Ph.D. 409 pp. (History)
Berry traces the 19th century Mexican Reform movement as it affected the Central District of Oaxaca, primarily expressing itself as an anticlerical campaign with the suppression of monasteries and convents, imprisonment and exile of priests, confiscation of church property, etc. He argues that although the Reform movement succeeded in nullifying the Church's influence, the price was widespread destruction of property and savings, a disruption of the economy, deep animosity, political schism, and the disruption of lives by a decade of civil war.

200   Brack, Gene Martin. *Imperious Neighbor: The Mexican View of the United States, 1821–1846*. Ph.D. 258 pp. (History)
The questionable conduct of the United States during the Texas Revolution convinced an already suspicious Mexico, after their first illusions of the liberal, prosperous neighbors had faded, that the Revolution was nothing but a thinly disguised American plot to acquire Mexican territory. Subsequent events convinced them that Americans considered them inferior and that their civilization would be endangered by surrendering territory to the United States. Thus they chose to fight rather than make concessions in 1846.

201   Castañeda, Alberta Maxine Mondor. *The Differential Effectiveness of Two First Grade Mathematics Programs for Disadvantaged Mexican-American Children*. Ph.D. 280 pp. (Education)
A group of Mexican-American first graders in an experimental mathematics class which capitalized on the learner's competency drive and on the intrinsic motivation of success and of structured learning showed greater gains than a control group taught the regular textbook-oriented program. The experimental program attempted to show that anticipated ineffectiveness of external motivation with disadvantaged children can be counterbalanced by inner motivation and proper teaching techniques. Castañeda also concludes that the experimental program made better provision for individual differences than did the control program.

202   Chrisitan, Chester Carsel, Jr. *Literary Representation and Sociological Analysis. Social Class in Latin America.* Ph.D. 364 pp. (Latin American Studies: Literature)

The novel is related to a work of art as sociology is to a science showing how the formal study of society can contribute to the appreciation of the novel and how the study of the novel contributes to the understanding of technical analysis of social structure and cultural values. The focus is on the reaction, as portrayed in novels, of members of all Latin American social classes to contemporary urban middle-class cultural values, especially as represented in the United States.

203   Davidson, Margaret Ruth Ashe. *A Comparative Pilot Study of Two First-Grade Programs for Culturally Deprived Mexican-American Children.* Ph.D. 233 pp. (Education)

Davidson attempts to design and implement a teaching program on ideas in the social and natural sciences for Mexican-American children, using experimental and control groups in Austin, Texas. The basic premise was that language growth would accompany concept formation and be manifest in the children's reading achievement. The null hypothesis posited that there would be no significant differences in mean score on reading achievement and total achievement.

204   Evans, James Leroy. *The Indian Savage, the Mexican Bandit, the Chinese Heathen—Three Popular Stereotypes.* Ph.D. 300 pp. (Romance Languages—Literature)

This study traces the 19th century development and use of popular stereotypes for three unassimilated ethnic groups, the Indian savage, the Mexican bandit, and the Chinese heathen, in the American West. Evans says that when each group began to diminish in number and/or economic value to the Anglo-Saxon community, the stereotype was discarded.

205   Hann, John Henry. *Brazil and the Rio de la Plata, 1808–1828.* Ph.D. 490 pp. (History)

Platine policy of the Portuguese and Brazilian governments from 1808–1828 is analyzed as to the principles which guided their relations with the governing elements in Uruguay, Paraguay, and Argentina. Hann contends that this policy was not a single-minded pursuit of imperialist expansionism but rather a response to a variety of impulses not only moved forward but temporized and retracted at times in order to pursue alternative policy objectives.

206   Harrison, Helen Westbrook. *A Methodological Study in Eliciting Data from Mexican-American Bilinguals.* Ph.D. 127 pp. (Romance Languages—Linguistics)

This study used a questionnaire consisting of twenty-five emotionally sensitive and twenty-five neutral stimuli to elicit lexical data from ninety-six bilingual Mexican–Americans in a face-to-face interview situation. Results showed that the female informants gave more numerous responses, especially to sensitive stimuli, when the test was administered in Spanish; the male informants gave more numerous responses when the test was in English.

207   Hensey, Frederick Gerald. *Linguistic Consequences of Culture Contact in a Border Community.* Ph.D. 208 pp. (Romance Languages-Linguistics)

This sociolinguistic study of four communities on the Brazilian-Uruguayan border—Jaguarao, Rio Branco, Livramento, and Rivera—(1) outlines the socioeconomic structure of each community, (2) defines culture contact with this particular milieu, and (3) determines the extent and distribution of bilingualism. Bilinguals were studied in regard to habitual language use, and the author recommends Portuguese be taught as a second language in Rivera to stimulate the growth of bilingualism to increase social mobility.

208   Jameson, Gloria Ruth. *The Development of a Phonemic Analysis for an Oral English Proficiency Test for Spanish-Speaking School Beginners.* Ph.D. 196 pp. (Education)

Pre-literate Spanish-speaking children are handicapped in their progress in American schools by the lack of adequate language tests to diagnose their problems in mastering oral English. The objective of the study was to develop a phonemic analysis, Part A of an Oral English Proficiency Test, designed to help the teacher recognize errors and increase her effectiveness in working with the pupil to overcome them.

209   Juarez, Joseph Robert. *Conflict and Cooperation between Church and State: The Archbishop of Guadalajara during the Porfiriato, 1876–1911.* Ph.D. 324 pp. (History)

Sources in the *cabildo* and the archepiscopal archives of Guadalajara indicate that in spite of the Reforma Laws, the Church in the state of Jalisco fared well during the dictatorship of Porfirio Díaz (1876–1911). Although the state government at times opposed the Church, the federal government generally allowed the clergy to continue buying and selling property. Although its income did not reach pre-revolutionary heights, it rose from

82.5 to 240 thousand pesos by 1906 with the major portion benefitting the archbishop, canons and public worship in the city of Guadalajara.

210   Loos, Eugene Emil. *The Phonology of Capanahua and its Grammatical Basis.* Ph.D. 242 pp. (Romance Languages-Linguistics)

The systematic phonemes of Capanahua, a Panoan language of eastern Central Peru, are distinguished by the distinctive features of consonantality, syllabicity (instead of vocality), and obstruence. Loos claims that the principles of generality and predictiveness suggest for the simplicity metric that alpha variables be given a unit value, and that phonological features be more highly valued than morpheme features.

211   McDaniel, Elizabeth Alice Logan. *Relationships between Self-Concept and Specific Variables in a Low-Income Culturally Different Population.* Ph.D. 218 pp. (Education-Educational Psychology)

The purpose of this investigation was to determine functional relationship which exist between the self-concept of low-income culturally different children and specific organismic and behavioral variables such as sex, race, family size, birth order, and grade level. Changes in self-concept after six months of school attendance were also examined. Analysis of the data reveals that the self-concept of these children in the elementary school setting is scored as "positive," be they Anglos, Mexican-Americans or Negroes. The only significant difference obtained was between races, with Anglos having a self-concept significantly different from Mexican-Americans, but not significantly different from Negroes.

212   Maynard, Betty Janette. *Economic Development and the Division of Labor in Metropolitan Guatemala, Mexico, and the U.S.A.* Ph.D. 217 pp. (Sociology)

The findings of this study substantiate in general the usefulness of a broad interpretation of division of labor—the occupational division of labor with industries and the breaking down of the total labor force into particular "sustenance" activities—as an indicator of differential levels of economic development. For example, metropolitan Mexico in the mid-stage of development has 7.4% of its total labor force in 19 industries of its leading sector, while less developed metropolitan Guatemala has 4.6% of its labor force in the 10 industries of its leading sector.

213   Micklin, Michael Thomas. *Urban Life and Differential Fertility in Guatemala: A Study in Social Demography.* Ph.D. 414 pp. (Sociology)

This investigation of the inverse relationship between urban residence and fertility concludes that of all potential causes in fertility variation, including social mobility, value orientation, number of children, etc., "concern with family limitation" is the best predictor. If respondents are "concerned," Micklin continues, the next step in combating the problem of population growth seems to be an educational program on the efficient use of contraceptive methods.

214   Minick, Robert Arthur, Jr. *An Analysis of the Contribution of Foreign Investment into the Brazilian Economy.* Ph.D. 268 pp. (Economics)
Minick concludes that foreign investment had not contributed to the economic development of Brazil except in a peripheral manner, in spite of that country's strong tendency to look outside its own borders for its economic prosperity. The 1964 foreign investment in Brazil is estimated at about equivalent to $5 billion. It has been inefficient as a device for contributing to economic development, either in transferring capital resources or in transferring technology, since the large percentage of the funds since 1822 has been used to finance debts payments.

215   Ott, Elizabeth Haynes. *A Study of Levels of Fluency and Proficiency in Oral English of Spanish-Speaking School Beginners.* Ph.D. 192 pp. (Education)
The results of tests given to two groups of disadvantaged Spanish-speaking school beginners in San Antonio, Texas, implies that the language power developed through varied and interesting learning experiences added to effective oral-aural techniques in English as a second language, and can produce significant gains in achievement.

216   Peña, Albar Antonio. *A Comparative Study of Selected Syntactical Structures of the Oral Language Status in Spanish and English of Disadvantaged First-Grade Spanish-Speaking Children.* Ph.D. 152 pp. (Education)
Of four groups of disadvantaged Spanish-speaking first-grade children, two received intensive oral instruction in Spanish and English, using science-based materials for one year; one received no oral instruction but used the science materials; one followed the regular school teaching program. The intensive comparative analysis of selected basic sentence patterns showed no significant difference in the language used, but each group utilized basic sentences and transformation of both languages in varying degrees.

217   Ross, William John, III. *The Role of Manuel Doblado in the Mexican Reform Movement, 1855–1860.* Ph.D. 376 pp. (Latin American Studies: History)

Manuel Doblado, governor of the wealthy and strategically located state of Guanajuato, supported the mid-19th century Reform movement in Mexico by trying to persuade the decision makers to stress common values and adopt a moderate approach to problems. According to Ross, Doblado took to the battlefield to sustain the federal government when subversion and revolt threatened. He set a pattern for the implementation of the Reform philosophy by personal example.

218  Sanders, Richard Dewayne. *An Econometric Model of Guatemala, 1950 to 1963.* Ph.D. 165 pp. (Economics)

This ten equation marco-model of the Guatemalan economy for the period 1950 to 1963 was directed toward two goals: acquisition of forecasting equations and estimates of various economic parameters. Forecasts were generated for a period of five years and model forecasts of total product, private investment, and imports were then compared to their respective counterparts in the projected development plan. The model projected a significantly higher rate of imports than that allowed for by the government economists, resulting in a wide discrepancy in the respective forecasts of foreign exchange requirements.

219  Stenning, Walter Francis. *The Relationship of Birth Order to Affiliation and Achievement in Children of Two Cultures.* Ph.D. 176 pp. (Psychology)

In this segment of the ongoing research project, "Coping Styles and Achievement: A Cross-National Study," first born children in the United States were higher in achievement, both in grade point average and projective achievement than other ordinal positions. No consistent relationships between ordinal position and achievement were found in Mexico. Stenning suggests that the definition and rigidity of the parent-child relationship in family structure of each respective culture may be responsible.

220  Weaver, Charles Norris. *A Comparative Study of Selected Significant Factors in the Job Performance of the Spanish-Surname Employee in Selected Organizations.* Ph.D. 106 pp. (Business Administration)

The job performance of Mexican-Americans and Anglo-Americans is contrasted according to the personnel records of the Main Post Office, a large retailer, the Housing Authority, and the Police Department of San Antonio, Texas. Weaver contends that information from sources such as supervisory evaluations, accident, annual leave, and sick leave reports tends to negate the belief that Mexican-Americans are unable to perform adequately in an industrial society.

[ 83 ]

221 Balán, Mrs. Elizabeth Jelin. *Men and Jobs: Lifetime Occupational Changes in Monterrey, Mexico.* Ph.D. 277 pp. (Sociology)

The manpower relocation necessary for transformations in a rapidly industrializing society can be met through inter- and intra-cohort occupational changes. In Monterrey, Mexico, the large intercohort difference in education and the surplus of labor in the city have resulted in the better educated but inexperienced younger worker having more chances for occupational advancement than the experienced but uneducated older worker. The intercohort difference in education will diminish with further increases in the general level of education in the society. Experience may be once again an important criterion for job allocation.

222 Balán, Jorge. *The Process of Stratification in an Industrializing Society: The Case of Monterrey, Mexico.* Ph.D. 324 pp. (Sociology)

By measuring the set of influences affecting a man's adult occupational status, this study outlined the process by which men are located in stratified positions in the society of Monterrey, Mexico. A sample of 1,640 adult male residents of Monterrey were interviewed in 1965. Information was obtained on education and the complete occupation histories of the men, including parents' socio-economic status, migratory history, marriage, family formation and the education attainment of adult sons. Education is the main determinant of occupational status from the beginning of a man's occupational history. The socioeconomic status of the parents or the grandparents yields a negligible impact on a man's opportunity for education or his occupation.

223 Benfer, Robert Alfred, Jr. *An Analysis of a Prehistoric Skeletal Population, Casas Grandes, Chihuahua, Mexico.* Ph.D. 156 pp. (Anthropology)

This report presents descriptive statistics and observations on the skeletal remains from Casas Grandes and nearby areas in Chihuahua, Mexico. Comparisons show slight but consistent morphological differences between the three subdivisions suggested by archeological evidence. Comparisons of this sample with others of approximately the same time period in the region illustrate possible morphological effects of isolation. Functional relationships between certain anatomical features are suggested for the tentative establishment of biological and cultural sources of variability.

224 Burke, Linda Lou Waite. *Coping Effectiveness as a Function of the Social Environment.* Ph.D. 225 pp. (Education-Educational Psychology)

Coping effectiveness scores were obtained from a sentence completion instrument. Demographic, parental, and child behavior data were obtained from individual interviews with the mothers whose children were subjects. Results obtained showed that (1) Anglo-American children residing in the upper-middle socioeconomic status group will exhibit significantly more effective coping responses than will Anglo-American children residing in the upper-lower socioeconomic group. (2) Anglo-American children of the upper-lower socioeconomic group did not exhibit more effective coping responses than Negro or Latin American children of the same socioeconomic group. (3) There was no significant difference in effective coping responses between Blacks and Latin Americans of the upper-lower socioeconomic groups.

225   Cretien, Paul Dudley, Jr. *Deposit Bank Response to Changes in Central Bank Policy: Mexico: 1945–1965.* Ph.D. 216 pp. (Business Administration)

During the period 1945 to 1965, Mexican monetary authorities developed a system of qualitative controls which were directed towards modification of bank asset structures. The banks were given the alternative of investing in specific earning assets or in reserve deposits in the central bank. Two goals were emphasized: (1) establishment of an increased flow of funds into securities, and (2) increase of bank lending for "productive" purposes. The study concludes that the qualitative controls of Banco de México were effective in changing bank asset structure and in redirecting the flow of bank credit.

226   Frankman, Myron Joseph. *Export Promotion and Developmental Priorities in Peru 1946–1965.* Ph.D. 278 pp. (Economics)

In contrast to many developing nations in the post World War II period, Peru did not experience a relative stagnation of exports. Peru maintained its percentage share on the cotton and sugar world export market; increased sharply its share in copper, lead, silver and zinc exports; and became the leading exporter of fishmeal. The author examined tax policy, the credit policy, tariff exemptions for imported inputs, and exchange rate policy to determine how Peruvian government policies affected these exports. He concludes that Peru's exchange policy has favored export producers, and little recourse has been made to control exchange. Moreover, several of the policies have had adverse consequences for the domestic sector of the economy without having directly contributed to expansion of export production.

227   Greding, Edward James, Jr. *Geographical and Reproductive Isolation in Frogs of the Genus* RANA *in Lower Central America.* Ph.D. 126 pp. (Zoology)

[ 85 ]

Reproductive and geographical isolating mechanisms are studied in the four species of frogs in the genus *Rana* known to inhabit southern Nicaragua, Costa Rica and Panama. Some factors studied are: size cline from low to high altitude; genetic compatibility; temporal isolation; and mechanical isolation. A series of artificial crosses, with controls, in every combination produced no viable interspecific hybrids; postmating reproductive isolation is therefore complete. The known geographical ranges of all four species are defined more accurately than was possible before. The presently recognized groups of Mexican and Central American *Rana* are evaluated on the basis of their external morphology, known hybridization patterns, and call characteristics.

228 Hardt, Annanelle. *The Bi-Cultural Heritage of Texas.* Ph.D. 307 pp. (Education-History and Philosophy)

To assume their responsibilities in the area of intercultural relations, educators must begin changing cultural attitudes in the elementary school level. Facts must be substituted for long-held myths. The author believes that the bi-cultural heritage of Texas would be an excellent example of specific lessons or units that could be taught. Every aspect of the Texas elementary school (teacher education, state-approved curriculum guide, state-adopted textbooks) is studied in relation to its role in the intercultural education of Texas. Unfortunately, concludes the author, Texas has not fulfilled her obligation for an improved intercultural education. The cultural heritage of the *mexicanos* in Texas must be recognized by Texas educators and drastic educational changes made accordingly.

229 Harris, Charles Houston, III. *A Mexican Latifundio: The Economic Empire of the Sánchez Navarro Family, 1765–1821.* Ph.D. 408 pp. (History)

The success story of how the Sánchez Navarro family of Coahuila created, managed, and profited from their *latifundio* does not fit the stereotype version of the *latifundio* story. The Sánchez Navarro's were practical businessmen who built their *latifundio* as a profit-making enterprise rather than for the prestige of owning land. Moreover, family commercial enterprises produced liquid assets which enabled the family to buy out neighboring *hacendados*. The priest, José Miguel, who started the family fortune with commercial enterprises, organized and mobilized the whole family to prevent dissipation of the family's growing assets. When revolution threatened their holdings, family members fought back and captured insurgent chieftains in 1811.

230 Hines, Calvin Warner. *United States Diplomacy in the Caribbean during World War II.* Ph.D. 434 pp. (History)

Detailing the policies the United States followed in the Caribbean during World War II, this study stresses the gravitation of diplomacy toward a coordinated defense effort. It seeks to place the history of this diplomacy within the context of inter-American relations, military operations and the diplomacy of coalition warfare by reviewing the significant inter-American conferences and relations with France, Great Britain and Holland.

231   Lane, John Hart, Jr. *Voluntary Associations among Mexican-Americans in San Antonio, Texas: Organizational and Leadership Characteristics.* Ph.D. 220 pp. (Sociology)

The findings of this study indicate that Mexican-Americans in a metropolitan setting can and do organize. A partial count identified over 500 associations in San Antonio that were predominantly Mexican-American in their membership. The characteristics of the leadership demonstrate that not all acculturated Mexican-American talent is being siphoned off by the dominant Anglo community. The heterogeneous elements to be found in the Mexican-American community may interfere with the emergence of an effective political bloc, but ethnic qualities have not deterred many Mexican-Americans from actively participating in formally organized voluntary associations.

232   Lockett, Landon Johnson, III. *Use of the Infinitive in a Corpus of Colloquial Brazilian Portuguese.* Ph.D. 118 pp. (Linguistics)

The corpus consists of recorded conversations by four Brazilian informants, all of whom have some university education, and are, respectively, natives of Rio de Janeiro, Belo Horizonte, São Paulo state, and Recife. The dissertation consists of a syntactic analysis of the various functions of the infinitive: (1) as subject and as predical nominal, (2) as objects of a ruling verb, and (3) as ruled by a preposition. These three usages describe 96% of all infinitive used in the corpus. Concurrent with the description of each function is a description of the word order of the various constructions in which the infinitive appears.

233   Maddox, Robert Casey. *A Study of the Wage Differences between United States and Guatemalan Industrial Firms in Guatemala.* Ph.D. 185 pp. (Business Administration)

The hypothesis that wages in United States firms operating in Guatemala were actually higher than in Guatemalan firms was found to be true, using date from 1964. Rank correlation, however, failed to show (1) that this higher average wage resulted from a concentration of American firms in high-paying industries, physical location, etc., and (2) any strong correlation, which would ordinarily be expected, between wages and several independent variables such as total assets, total production, productivity per employee, etc.

234   Pauck, Frederick Glen. *An Evaluation of the Self-Test as a Predictor of Reading Achievement of Spanish-Speaking First Grade Children.* Ph.D. 197 pp. (Education—Curriculum and Instruction)

The primary purpose of this study was to determine the effectiveness of Part II, Oral English Fluency, of the Ott-Jameson Test of Spoken English as a predictor of reading achievement of Spanish-speaking first-grade childrent. In addition, this study also sought to determine the predictive effectiveness of the Metropolitan Readiness Tests, Form A, for this same population. Comparisons were made to determine if there was a significant difference between the two tests as effective and meaningful predictors of reading achievement. Data revealed that there is high correlation between the two tests.

235   Porter, Mary Erin. *Oratory of the South American Independence: An Analysis of Speeches by Antonio Nariño and Francisco de Paula Santander.* Ph.D. 228 pp. (Education—Curriculum and Instruction)

The purposes of this study are to (1) describe briefly the prevailing conditions during the revolutionary period in Colombia from 1800 to 1830, (2) highlight pertinent biographical facts about Nariño (1760–1823) and Santander (1792–1840), (3) conduct a critical study of "invention, arrangement and style" in selected speeches by Nariño and Santander, and (4) draw conclusions, comparisons and recommendations based on the results of this study. In general, the oratory of the two speakers reflected important issues of the period, the basic classical principles applied by orators of the day and the individual differences of Nariño and Santander as public speakers.

236   Saville, Thomas Keith. *A Cross-Cultural Investigation of the Role of a Personality Parameter in Choice of Mode of Dissonance Reduction.* Ph.D. 117 pp. (Psychology)

This experiment was based on the dissonance theory paradigm and utilized predictions from a cross-cultural theory of coping behavior. It was predicted that student subjects drawn from Mexico and the United States would differ on the measured personality parameter and in the methods which they use to reduce dissonance. Subjects received a disagreement from a "friendly fellow student" who has been expressing very similar attitudes. Changes from pre-to-post-measures were used to evaluate differences. Conclusions suggest that there are individual differences in reactions to dissonance, but there is no evidence here of cultural differences.

237 Sloan, John William. *The Electoral Game in Guatemala*. Ph.D. 260 pp. (Government)

Based on data concerning elections in the 1957–1966 period, the author examined the contestants for political power, laws which govern elections, statistics of elections and events of election campaigns for the March 1966 election. The study shows that top leaders are usually lawyers or military men, whose party loyalties are weak and temporary. Guatemalans have not learned to share power and reconcile conflicts within a single political organization. Finally, the Revolutionary parties are found to have most support in Guatemala City and *municipios* with high percentages of literates, *ladinos* and in-migration, the latter a land-hungry and low status group which is especially receptive to revolutionary political propaganda.

238 Treviño, Mrs. Bertha Alicia Gamez. *An Analysis of the Effectiveness of a Bilingual Program in the Teaching of Mathematics in the Primary Grades*. Ph.D. 116 pp. (Education—Curriculum and Instruction)

A set of hypotheses on achievement levels in arithmetic fundamentals and arithmetic reasoning of children taught in English and bilingually was tested on separate groups of first and third grade English-speaking and Spanish-speaking children. No significant differences were noted between the achievement of the English group and the Spanish group in the bilingual program. Although Spanish-speaking children were generally below the grade level at the end of the first year in the bilingual program, they were generally above the grade level by the end of the third year.

239 Von Bertrab Erdmann, Hermann Raimund. *The Transfer of Technology: A Case Study of European Private Enterprises Having Operations in Latin America with Special Emphasis on Mexico*. Ph.D. 314 pp. (Economics)

The most important considerations of a European firm investing in Latin America refer to expectations of market growth or to fear of market loss, the latter due to governmental restrictions. The adaptation of techniques to smaller-scale production is the greatest concern of the European industry in Latin America. The proportion of foreigners in European subsidiaries does not generally block assimilation of technology by local personnel, but rather contributes to the assimilation of technical know-how. Investment originating in European Economic Community countries has increased considerably since 1955, while the inflow of foreign technical knowledge has grown more rapidly than foreign capital inflow.

240 Wogart, Jan Peter. *Demand-Pull, Corrective, and Cost-Push Inflation: The Case of Brazil (1964–1966)*. Ph.D. 437 pp. (Economics)

Despite earlier attempts from 1958–1963 to stop price increases, the Brazilian Action Program (1964–1966) instituted by the military government which took power in 1964 was the first comprehensive plan to stop inflation and resume economic growth. Fiscal and monetary policies between 1964 and 1967 support two hypotheses: (1) the stabilization attempt represented a well conceived synthesis of "monetarist" and "structuralist" elements, and (2) a gradual stabilization effort, which includes "corrective inflation" and a passive monetary policy, cannot succeed in curbing inflation substantially. Most of the inflationary pressure seems to have been caused by excess money supply in 1965 and low agricultural output in 1966.

## 1969

241 Anderson, Thomas Howard. *Geology of the San Sebastian Huehuetenango Quadrangle, Guatemala, Central America.* Ph.D. 218 pp. (Geology)

This is the first detailed report and description of a 500 square kilometer area in northwestern Guatemala. The oldest exposed rocks are of pre-Permian age. Most recent displacement along the east-west zone have shown left-lateral separation. Subsequent displacements occurred along northeasterly-trending normal faults.

242 Bills, Garland Dee. *On Case in Quechua.* Ph.D. 129 pp. (Linguistics)

This study explores three areas of case-related phenomena in Bolivian Quechua: the most important overt case markers; several case related verbal suffixes; and some major aspects of the causative construction which are relevant to case. Discoveries resulting from the examination of these three fields lead the author to two important implications for general linguistics theory and for future research in this area. First, conceptually-based case notions should be recognized as substantive terms of the theory. Second, the formalization of these case terms may best be accomplished through the use of case features.

243 Boren, James Harlan. *The Partners of the Alliance—A Documentary.* Ph.D. 241 pp. (Education—History and Philosophy)

This study documents the founding of the Alliance for Progress. The author discusses the administrative mechanisms created to manage the program, the resources that were pooled to insure the program's effective operation and the program's contributions at its advent.

244 Clegg, Joseph Halvor. *Fonética y fonología del español de Texas.* Ph.D. 87 pp. (Spanish)

This study investigates the segmental phonemes and allophones of the Spanish spoken in Texas. The examination is based on the theory that there are in practice indivisible entities. The author finds that the phonemes of Texas Spanish are the same as in Latin American Spanish. However, distinctive phenomena are allophonic.

245   Cornejo, Ricardo Jesús. *Bilingualism: Study of the Lexicon of the Five-Year-Old Spanish-Speaking Children of Texas.* Ph.D. 219 pp. (Education—Curriculum & Instruction)

The lexicon of Spanish-English bilingual children in Texas just before they enter first grade indicates: (1) a high frequency of "baby talk" and (2) the predominance of English over Spanish, especially in the lexical and syntactical levels, although Spanish is still strong in the phonological level. This language situation has important implications in the preparation of teaching materials for bilingual education programs. In order to improve the language skills of these children, a language program must provide for their needs in terms of their socioeconomic status, family background, environment and intellectual development.

246   Denton, Charles Frederick. *The Politics of Development in Costa Rica.* Ph.D. 277 pp. (Government)

The *Partido Liberación Nacional* (PLN) has consistently backed policies which have strengthened Costa Rica's public administration. As a result, the bureaucracy has amassed much administrative and political strength. A process of cooptation of personnel has occurred between the PLN and the public administration; the net effect has been *"imobilismo"*: a deadlock between politics and administration and an unnecessary lag in Costa Rica's development efforts. The various "environments" of the bureaucracy, the relationship between the bureaucracy and the environment, and the Central American Common Market, are other topics of consideration in this study.

247   Flores Caballero, Romeo Ricardo. *Los españoles en la vida política, económica y social de México: 1804–1838.* Ph.D. 347 pp. (History)

This study is an analysis of the *Real Cédula de Consolidación* of December 26, 1804 and its effects upon the economy, society and politics of New Spain. It also analyzes the way in which the Spaniards in the upper levels of government, the Church, the army, the judiciary and the oligarchy were affected by the *Cédula de Consolidación* after the French invasion of Spain, Mexico's War of Independence, the execution of the liberal constitution of 1812 and the achievement of Independence in 1821. This study further analyses the role of the Spaniards during Iturbide's empire and the first republican governments.

248   Fowler, Mrs. Elaine Louise Danielson. *An Evaluation of the Brengelman-Manning Linguistic Capacity Index as a Predictor of Reading Achievement of Spanish-Speaking First Grade Children.* Ph.D. 159 pp. (Education—Curriculum & Instruction)

Using the Brengelman-Manning Linguistic Capacity on a random sample of Spanish-speaking first grade children in the most economically disadvantaged area of San Antonio, Texas, the author found a definite correlation between receptive language capacity of these children and their reading achievement. This conclusion in turn confirms the Brengelman-Manning Index as a useful and effective instrument in predicting reading achievement of Spanish-speaking first grade children.

249   Hill, Floyd William. *A Study of the Influence of Socialization Anxiety on the Achievement of First Grade Mexican-American Children.* Ph.D. 239 pp. (Education)

This study on the place of socialization anxiety as an acquired drive in a hierarchy of requisites for academic success in beginning Mexican-American first-graders concludes that: (1) socialization anxiety can be measured by Lambert and Bowers' (1961) Self Rating of Behavior (The Picture Game); (2) auditory perception was the variable most important to academic success; (3) socialization anxiety ranked low in a hierarchy of requisites for academic success; and (4) academic achievement of these Mexican-American children is affected more by cultural deprivation and bilingualism than by socialization anxiety associated with class- or culture-typed child rearing practices.

250   Hilton, Stanley Eon. *Brazil and Great Power Trade Rivalry in South America, 1934–1939.* Ph.D. 447 pp. (History)

Brazil provides an outstanding example of the success of German efforts in the commercial struggle between the liberal system championed by the Roosevelt Administration and the bilateralism of Nazi Germany. From 1934 to 1939, the Reich doubled its exports to, and imports from, Brazil, replacing Great Britain as Brazil's leading European trade partner and challenging the United States as a supplier of goods to that country.

251   Lillard, William Clair. *Cattle Feeding in El Salvador: An Economic Feasibility Study.* Ph.D. 138 pp. (Economics)

In spite of the lack of a modernized livestock sector, cattle is a major source of income in a large part of El Salvador, although beef has not yet become an export commodity. This study evaluated the cost of feeding cattle at the current costs of input, with the present market price of beef, and concludes that with the necessary technological change, El Salvador can profitably increase beef production in the short run for either the domestic or the foreign market.

252   Natalicio, Mrs. Eleanor D. S. *Formation of the Plural in English: A Study of Native Speakers of English and Native Speakers of Spanish.* Ph.D. 181 pp. (Linguistics)

This study examines the formation of English plurals, a restricted area of language acquisition phenomena. Emphasis was placed on carefully controlled sampling, data collection and analysis procedures in an attempt to provide a useful methodological model for investigators examining similar phenomena. The principal sample was composed of nonsense syllables which permitted simulation of nouns in English, provided the phonological variation required for a complete analysis, and eliminated the possible biases introduced by the use of actually existing English nouns. The study finds that although there is no significant difference in the performance by English- and Spanish-speaking groups at the first grade level, by the tenth grade the difference is highly significant.

253   Seay, Stiles Noel. *The Construction and Initial Classroom Tryout of an Instructional Unit on Latin America for the Middle Grades.* Ph.D. 213 pp. (Education—Curriculum & Instruction)

An instructional unit with Latin American content utilizes a multi-discipline approach. Key or main ideas provide the organizational framework for the unit's content, activities and reading selections. The unit's classroom tryout showed that: (1) This unit was feasible as a teacher-learning instrument for grade seven. (2) Pupils were interested in a Latin American study which emphasizes people. (3) The reading selections had meaningful content. And (4) the suggested activities encouraged pupils to examine their attitudes towards Latin America and their own culture.

254   Taylor, Thomasine Hughes. *A Comparative Study of the Effects of Oral-Aural Training on Gains in English Language for Fourth and Fifth Grade Disadvantaged Mexican-American Children.* Ph.D. 142 pp. (Education— Curriculum & Instruction)

This study examines the effects of continuous oral-aural language teaching techniques used with low socio-economic urban Spanish-speaking children. Six treatment groups were considered. Findings suggest that some instruction in Spanish is beneficial to English language proficiency.

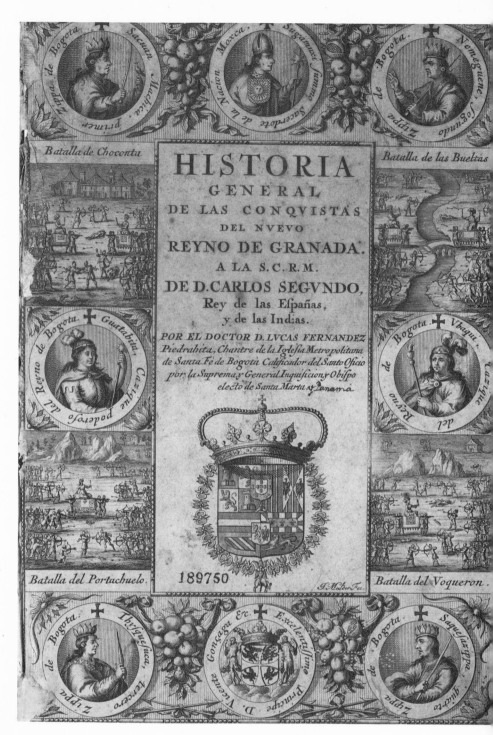

HISTORIA GENERAL DE LAS
CONQVISTAS DEL NVEVO REYNO DE GRANADA
(1688)
*Lucas Fernández de Piedrahita*

# Masters Theses of Latin American Interest
## 1893–1969

### 1893

255  Bugbee, Lester Gladstone. *Austin's Colony.* M.A. 69 pp. (History)

### 1897

256  McCaleb, Walter Flavius. *The Spanish Mission of Texas.* M.A. 110 pp. (History)

### 1901

257  Clark, Robert Carlton. *The Beginnings of Texas: Fort St. Louis and Mission San Francisco de los Tejas.* M.A. 39 pp. (History)
258  West, Elizabeth Howard, *The Cartography of French and Spanish Expansion in North America.* M.A. 80 pp. (History)
259  Winkler, Ernest William. *The History of the Cherokee Indians in Texas.* M.A. 150 pp. (History)

### 1902

260  Rather, Ethel Zivley. *DeWitt's Colony.* M.A. 191 pp. (History)

### 1903

261  Crane, Olatia. *The Gutierres-Magee Expedition.* M.A. 114 pp. (History)
262  Hatcher, Mrs. Mattie Alice. *Municipal Government of San Fernando de Béxar.* M.A. 96 pp. (History)

### 1905

263  Worley, John Lewis. *The Diplomatic Relations of England and The Republic of Texas.* M.A. 66 pp. (History)

### 1906

264  Morse, Frederic C. *The Commerce and the Commercial Policy of The Republic of Texas.* M.A. 64 pp. (History)

[ 95 ]

265   Bell, Holland Edward. *The Texas Convention of 1832.* M.A. 94 pp. (History)

266   Vázquez, Antonio C. *Lead Roasting at the Torreón Smelting Plant.* M.A. 44 pp. (Engineering)

267   Brown, Elise Denison. *The History of the Spanish Settlements at Orcoquisac, 1746–1772.* M.A. 116 pp. (History)
268   Householder, Fred Walter. *Sources of the Texas Law of Married Women.* M.A. 66 pp. (Government)
269   Neu, Charles Louis Ternay. *The Eastern Boundary of Texas from the Gulf of Mexico to the Red River.* M.A. 84 pp. (History)

270   Gibson, Louise. *Efforts of the Texas Government to Obtain Peace with Mexico through Santa Anna; 1836–1837.* M.A. 79 pp. (History)

271   Birge, Mamie. *The Casas Revolution, 1811; The First Period of Independence in Texas.* M.A. 43 pp. (History)

272   Brandenberger, William Samuel. *The Administrative System of Texas, 1821–1836.* M.A. 87 pp. (History)
273   Condron, Stuart Harkins. *The First Texas Agency at New Orleans in 1836.* M.A. 106 pp. (History)

274   Sandbo, Mrs. Anna Irene. *Beginnings of the Secession Movement in Texas.* M.A. 131 pp. (History)

275   Edwards, Herbert Rook. *The Diplomatic Relations between France and The Republic of Texas.* M.A. 91 pp. (History)

## 1918

276  McArthur, Daniel Evander. *The Cattle Industry of Texas, 1685–1918.* M.A. 428 pp. (History)

## 1919

277  Muckleroy, Anna. *The Indian Policy of The Republic of Texas.* M.A. 202 pp. (History)

278  Smith, Ruby Cumby. *James W. Fannin, Jr., in the Texas Revolution.* M.A. 158 pp. (History)

## 1920

279  Luker, Julia Eugenia. *The Diplomatic Relations between Texas and Mexico, 1836–1842.* M.A. 167 pp. (History)

280  Middleton, Annie Laura. *The Formation of the Texas Constitution of 1845.* M.A. 148 pp. (History)

281  Sparks, Earle Sylvester. *A Survey of Organized Labor in Austin.* M.A. 149 pp. (Economics)

282  Spell, Jefferson Rea. *The History of Spanish Teaching in the United States.* M.A. 165 pp. (Romance Languages)

283  Webb, Walter Prescott. *The Texas Rangers in the Mexican War.* M.A. 160 pp. (History)

## 1921

284  Cockrell, Myrtle. *Education in Texas, 1836–1860.* M.A. 112 pp. (Education)

285  Whatley, William Archibald. *The Formation of the Mexican Constitution of 1824.* M.A. 163 pp. (History)

## 1922

286  Curlee, Abigail. *The History of a Texas Slave Plantation, 1831–1863.* M.A. 99 pp. (History)

287  Greer, James Kimmins. *Louisiana and the South, 1848–1860.* M.A. 174 pp. (History)

288  Harris, Townes Malcolm. *The Labor Supply of Texas.* M.A. 115 pp. (Economics)

289  McDonald, Johnnie Belle. *The Soldiers of San Jacinto.* M.A. 450 pp. (History)

290  Ryan, Frances Dora. *The Election Laws of Texas, 1827–1875*. M.A. 82 pp. (Government)

291  Smither, Harriet. *The Diplomatic Service of Ashbel Smith of The Republic of Texas, 1842–1845*. M.A. 161 pp. (History)

292  Watkins, Mrs. Willye Ward. (trans.) *Memoirs of General Antonio López de Santa Anna: Translation with Introduction and Notes*. M.A. 297 pp. (History)

293  Young, William Harvey. *Banking in Mexico*. M.A. 58 pp. (Business Administration)

## 1923

294  Castañeda, Carlos Eduardo. *A Report on the Spanish Archives in San Antonio, Texas*. M.A. 349 pp. (History)

295  Chávez, David Julián. *Civic Education of the Spanish American*. M.A. 143 pp. (Education)

296  Cravens, Mattie Ella. *The Diplomacy between the U.S. and Mexico Concerning the Mixed Claims Commission, 1868–1892*. M.A. 123 pp. (History)

297  Eaves, Robert Lee. *President Roosevelt and the Panama Canal*. M.A. 157 pp. (History)

298  Gesche, Irma. *The Color Preferences of One Thousand One Hundred and Fifty-two Mexican Children*. M.A. 136 pp. (Psychology)

299  Price, Anne Broyles. *The Diplomacy between the United States and Mexico Growing Out of the Mexican Free Zone, 1858–1905*. M.A. 169 pp. (History)

## 1924

300  Brown, Maury Bright. *The Military Defenses of Texas and the Río Grande Region about 1766*. M.A. 234 pp. (History)

301  Holden, William Curry. *Fray Vicente Santa María: Historical Account of the Colony of Nuevo Santander and the Coast of the Seno Mexicano: With Introduction and Annotations*. M.A. 276 pp. (History)

302  McClendon, Robert Earl. *Daniel Webster and Mexican Relations, 1841–1843*. M.A. 178 pp. (History)

303  Stambaugh, Jacob Lee. *The Marketing of Perishable Farm Products Grown in the Lower Río Grande Valley of Texas*. M.A. 151 pp. (Economics)

304  Timm, Charles August. *The Diplomatic Relations between Brazil and the U.S.* M.A. 258 pp. (History)

305 Weaver, A. J. S. *The Agrarian Problem of Mexico.* M.A. 106 pp. (History)

306 Webb, Jesse Owen. *The History of Galveston to 1865.* M.A. 114 pp. (History)

307 Wilson, Robert Newton. *A History of the Educational Policy of the United States in Porto Rico: A Phase of Our Later Colonial Policy.* M.A. 108 pp. (History)

308 Wood, William Baker. *Production of Cotton in Mexico.* M.B.A. 103 pp. (Business Administration)

## 1925

309 Allen, Winnie. *The History of Nacogdoches, 1691–1830.* M.A. 148 pp. (History)

310 Bridges, Clarence Allen. *Texas and the Crisis of 1850.* M.A. 197 pp. (History)

311 Browne, Philip Dale. *The Early History of Freestone County to 1865.* M.A. 179 pp. (History)

312 Butler, May Angie. *Principles of Modern Foreign Language Study with Particular Reference to Their Application to Spanish.* M.A. 179 pp. (Education)

313 Carter, Eula Lee. *The Education Program of the Mexican Government, 1920–1924.* M.A. 150 pp. (History)

314 Connell, Earl Monroe. *The Mexican Population of Austin, Texas.* M.A. 65 pp. (Economics)

315 Crawford, Polly Pearl. *The Beginnings of Spanish Settlement in the Lower Río Grande Valley.* M.A. 165 pp. (History)

316 Hunnicutt, Helen Margaret. *The Relations between Antonio López Santa Anna as President and Valentín Gómez Farías as Vice-President of Mexico, April, 1833–January, 1835.* M.A. 85 pp. (History)

317 Kellam, Frances Wade. *Economic and Commercial History of Texas, 1821–1835.* M.A. 249 pp. (History)

318 Moore, Vera Lee. *The Motivation of Spanish Teaching in High Schools.* M.A. 130 pp. (Education)

319 Phipps, Pella. *The Mysticism of Amado Nervo.* M.A. 165 pp. (Romance Languages)

## 1926

320 Brenizer, Lester C. (trans.) *Translation of Book II of Cervantes de Salazar's "Crónica de la Nueva España."* M.A. 246 pp. (Romance Languages)

321 Cowling, Annie. *The Civil War Trade of the Lower Río Grande Valley*. M.A. 162 pp. (History)

322 Ellis, Mildred. *Some Problems in the Diplomatic Relations between the United States and the Five Republics of Central America*. M.A. 230 pp. (Government)

323 Garretson, Oliver Kelleam. *Causes of the Retardation of Mexican Children in American Schools*. M.A. 174 pp. (Education)

324 Henderson, Mary Virginia. *Minor Empresario Grants in Texas, 1825–1834*. M.A. 113 pp. (History)

325 Ingenhuett, Arthur Hilmer. *La Influencia de Horacio Mann en la Obra de Domingo Faustino Sarmiento*. M.A. 113 pp. (Romance Languages)

326 Jackson, Lola. *The Life and Work of Genaro García; An Estimate of His Contribution to Mexican Historiography*. M.A. 111 pp. (History)

327 Maris, Wiley Dee. *Diplomatic Aspects of the Controversy between the United States and Mexico over Petroleum*. M.A. 118 pp. (History)

328 Robertson, Martha Ann. *The Cuban Sugar Situation and Its Effect on Cuban Banking in 1920*. M.A. 159 pp. (Business Administration)

329 Williams, Amelia. *The Siege and Fall of the Alamo*. M.A. 258 pp. (History)

1927

330 Blocker, William Robert. *The Diplomatic Relations between the United States and Haiti since 1915*. M.A. 131 pp. (Government)

331 Charlton, Agnes Adalyn. *Ignacio Comonfort and the Mexican Constitution of 1857*. M.A. 111 pp. (History)

332 Cravens, Lucy Elizabeth. *The Congressional History of the Annexation of Texas*. M.A. 225 pp. (History)

333 Curry, Ora Mae. *The Texan Siege of San Antonio, 1853*. M.A. 151 pp. (History)

334 De Burgos, Francis. *The Administration of Teodore de Croix, Commander General of the Provincias Internas de México, 1776–83*. M.A. 422 pp. (History)

335 Harris, James Kilbourne. *A Sociological Study of a Mexican School in San Antonio, Texas*. M.A. 98 pp. (Economics)

336 Hughes, Vernon. *Currency of the Republic of Texas*. M.A. 109 pp. (History)

337 Ivey, Alfred Joe. *A Study of the Vocabulary of Newspapers Printed in the Spanish Language in Texas*. M.A. 137 pp. (Romance Languages)

338  Jones, Albert Pearson. *History of the Kansas City, Mexico, and Orient Railway*. M.A. 80 pp. (History)

339  Knox, William John. *The Economic Status of the Mexican Immigrant in San Antonio, Texas*. M.A. 66 pp. (Economics)

340  McGill, Mary. *The Life and Works of José Enrique Rodó*. M.A. 135 pp. (Romance Languages)

341  Mercer, Claudia. *The Role of Germany in the Venezuelan Crisis of 1903*. M.A. 191 pp. (History)

342  Nelson, Mary. *The Mexican Historical Novel*. M.A. 114 pp. (Romance Languages)

343  Rogers, Thomas Guy. *The Housing Situation of the Mexicans in San Antonio, Texas*. M.A. 65 pp. (Economics)

344  Shelby, Charmion Clair. *St. Denis's Second Expedition from Louisiana to the Rio Grande, 1716–1719*. M.A. (History)

345  Smith, Mrs. Elizabeth Parkes. *The History and Culture of the Pueblo of Pecos, New Mexico*. M.A. 136 pp. (History)

346  Stephens, Andrew Jackson. *A Calendar of the Writings of Sam Houston in the Various Collections in Austin*. M.A. 246 pp. (History)

347  Whittaker, Annie Eikel. *The Frontier Policy of the United States in the Mexican Cession, 1845–1860*. M.A. 226 pp. (History)

348  Wright, Mrs. Carrie Elizabeth. *An Experiment with a Spanish Reading Test*. M.A. 155 pp. (Education)

### 1928

349  Arnold, Charles August. *The Folklore, Manners, and Customs of the Mexicans in San Antonio, Texas*. M.A. 71 pp. (Sociology)

350  Avrett, William Robert. *Philosophical and Mystical Elements in the Poetry of Enrique González Martínez*. M.A. 129 pp. (Romance Languages)

351  Brown, Mrs. Alma Howell. *The Consular Service of the Republic of Texas*. M.A. 124 pp. (History)

352  Evans, Kenneth. *The Administration of Manuel de Sandoval, Governor of Texas, 1734 to 1736*. M.A. 101 pp. (History)

353  Gerhardt, Mrs. Haidee Williams. *The History of the University of Mexico*. M.A. 90 pp. (History)

354  Goldthorp, Audrey G. *Castro's Colony*. M.A. 133 pp. (History)

355  Gonzales, Kathleen May. *The Mexican Family in San Antonio, Texas*. M.A. 69 pp. (Sociology)

356  Hughes, Mrs. Lois Spears. *A Comparative Study of the Intelligence of Mexican and Non-Mexican Children*. M.A. 78 pp. (Education)

357  Johnson, Harvey Leroy. *The Life and Customs of the Gaucho.* M.A. 70 pp. (History)

358  Laurence, Marion Sidney. *A Study of the Chilean Epic by a Comparison of "La Araucana" and "Arauco Domado."* M.A. 82 pp. (Romance Languages)

359  McGill, Margaret. *The Administration of Carlos Franquis de Lugo, Governor of Texas, 1736–1737.* M.A. 109 pp. (History)

360  Mansell, Mabel Jeanette. *Ignacio Manuel Altamirano: A Biographical and Critical Study.* M.A. 81 pp. (Romance Languages)

361  Montgomery, Mary. *El elemento elegíaco en la lírica cubana.* M.A. 166 pp. (Romance Languages)

362  Patterson, John Clarke. *José María Morelos, Mexican Revolutionary Patriot.* M.A. 140 pp. (History)

363  Perron, Marius. *Employment Agencies on the Mexican Border.* M.A. 50 pp. (Economics)

364  Skelton, Byron G. *Electoral Theories and Practices in Mexico, as Illustrated by Presidential Elections since 1857.* M.A. 234 pp. (Government)

365  Smith, Cecil Bernard. *Diplomatic Relations between the United States and Mexico Concerning Border Disturbances during the Díaz Regime, 1876–1910.* M.A. 186 pp. (History)

366  Streeter, Vivian. *The Development of the Teaching of Spanish in Texas Public Schools.* M.A. 125 pp. (Education)

1929

367  Barker, Bernice. *The Texas Expedition to the Río Grande in 1842.* M.A. 132 pp. (History)

368  Buckner, Dellos Urban. *Study of the Lower Río Grande Valley as a Culture Area.* M.A. 130 pp. (Sociology)

369  Coor, Minnie. *Relations between the United States and Spain Preceding the Spanish American War.* M.A. 128 pp. (History)

370  Covington, Nina. *The Presidential Campaigns of the Republic of Texas of 1836 and 1838.* M.A. 120 pp. (History)

371  Furnish, Mrs. Alice Gray. *A Comparative Study of the Materials and Methods Appearing in Twenty-six Spanish Grammars Published within the last Fifty Years.* M.A. 157 pp. (Education)

372  Goldmann, Mary Ernestine. *A Study of the Adequacy and Economy of Some Mexican Dietaries.* M.A. 128 pp. (Home Economics)

373  Lozano, Dolores Dora. *"El Peregrino Indiano" y algunas relaciones del siglo XVI de la Conquista de México.* M.A. 94 pp. (Romance Languages)

374 Moore, Wilma Harper. *A History of San Felipe de Austin, 1824–1836.* M.A. 167 pp. (History)

375 Myers, Mrs. Minnie Moore Porter. *The Origin and Beginning of the University of Mexico from 1553 to 1580.* M.A. 108 pp. (History)

376 Splawn, Mary Ruth (trans.). *Don José Antonio Pichardo: Investigation Concerning the True Boundaries of the Provinces of Louisiana and Texas. Translation of Volume One with Introduction and Notes.* M.A. 389 pp. (History)

## 1930

377 Allemand, Paul. *Rafael Delgado, costumbrista mexicano.* M.A. 165. pp. (Romance Languages)

378 Cavness, Raymond McCarey. *The Social Principles of Hugo Wast (Martínez Zuviría).* M.A. 97 pp. (Romance Languages)

379 Coon, Ruby Irene. *The History of the Teaching of Spanish in Texas.* M.A. 95 pp. (Education)

380 Darnell, William Leonard. *The Services of Francisco de Urdiñola in Nueva Viscaya, 1575–1612.* M.A. 104 pp. (History)

381 Dodd, Elmer Cecil. *A Comparison of Spanish-speaking and English-speaking Children in Brownsville, Texas.* M.A. 108 pp. (Education)

382 Edman, Grace Augusta (trans.). *A Compilation of Royal Decrees in the Archivo General de la Nación Relating to Texas and Other Northern Provinces of New Spain, 1719–1799: Translated and Edited with Introduction and Notes.* M.A. 509 pp. (History)

383 González, Jovita. *Social Life in Cameron, Starr and Zapata Counties.* M.A. 113 pp. (History)

384 Hoffmann, Fritz Leo. *The First Three Years of the Administration of Juan María, Barón de Ripperdá, Governor of Texas, 1770–1778.* M.A. (History)

385 MacManus, Sister Mary Borromeo (trans.). *"Life of Pedro Moya de Contreras" by Cristóval Gutiérrez de Luna—A Translation with Introduction and Notes.* M.A. 69 pp. (Romance Languages)

386 Morey, Elizabeth May. *Attitude of the Citizens of San Fernando toward Independence Movements in New Spain, 1811–1813.* M.A. 130 pp. (History)

387 Roberts, Lillian. *The Diplomatic and Commercial Relations of the United States and Argentina from 1811 to 1928.* M.A. 160 pp. (Government)

388 Smith, Helen Perrin. *Health and Nutrition of the Mexican Infant and Preschool Child.* M.S. 95 pp. (Home Economics)

389  White, Robert Leon. *Mission Architecture of Texas Exemplified in San Joseph de San Miguel de Aguayo.* M.A. 127 pp. (Architecture)

390  Woolsey, Arthur Wallace. *The Novels of Federico Gamboa.* M.A. 131 pp. (Romance Languages)

## 1931

391  Cleaves, Wilbur Shaw. *The Political Career of Lorenzo de Zavala.* M.A. 173 pp. (History)

392  Davenport, Everard Lee. *A Comparative Study of Mexican and Non-Mexican Siblings.* M.Ed. 60 pp. (Education)

393  Davis, James William. *The Joint Intervention of the United States and Mexico in Central America in 1906 and 1907.* M.A. 149 pp. (History)

394  Huston, Edgar. *La obra dramática de Adelardo López de Ayala.* M.A. 86 pp. (Romance Languages)

395  Johnston, Marjorie Cecil. *Rubén Darío's Knowledge of English and the English-speaking World as Revealed by His Works.* M.A. 137 pp. (Romance Languages)

396  Kress, Dorothy Margaret. *Catalina de Erauso, su personalidad histórica y legendaria.* M.A. 100 pp. (History)

397  Long, Grace. *The Anglo-American Occupation of the El Paso District.* M.A. 287 pp. (History)

398  Oliver, Winfred Allen, Jr. *The Early History of the Mission of Espíritu Santo de Zúñiga and the Presidio of Nuestra Señora de Loreto, 1718–1751.* M.A. 138 pp. (History)

399  Parker, Lydia Edith. *Public Education in Colombia, South America.* M.A. 243 pp. (Education)

400  Perry, Elsie Adele. *A Comparison of the Content Material in Mexican and United States Readers.* M.A. 443 pp. (Education)

401  Roy, Addie May. *History of "Telegraph and Texas Register," 1835–1846.* M.A. 149 pp. (History)

402  Sánchez, George Isidore. *A Study of the Scores of Spanish-speaking Children on Repeated Tests.* M.Ed. 74 pp. (Education)

403  Sparks, Dade. *The Career of Henry Lane Wilson as United States Ambassador to Mexico (1910–1913).* M.A. 251 pp. (History)

404  Stolz, Alberta Louise. *A Comparative Study of the Art Judgment of Spanish-speaking and English-speaking Children.* M.A. 57 pp. (Education)

## 1932

405  Cogdell, Ava Consuelo. *The Diplomatic and Commercial Relations between the United States and Chile from 1810 to 1830.* M.A. 172 pp. (History)

406 Ellis, Christine Evangeline. *The Relation of Socioeconomic Status to the Intelligence and School Success of Mexican Children.* M.A. 81 pp. (Education)

407 Glick, Walter Reid. *United States' Occupation of Haiti, 1915–1922.* M.A. 117 pp. (History)

408 González, Aurora Marjorie. *A Study of the Intelligence of Mexican Children in Relation to Their Socioeconomic Status.* M.A. 45 pp. (Education)

409 Hogan, William Ransom. *The Life and Letters of Henry Austin, 1782–1852.* M.A. 423 pp. (History)

410 Jackson, Mrs. Lillis Tisdale. *Sam Houston in the Texas Revolution.* M.A. 188 pp. (History)

411 Johnson, Roberta Muriel. *History of the Education of Spanish-speaking Children in Texas.* M.A. 121 pp. (Education)

412 Kerbow, Frances Virginia. *A Study of Color, Sound, and Odor in the Works of Gutiérrez Nájera.* M.A. 222 pp. (Romance Languages)

413 Lozano, Amparo Augusta. *An Experiment in Teaching Spanish and English to Spanish-speaking Children.* M.A. 48 pp. (Education)

414 Moore, Richard Roy Woods. *The Rôle of the Baron de Bastrop in the Anglo-American Settlement of the Spanish Southwest.* M.A. 135 pp. (History)

415 Philibert, Thomas Warren. *The Social Principles of Florencio Sánchez.* M.A. 68 pp. (Romance Languages)

416 Poag, Goldsby May. *The Novels of Mariano Azuela.* M.A. 134 pp. (Romance Languages)

417 Rigler, Frank Clement. *The History of "The San Antonio Express."* M.J. 112 pp. (Journalism)

418 Terry, Zula. *State Control of Education in Brazil during the Empire, 1822–1889.* M.A. 139 pp. (History)

419 Wackerbarth, Allie Mae. *A Comparison of Spanish and English Primers.* M.A. 69 pp. (Education)

420 Ward, Berta Elena. *Un estudio de la vida bonaerense pintada en las novelas argentinas de Carlos María Ocantos.* M.A. 100 pp. (Romance Languages)

## 1933

421 Baugh, Lila. *A Study of the Preschool Vocabulary of Spanish-speaking Children.* M.Ed. 129 pp. (Education)

422 Brooks, Richard Sinclair. *An Inquiry into the Effect of the Geographical Discoveries upon Spanish Thought Prior to the Year 1601, Being a List of the Sources.* M.A. 162 pp. (History)

423　Cezeaux, Louise Catherine. *Social Life in the Republic of Texas, 1836–1845.* M.A. 172 pp. (History)

424　Coplen, Mrs. Cora Elna Reese. *Manuel Gálvez: The Voice from the Argentine.* M.A. 60 pp. (Romance Languages)

425　Deviney, Marvin Lee. *The History of Nueces County to 1850.* M.A. 134 pp. (History)

426　Fullinwider, Elizabeth. *English Translations from Spanish, 1575–1600.* M.A. 113 pp. (English).

427　Garrett, Julia Haughton. *United States-Mexican Relations during the First Administration of Porfirio Díaz, 1876–1880.* M.A. 111 pp. (History)

428　Hackett, Bess Greer. *The Diplomatic and Commercial Relations between the United States and Argentina from 1810 to 1830.* M.A. 120 pp. (History)

429　Henderson, Seth Ward. *Doctor José María Luis Mora and the Mexican Church Problem.* M.A. 108 pp. (History)

430　Johnson, Richard Abraham. *The Preliminaries and Causes of the Mexican Revolution of Ayutla, 1853–1854.* M.A. 151 pp. (History)

431　Keefe, Edgar S. *Denial of Justice as Interpreted and Applied by the United States-Mexican General Claims Commission under the Convention of September 8, 1923.* M.A. 199 pp. (Government)

432　Love, Johnnie Andrew. *Mexico as a Market for United States Farm Machinery.* M.B.A. 108 pp. (Business Administration)

433　McCollom, Ina Mae. *United States Mediation between Colombia and Panamá, 1903–1924.* M.A. 92 pp. (History)

434　Mahler, Theodor. *Life and Work of Ángel de Campo.* M.A. 71 pp. (Romance Languages)

435　Parry, Esther Louise. *A Comparison of the Abilities of Spanish-speaking and English-speaking Children in Ninth-grade Algebra.* M.A. 62 pp. (Education)

436　Pridgen, Mrs. Velma Hill. *The Administration of Don Jacinto de Barrios y Jáuregui as Governor of Texas, 1751–1759.* M.A. 101 pp. (History)

437　Roy, Mary Marguerite. *Relations between the United States and Mexico during the Administration of Lerdo de Tejada, 1872–1876.* M.A. 113 pp. (History)

438　Slaughter, Mrs. Grace McClain. *Relations between the United States and Mexico during the Madero Regime.* M.A. 139 pp. (History)

439　Sprague, William Forrest. *The Career of Vicente Guerrero in the Mexican War for Independence, 1810–1821.* M.A. 104 pp. (History)

## 1934

440 Arrowood, Mrs. Flora Register. *United States-Mexican Relations from 1867 to 1872.* M.A. 125 pp. (History)

441 Brinsmade, Robert Turgot. *The Effect of the Agrarian Reforms upon the Peon in San Luis Potosí.* M.A. 93 pp. (Economics)

442 Brown, Willie Leonzo. *Knowledge of Social Standards among Mexican and Non-Mexican Children.* M.Ed. 76 pp. (Education)

443 Brownlee, Haskell. *United States-Mexican Relations, 1900–1910.* M.A. 117 pp. (History)

444 Burrell, Dick Múzquiz. *The Life and Political Ideas of Father Mier.* M.A. 147 pp. (History)

445 Callicutt, Laurie Timmons. *Word Difficulties of Mexican and Non-Mexican Children.* M.A. 196 pp. (Education)

446 Davis, Lorena Hood. *An Annotation and an Analysis of Sixty Spanish Grammars Published in the United States since 1880.* M.A. 162 pp. (Education)

447 Dixon, Helen Miller. *The Middle Years of the Administration of Juan María, Barón de Ripperdá, Governor of Texas, 1773–1775.* M.A. 97 pp. (History)

448 Jennings, Vivian. *History of Sam Houston's Governorship of Texas.* M.A. 189 pp. (History)

449 LeFevers, Riley Harlan. *The Diplomatic and Commercial Relations between the United States and Colombia from 1810 to 1830.* M.A. 127 pp. (History)

450 Morton, Ward McKinnon. *Foreign Landholdings in the Mexican Agrarian Revolution, 1915–1927.* M.A. 259 pp. (Government)

## 1935

451 Barton, Mable Exa. *The Diplomatic Relations between the United States and Mexico from 1892 to 1900.* M.A. 107 pp. (History)

452 Belaunde, Rafael, Jr. *Santa Cruz and the Peru-Bolivian Confederation, 1836–1839.* M.A. 176 pp. (History)

453 Brown, Mary Sue. *The Development of Secondary Education in Brazil.* M.A. 98 pp. (Education)

454 Browning, Vivian Alma. *Wilson's Policy toward Huerta, 1913–1914.* M.A. 98 pp. (History)

455 Catterton, Conn DeWitt. *The Political Campaigns of the Republic of Texas of 1841 and 1844.* M.A. 143 pp. (History)

456 Greene, Lila Thrace. *A Study of the Women Characters of the South American Novel.* M.A. 115 pp. (Romance Languages)

457 Gunn, Ewing Leyton. *An Eye-movement Study of the Reading Habits of Spanish-speaking Children.* M.A. 116 pp. (Education)

458 Hammond, John Hays. *The Prose Works of Don José María Roa Bárcena.* M.A. 113 pp. (Romance Languages)

459 Hodges, Claudus Grashier. *Diplomatic Relations between the United States and the Republic of Panama, 1903–1918.* M.A. 219 pp. (History)

460 Parsley, Rosa Frances. *A Study of the Expenditure for Food of Some Urban Latin American Families on Work Relief in Austin, Texas.* M.S. in H.E. 68 pp. (Home Economics)

461 Robertson, Clyde Reeves. *A Comparative Study of the Progress of American and Mexican Pupils in Certain Elementary Schools in Texas.* M.A. 46 pp. (Education)

462 Scott, Mrs. Florence Johnson. *Spanish Land Grants in the Lower Río Grande Valley.* M.A. 177 pp. (History)

463 Smith, Rosaileen May. *The Diplomatic Relations between the United States and Mexico from 1884 to 1892.* M.A. 110 pp. (History)

464 Thurston, Raymond LeRoy. *The Colorado River as a Factor in United States-Mexican Relations.* M.A. 270 pp. (Government)

465 Walsh, Sister Natalie. *The Founding of Laredo and St. Augustine Church.* M.A. 122 pp. (History)


1936

466 Benson, Nettie Lee. *The Preconstitutional Regime of Venustiano Carranza, 1913–1917.* M.A. 132 pp. (History)

467 Boxley, Katie Clara. *"Doña Isabel de Solís": An Historical Novel by Francisco Martínez de la Rosa.* M.A. 76 pp. (Romance Languages)

468 Bristow, Robert B. *Internal Improvements in Texas, 1836–1845.* M.A. 107 pp. (History)

469 Clark, Madeline. *A Preliminary Survey of the Employment Possibilities of the Spanish-American Girls Receiving Commercial Training in the San Antonio Secondary Schools.* M.A. 97 pp. (Education)

470 Coan, Bartlett E. *A Comparative Study of the American and Mexican Children in the "Big Bend" Area for 1935–36.* M.Ed. 47 pp. (Education)

471 Graham, Nora Agnes. *Chile's Foreign Policy, 1810–1823.* M.A. 123 pp. (History)

472 Kerbow, Mrs. Blewett Barnes. *The Early History of Red River County, 1817–1865.* M.A. 141 pp. (History)

473 King, Genevieve. *The Psychology of Mexican Community in San Antonio, Texas.* M.A. 85 pp. (Education)

474 Kubela, Marguerite Evelyn. *History of Fort Concho, Texas.* M.A. 123 pp. (History)

475 LeSueur, Hardeman David. *A Contribution to the Knowledge of the Flora of the State of Chihuahua, Mexico: A List.* M.A. 15 pp. (Botany)

476 Lynn, Vela Leatrice. *Chilean-United States Diplomatic Problems Arising from the Chilean Revolution of 1891.* M.A. 90 pp. (History)

477 Morales-Carrión, Arturo. *The Expedition of Francisco Xavier Mina.* M.A. 144 pp. (History)

478 Richards, Hons Coleman. *The Establishment of the Candelaria and San Lorenzo Missions on the Upper Nueces.* M.A. 75 pp. (History)

479 Roberts, Mary Lake. *An Analysis of the Professional Literature Dealing with Latin and Spanish Clubs.* M.A. 109 pp. (Education)

480 Steakley, Dan Lewis. *The Border Patrol of the San Antonio Collection District.* M.A. 131 pp. (History)

481 Wildenthal, Mary Louise. *The Expression of Modernism in the "Revista Azul."* M.A. 108 pp. (Romance Languages)

## 1937

482 Cerda, Evangelina. *La Revolución Mexicana en la novela mexicana.* M.A. 200 pp. (Romance Languages)

483 Drennan, Davy Deolece. *The Progress in Reading of Fourth Grade Spanish-speaking and English-speaking Pupils.* M.A. 130 pp. (Education)

484 Gavaldón-Salamanca, Ignacio. *The Mexican Writ of "Amparo."* M.A. 167 pp. (Government)

485 Griffith, Verona Theresa. *The Short Story in Mexico.* M.A. 79 pp. (Romance Languages)

486 Hunley, Josephine Keller. *A Documentary History of Texan Sentiment for Annexation to the United States, 1835–1838.* M.A. 127 pp. (History)

487 Johnston, Edith Louise. *The Use of Mexican Folk Dances in School Activities.* M.A. 86 pp. (Education)

488 Kahle, Louis George. *The Life and Literary Works of Manuel Payno.* M.A. 107 pp. (Romance Languages)

489 Strieber, Mrs. Mary Esther. *Cédulas Relating to the Early Spanish Exploration of the Shoreline of North America, 1512–1523; Translated with Introduction and Notes.* M.A. 95 pp. (History)

490    Anthony, Samuel Cooper. *The Diplomatic Protection of American Nationals in the Island Republics of the Caribbean Area, 1900–1938.* M.A. 152 pp. (History)

491    Bernhardt, George Marcellus. *The Foreign Oil Interests in Mexico.* M.A. 111 pp. (Economics)

492    Blazek, Leda Frances. *Food Habits and Living Conditions of Mexican Families on Four Income Levels in the Upper Río Grande Valley.* M.S. in H.E. 233 pp. (Home Economics)

493    Clark, Daniel Hendricks. *A Comparison of the Factors Related to Success in Problem Solving in Mathematics for Latin American and Anglo American Students in the Junior School.* M.A. 68 pp. (Education)

494    Coole, Mrs. Ruth Musgrave. *A Comparison of Anglo-American and Latin American Girls in Grades V–XI with Reference to their Vocational, Academic, and Recreational Preferences and Aversions.* M.Ed. 63 pp. (Education)

495    Crawford, Helen Royse. *The Contribution of Benito Juárez to Education.* M.A. 84 pp. (Education)

496    Doerr, Marvin Ferdinand. *Problem of the Elimination of Mexican Pupils from School.* M.Ed. 76 pp. (Education)

497    Hernández, Arcadia. *A Study of Retarded Spanish-speaking Children in the Second Grade.* M.A. 138 pp. (Education)

498    Jackson, Mrs. Lucile Prim. *An Analysis of the Language Difficulties of the Spanish-speaking Children of the Bowie High School, El Paso, Texas.* M.A. 170 pp. (Education)

499    Kaderli, James Nicholas. *A Study of Mexican Education in Atascosa County with Special Reference to Pleasanton Elementary School.* M.Ed. 77 pp. (Education)

500    Rehn, Dorothy. *San Antonio and the Missions in the Literature of the Southwest.* M.A. 99 pp. (English)

501    Story, Anna B. *The Alamo from Its Founding to 1937.* M.A. 135 pp. (History)

## 1939

502    Barbour, Lizzie Messick. *Federal Participation in Public Education in Mexico, 1934–1937.* M.Ed. 132 pp. (Education)

503    Bennett, Catherine. *The History of Education in Laredo, Texas, to 1870.* M.A. 169 pp. (Education)

504 Carroll, Edward Leroy. *Eduardo Barrios as a Literary Artist.* M.A. 80 pp. (Romance Languages)

505 Castillo, Henrietta Amparo. *The Life and Works of María Enriqueta.* M.A. 104 pp. (Romance Languages)

506 Cotner, Thomas Ewing. *Diplomatic Relations between the United States and Mexico Concerning a Tehuantepec Transit Route, 1823–1860.* M.A. 152 pp. (History)

507 Coy, Edna. *Cultural Relations between South America and the Old World with Reference to Possible Contacts across the Pacific Ocean.* M.A. 136 pp. (Anthropology)

508 Drennan, Orlena Pink. *The Progress in Reading of Second Grade Spanish-speaking and English-speaking Pupils.* M.Ed. 115 pp. (Education)

509 Filizola, Umberto Daniel. *Correspondence of Santa Anna during the Texas Campaign, 1835–1836; Translated, with Introduction and Notes.* M.A. 89 pp. (History)

510 Gámez, Luis Ezequiel. *Justo Sierra: historiador, educador, y literato.* M.A. 157 pp. (Romance Languages)

511 Grace, Mrs. Delfina Gómez. *Heriberto Frías y la novela nacional.* M.A. 93 pp. (Romance Languages)

512 McIver, Mrs. Zadie Runkles. *Linguistic Borrowings from the Spanish as Reflected in Writings of the Southwest.* M.A. 77 pp. (English)

513 McLennan, LeRoy. *A Comparison of the Spanish-speaking and English-speaking Children in Nine Schools over a Five-year Period.* M.Ed. 55 pp. (Education)

514 Medley, Gladys. *A Study of the Historical Novel in Argentina.* M.A. 100 pp. (Romance Languages)

515 O'Bannion, Mrs. Jessie May Traylor. *A Comparative Study of Four South American Novelists of this Generation.* M.A. 73 pp. (Romance Languages)

516 Passmore, Helen Fay. *Women Printers, Publishers, and Journalists in Colonial Mexico.* M.A. 124 pp. (Romance Languages)

517 Roots, Floy Eula. *Methods and Materials for Teaching Spanish to Spanish-speaking Students in Texas High Schools.* M.A. 175 pp. (Education)

518 Shannon, Fain Gillock. *A Comparative Study of Desirable Teacher Traits as Listed by Anglo American and Latin American Pupils.* M.A. 76 pp. (Education)

519 Williams, Albert Calvin. *The Route of Cabeza de Vaca in Texas: A Study in Historiography.* M.A. 99 pp. (History)

520 Yager, Hope. *The Archive War in Texas.* M.A. 97 pp. (History)

521  Apstein, Theodore. *A Modern Mexican Playwright: José Joaquín Gamboa.* M.A. 250 pp. (Romance Languages)

522  Cockrum, Amil Blake. *Some Laboratory Procedures and a Preliminary Study of Río Grande River Sediments.* M.A. 85 pp. (Geology)

523  Fussell, William Durwood. *Comparable Norms for Anglo and Latin American Pupils on a Scholastic Aptitude Test.* M.Ed. 62 pp. (Education)

524  Jackson, Dorothy Jean. *Pershing's Expedition into Mexico.* M.A. 143 pp. (History)

525  Kaderli, Albert Turner. *The Educational Problem in the Americanization of the Spanish-speaking Pupils of Sugarland, Texas.* M.A. 71 pp. (Education)

526  Langham, Loucille Grace. *The Ascorbic Acid of Metabolism of Mexican Women on a Low Income Level.* M.S. in H.E. 64 pp. (Home Economics)

527  Moran, Mrs. Mattie Belle Sauer. *A Study of the Oral and Reading Vocabularies of Beginning Spanish-speaking Children.* M.A. 109 pp. (Education)

528  Roach, Sister Mary Baptista. *Diplomatic Relations between the United States and Central America and the Ministership of Mirabeau B. Lamar, 1850–1860.* M.A. 200 pp. (History)

529  Smith, Mary Avis Dowis. *Comparative Study of Some Attitudes and Interests of Latin American and Anglo American Boys.* M.Ed. 82 pp. (Education)

530  Christie, Christina Cloe. *The Jesuits in Brazil, 1549–1568.* M.A. 134 pp. (History)

531  Collins, James William. *The Attitude of South America toward the Belligerency of the United States in the First World War.* M.A. 136 pp. (Government)

532  Foerster, Viola Marguerite. *Hidalgo and the Mexican Revolution of 1810.* M.A. 126 pp. (History)

533  Guerra, Fermina. *Mexican and Spanish Folklore and Incidents in Southwest Texas.* M.A. 139 pp. (Romance Languages)

534  Jáuregui Fernández, Beatriz. *Carlos Loveira: Su Vida y Sus Obras.* M.A. 81 pp. (Romance Languages)

535  Keen, Marvin Spruce. *A Comparative Study of the Motor Ability of Latin American and Anglo American Boys.* M.Ed. 82 pp. (Education)

536 Neal, Joe West. *The Policy of the United States toward Immigration from Mexico.* M.A. 251 pp. (Government)

537 Saenz, Pilar. *Learning Units in Secondary-School Spanish: First Year.* M.A. 237 pp. (Education)

538 Studhalter, Margaret Ruth. *An Index of the Literary Materials in "El Tiempo."* M.A. 320 pp. (Romance Languages)

## 1942

539 Ambía, Sister María de la Paz. *La obra poética de Alfonso Junco.* M.A. 153 pp. (Romance Languages)

540 Cole, Ruth. *The Works of Rómulo Gallegos.* M.A. 95 pp. (Romance Languages)

541 Covington, Mrs. Carolyn Callaway. *The "Runaway Scrape": An Episode of the Texas Revolution.* M.A. 104 pp. (History)

542 Dailey, Mrs. Mauryne Phelps. *A Study of Achievement in Spanish in Relation to Intelligence and Other Traits.* M.A. 49 pp. (Education)

543 Goodstein, Barnett Morris. *Sugar in Inter-American Trade.* M.A. 117 pp. (Economics)

544 Newberry, Josephine. *Legends and Festivals Associated with Indigenous Dances of Mexico.* M.Ed. 98 pp. (Education)

545 Newton, Margaret Elizabeth. *The Texas Cowboy and the Argentine Gaucho in Literature, as Found in Andy Adams' Novels, Badger Clark's Poetry, Ricardo Güiraldes' "Don Segundo Sombra," and José Hernández' "Martín Fierro."* M.A. 130 pp. (English)

546 Ochoa, Hermelinda. *Linguistic Errors Made by Spanish-speaking Children in Written English.* M.A. 85 pp. (Education)

547 Smith, Ola Lee. *The Influence of Misiones on the Life and Works of Horacio Quiroga.* M.A. 119 pp. (Romance Languages)

548 Valdés Pérez, Carlos Manuel. *Las ideas filosóficas en las novelas de A. Hernández Catá.* M.A. 117 pp. (Romance Languages)

549 Vetters, Mrs. Anna Hill. *Speech Correction among Spanish-speaking Children in an Elementary School.* M.Ed. 71 pp. (Education)

550 Willard, Mary Jean. *A Study of the Diet and Nutritional Status of Latin American Women.* M.S. in H.E. 90 pp. (Home Economics)

## 1943

551 Armas-Hernández, Salvador. *A Highway System for Venezuela.* M.S. in C.E. 112 pp. (Civil Engineering)

552 Cruz, Angelita María. *Spanish-speaking Children's Expressed Attitudes toward Money Value.* M.A. 49 pp. (Education)

553 England, Frances Hall. *A Translation, with Notes, of José Joaquín Fernández de Lizardi's "Don Catrín de la Fachenda."* M.A. 124 pp. (Romance Languages)

554 Terry, Hubert Hendrix. *The Origins of the Mexican Revolution of 1910.* M.A. 176 pp. (History)

555 Velasco Terres, Raoul. *Silver in Mexico during 1930–1940.* M.A. 199 pp. (Economics)

## 1944

556 Browning, Horace Noel. *A Comparison of the Spanish-speaking and English-speaking Children in Nine Schools over a Four-year Period.* M.Ed. 51 pp. (Education)

557 Farabee, Ethel Sadie. *The Career of William Stuart Parrott, Business Man and Diplomat in Mexico.* M.A. 348 pp. (History)

558 Martínez, Arnulfo Simeón. *A Study of the Scholastic Census of the Spanish-speaking Children of Texas.* M.A. 105 pp. (Education)

559 Walters, Paul Hugh. *Surveys of the History of La Bahía del Espíritu Santo, 1721–1821.* M.A. 148 pp. (Latin American Studies: History)

560 Wilson, Thomas Ray. *William Walker and the Filibustering Expedition to Lower California and Sonora.* M.A. 105pp. (History)

## 1945

561 Callicutt, Mrs. Dorothy Hinds. *A Study of the Socioeconomic Status of Puerto Rican School Children.* M.Ed. 92 pp. (Education)

562 Caro-Costas, Aída Raquel. *Porfirio Díaz and Beginning of the Mexican Political Stabilization.* M.A. 229 pp. (History)

563 Hutchison, Mrs. Cornelia. *A Comparative Study of the Teaching Materials for Six-year-old Children in Mexico and Texas.* M.A. 133 pp. (Education)

564 Klages, Roy Arthur. *Air Transportation in Latin America —Its Growth and Development.* M.B.A. 146 pp. (Business Administration)

565 Lado, Robert. *A Study of the Use of Motion Pictures in Teaching Spanish-speaking Adults to Read.* M.A. 115 pp. (Education)

566 Neal, Mary Mason. *The Career of Francisco Morazán, Liberator of Central America.* M.A. 143 pp. (Latin American Studies: History)

567 Pflucker, Eduardo Cabiese. *A Review of the Geology of the Oil Fields*

*of South America with Emphasis on Prospective Areas.* M.A. 423 pp. (Geology)

568 Sullivan, Ben Dell. *An Analysis of Evaluation of a Group of Spanish Textbooks Published since 1933.* M.A. 139 pp. (Education)

## 1946

569 Aikin, Mrs. Welma Morphew. *Works of Roberto Payró that Deal with His Own Times.* M.A. 111 pp. (Romance Languages)

570 Dickens, Betty Jane. *A Translation, with Notes, of Manuel Díaz Rodríguez's "Sangre Patricia."* M.A. 140 pp. (Romance Languages)

571 Fahrenkamp, Billie Mae. *The European Background of Certain Spanish American Novels.* M.A. 138 pp. (Romance Languages)

572 Fraser, William McKinley. *A Study of the Abilities of Spanish-speaking and English-speaking Children of Kinney County, Texas.* M.Ed. 102 pp. (Education)

573 González de Gueits, Mrs. Francisca. *A Study of the Child Development Program on the Secondary School Level in Texas, and Its Implication to Puerto Rico.* M.Ed. 93 pp. (Education)

574 Johnson, Mrs. Claudia Loris Parker. *The Re-organization of an Elementary School for Spanish-speaking Children.* M.Ed. 145 pp. (Education)

575 Lozano, Mrs. Dora Alice. *An Edition, with Introduction and Notes, of Fernando Calderón's "A Ninguna de las Tres."* M.A. 124 pp. (Romance Languages)

576 Marulanda, Juan Manuel. *La enseñanza del francés en Colombia.* M.Ed. 206 pp. (Education)

577 Mitchell, Mrs. Nan Jones. *An Evaluation of Provisions for the Education of the Spanish-speaking Children in San Marcos, Texas.* M.Ed. 91 pp. (Education)

578 Odell, Abrabella Gertrude. *Reopening the African Slave Trade in Texas.* M.A. 131 pp. (History)

579 Rodríguez-Pacheco, Osvaldo. *Social and Economic Conditions in Puerto Rico and Their Implications for Education.* M.Ed. 69 pp. (Education)

580 Scott, Elizabeth. *A Study of the Chronicles of Indian Captivity in the Southwest.* M.A. 112 pp. (English)

581 Shelton, Edgar Greer, Jr. *Political Conditions among Texas Mexicans along the Río Grande.* M.A. 126 pp. (Government)

582 Sobrino, Josephine. *Estudio crítico de las obras de Joaquín Edwards Bello.* M.A. 76 pp. (Romance Languages)

583 Vázquez, Diamantina Minerva. *The Historical Development of Ownership in the Subsoil Resources of Mexico.* M.A. 154 pp. (Government)

584 Willhauk, Ralph Clyde. *A Study of Inter-American Tests in Relation to the Stanford-Binet Tests.* M.A. 86 pp. (Education)

## 1947

585 Abat, Mary Lee. *Madama Lynch of Paraguay, Her Rise, Her Romance, Her Tragedy.* M.A. 176 pp. (History)

586 Aponte Rivera, Luz Loarina. *A Study of the School Lunch and Nutrition Education Program in the Schools of Puerto Rico.* M.Ed. 91 pp. (Education)

587 Bennett, Hazel Marylyn. *A Translation with Introduction and Notes of "El General Quiroga," by Manuel Gálvez.* M.A. 353 pp. (Romance Languages)

588 Cartagena Colón, Demetrio. *Emphasizing Character Education in the Curriculum of the Public Schools of Puerto Rico.* M.Ed. 158 pp.

589 Gerling, Charles Frederick. *Twenty Representative Contemporary Spanish American Cuentos in English Translation, with Introduction, Notes, and Bibliography.* M.A. 299 pp. (Romance Languages)

590 Gibson, Charles. *The Inca Concept of Sovereignty and the Spanish Administration in Peru.* M.A. 213 pp. (History)

591 Gilbert, Ennis Hall. *Some Legal Aspects of the Education of Spanish-speaking Children in Texas.* M.Ed. 144 pp. (Education)

592 Hedrick, Elinor May. *The Novels of Juan Antonio Mateos.* M.A. 100 pp. (Romance Languages)

593 Hestire, Bluford Bradford. *The Urges to a Texas Literature, 1526–1716.* M.A. 223 pp. (English)

594 Meyer, Samuel Alexander. *A Translation of Enrique López Albújar's "Cuentos Andinos," with Introduction and Notes.* M.A. 179 pp. (Romance Languages)

595 Neblett, Mrs. Myrtle Hargon. *Large Scale Food Service for the Tropics Adapted to Cuba.* M.S. in H.E. 245 pp. (Home Economics)

596 Oliphant, James William, Jr. *An Appraisal of the Consumer's Goods Industry in Mexico, 1940–1946.* M.A. 213 pp. (Latin American Studies: Economics)

597 Paul, Lewis Nelson. *Evolution of the Pan American Union (1890–1947) with Sketches of the Political Background.* M.A. 339 pp. (Government)

598 Walker, Elna La Verne. *Latin American Through Juvenile Literature: An Evaluated Bibliography.* M.Ed. 98 pp. (Education)

599 Weir, Avis. *Ciro Alegría's "Los Perros Hambrientos": A Translation, with Summaries, Notes, and Introduction.* M.A. 166 pp. (Romance Languages)

## 1948

600 Arrington, Frank Wade. *The Development of Oil Exclaves in Venezuela, January 1854 to April 1948.* M.A. 104 pp. (Latin American Studies: Economics)

601 Cabrera, María Guadalupe (ed.). *An Abridged, Annotated Edition of "La Calandria" by Rafael Delgado.* M.A. 337 pp. (Romance Languages)

602 Crain, Forest Burr. *A Study of Occupational Distribution of Spanish-name People in Austin, Texas.* M.A. 117 pp. (Sociology)

603 Crasilneck, Harold Bernard. *A Study of One Hundred Male Latin American Juvenile Delinquents in San Antonio, Texas.* M.A. 100 pp. (Sociology)

604 Daniel, James Manley. *La Junta de los Ríos and the Despoblado, 1680–1760.* M.A. 193 pp. (History)

605 Fogartie, Mrs. Ruth Ann Douglass. *Spanish-name People in Texas with Special Emphasis on Those Who Are Students in Texas Colleges and Universities.* M.A. 88 pp. (Education)

606 Havins, Mary Sue. *A Translation of José Rubén Romero's "Mi caballo, mi perro, y mi rifle," with Introduction and Notes.* M.A. 138 pp. (Romance Languages)

607 Lancaster, Mrs. Irene Knopp. *Spanish Culture in the Philippine Islands in the Sixteenth and Seventeenth Centuries as Revealed in Some of the Early Chronicles.* M.A. 188 pp. (History)

608 Martin, Marjorie Kathryn. *A Comparative Study of Class and Individual Instruction in Latin and Anglo American Music Classes.* M.Mus. 92 pp. (Music)

609 Roca, Pablo. *A Study of a Test of Word-Relations for Spanish-speaking Children.* M.Ed. 131 pp. (Education)

610 Rohr, Thurman Goodwin. *A Study of the Correction of English Pronunciation of Latin American Pupils.* M.Ed. 117 pp. (Education)

611 Rouse, Mrs. Lura Nelson. *A Study of the Education of Spanish-speaking Children in Dimmit County, Texas.* M.Ed. 89 pp. (Education)

612 Schiller, Mae Dell. *Selected Stories from Manuel Gutiérrez Nájera; A Translation with Introduction and Notes.* M.A. 165 pp. (Romance Languages)

613 Stasieluk, Laura Ann. *Significant Latin American Expropriations and Their Relation to International Law*. M.A. 165 pp. (Government)

614 Vigness, David Martell. *The Lower Río Grande Valley, 1836–1846*. M.A. 145 pp. (History)

615 Warren, Bonnie Davis. *A Translation of "Nuestros hijos" and an Index of the Characters in the Plays of Florencio Sánchez*. M.A. 157 pp. (Romance Language)

## 1949

616 Ashton, Price Richard. *The Fourteenth Amendment and the Education of Latin American Children in Texas*. M.Ed. 153 pp. (Education)

617 Bass, Thomas Edwin. *Standard Investment Aanlysis as Applied to Current U.S. Investments in Mexico*. M.B.A. 316 pp. (Business Administration)

618 Beresford, Martha. *The Role of Ignacio Rayón: Mexican Revolutionary*. M.A. 203 pp. (History)

619 Connor, Mrs. Ruth Patton. *Some Community-Home-School Problems of Latin American Children in Austin, Texas*. M.Ed. 93 pp. (Education)

620 Craddock, Vina Marie. *A Comparative Study of Anglo-American and Latin American Children in Preference and Performance of Arithmetic Problems*. M.Ed. 94 pp. (Education)

621 Cromack, Mrs. Isabel Charlotte Work. *Latin Americans: A Minority Group in the Austin Public Schools*. M.A. 100 pp. (Education)

622 Daniels, Marion Gordon. *Guano, Railroads, and the Peruvian Corporation*. M.A. 225 pp. (History)

623 Delk, Lois Jo. *Spanish Language and Literature in the Publications of American Universities: A Bibliography*. M.A. 114 pp. (Romance Languages)

624 Flood, Virginia Lee. *Teaching English as a Foreign Language to Spanish-speaking Students of the Other American Republics*. M.A. 93 pp. (Education)

625 Ford, Mrs. Lucile Catheryn Kirsch. *Books Listed in the "Gaceta de México" (1784–1809) with Bibliographical Annotations*. M.A. 153 pp. (Romance Languages)

626 Flores, Louis Sierra. *An Experimental Oral-Aural Test of Spanish*. M.A. 90 pp. (Education)

627 Galván, Robert A. *Un estudio geográfico de algunos vocablos usados por los habitantes de habla española de San Antonio, Texas*. M.A. 141 pp. (Romance Languages)

628 Glass, Nellie May. *A Study of Reading Performance of Anglo and Latin American Children.* M.A. 142 pp. (Education)

629 Glasscock, William Donley. *Fray Bernardino de Sahagún.* M.A. 78 pp. (Education)

630 Greer, Viola Ann. *Santiago Vidaurri, Cacique of Northern Mexico: His Relationship to Benito Juárez.* M.A. 155 pp. (History)

631 Handy, Mary Olivia. *A History of Fort Sam Houston.* M.A. 140 pp. (History)

632 James, George William. *The National Steel Industries of Latin America.* M.A. 226 pp. (Economics)

633 Lockwood, Dorothy Mae. *Commercial Education in Mexico.* M.B.A. 132 pp. (Business Administration)

634 McCrocklin, James Henry. *A Study: Latin American Attitude with Respect to World War I.* M.A. 217 pp. (Government)

635 Mack, Raymond DeElmont. *Constitutional Centralism in Mexico—A Study of the Constitutions of 1836 and 1843.* M.A. 279 pp. (Government)

636 Pérez, Soledad. *Mexican Folklore in Austin.* M.A. 152 pp. (English)

637 Pogson, Robert John. *Some Effects of the Second World War upon Latin American Agriculture.* M.A. 234 pp. (Economics)

638 Pope, Harold Clay. *Humberto Salvador: Present-day Ecuadorian Novelist.* M.A. 118 pp. (Romance Languages)

639 Riddle, María Isabel. *Ideario histórico de R. Blanco-Fombona a través de su obra.* M.A. 147 pp. (Romance Languages)

640 Sánchez, Mrs. Luisa G. G. *"Los de abajo": A Simplified Version for High Schools.* M.A. 224 pp. (Education)

641 Standefer, Harmon Bishop. *Some Economic Aspects and Consequences of Free-trade Zones in Mexican Border Cities.* M.B.A. 79 pp. (Business Administration)

642 Vaughan, Ernest Heath, Jr. *Some Aspects of Exchange Control in Latin America.* M.B.A. 76 pp. (Business Administration)

643 Vázquez, Elfida. *Grupos y tendencias literarias en México a partir de la Revista "Contemporáneos": Sus organos de expresión.* M.A. 116 pp. (Romance Languages)

1950

644 Abbott, Raymond Robert. *San Martín in Perú.* M.A. 226 pp. (History)

645 Ashby, Joe Charles. *Labor and the Argentine Revolution.* M.A. 215 pp. (Economics)

646 Bennett, Rosemary. *Positivism and the Escuela Nacional Preparatoria of Mexico.* M.A. 124 pp. (Education)

647 Brown-Wrinkle, Mary Helen. *Pitch Improvement in Anglo and Latin American Children.* M.Mus. 64 pp. (Music)

648 Burmeister, Sarah Eva. *Learning about Latin America in the Seventh Grade.* M.A. 82 pp. (Education)

649 Butler, Mrs. Carolyn Jane Matthews. *Prose Fiction of the Guayaquil Group.* M.A. 166 pp. (Romance Languages)

650 Cabaza, Berta. *The Spanish Language in Texas: Cameron and Willacy Counties, District* 10A. M.Ed. 183 pp. (Education)

651 Cerda, Gilberto. *The Spanish Language in Texas. No. 1: Val Verde, Edwards, and Kinney Counties.* M.A. 305 pp. (Romance Languages)

652 Cramer, Martin John. *Sir Walter Raleigh in the Caribbean.* M.A. 119 pp. (History)

653 Cunningham, Robert Emmet. *James Treat and His Mission to Mexico.* M.A. 95 pp. (History)

654 Davis, Richard Lee. *A Translation, with Notes, of Vito Alessio Robles' "Monterrey en la historia y en la leyenda."* M.A. 300 pp. (Romance Languages)

655 Elms, James Edwin. *Attendance of Mexican and Anglo Students in Two Austin, Texas, Schools.* M.Ed. 108 pp. (Education)

656 Ewing, Floyd Ford, Jr. *History of the Hemisphere Defense System.* M.A. 248 pp. (Latin American Studies: History)

657 Foster, William C. *The Postwar Sugar Problem.* M.A. 190 pp. (Economics)

658 García, Clotilde Pérez. *The Use of Readings from Spanish American Literature in High-school Spanish Classes: An Evaluated Bibliography.* M.Ed. 99 pp. (Education)

659 Garza, Alfonso Jesus. *The Economic and Business Aspects of Mexican Fruit Importing.* M.B.A. 134 pp. (Business Administration)

660 Giles, Geoffrey James. *Anglo-Spanish Hostilities, 1588–1604.* M.A. 225 pp. (History)

661 Haddick, Jack Allen. *The Administration of Viceroy José de Iturrigaray: The First Years.* M.A. 138 pp. (History)

662 Hay, Mrs. Gray Southern. *Argentine Dance Music with Particular Reference to the Gato.* M.Mus. 93 pp. (Music)

663 McLean, Robert Jack. *A Comparative Study of Anglo American and Spanish-name Children in the Austin Public Schools over a Seven-year Period.* M.Ed. 66 pp. (Education)

664   Martin, Mrs. Mary Etta Clift. *Improving the Teaching of Spanish in a Small High School of Texas.* M.A. 133 pp. (Education)

665   Near, Arthur Ward. *The Ordinances of Segovia of 1573 for New Entradas: A Translation with Notes and Historical Introduction.* M.A. 67 pp. (History)

666   Phillips, Mrs. Juanita Stroud. *The Spanish Folklore of Texas: No. 1, Cameron County,* M.A. 201 pp. (Romance Languages)

## 1951

667   Farías, María Julieta. *The Spanish Language in Texas. No. 3: Duval, Webb, and Zapata Counties.* M.A. 122 pp. (Romance Languages)

668   Gay, Robert Neill, Jr. *The Fuel and Power Resources of Brazil and Their Development.* M.A. 129 pp. (Economics)

669   Holden, Narcissa Jane. *Archaelogical Investigations at the Bonnell Site, Southeastern New Mexico.* M.A. 108 pp. (Anthropology)

670   Marshall, Mrs. Eleanor Jackson, *History of the Lancasterian Education Movement in Mexico.* M.A. 120 pp. (History)

671   Meador, Bruce Staffel. *Wetback Labor in the Lower Río Grande Valley.* M.Ed. 143 pp. (Education)

672   Niemeyer, E. Victor, Jr. *The Mexican Constitutional Convention of 1916–1917: The Constitutionalizing of a Revolutionary Ideology.* M.A. 311 pp. (Government)

673   Pandolfi de Rinaldis Lara, Dino. *Administrative Trends in the Educational System of Puerto Rico.* M.Ed. 216 pp. (Education)

674   Pease, Jay Jesse, Jr. *Highlands in Intra-Latin American Trade.* M.A. 105 pp. (Business Administration)

675   Pike, Frederick Braun. *Antecedents of the Spanish Municipality in America.* M.A. 232 pp. (History)

676   Ramírez, Alfonso René. *A Study of the Reactions of Latin American Pupils to English and Spanish Film Commentaries.* M.Ed. 136 pp. (Education)

677   Ramírez, Mrs. Emilia Schunior. *"Wetback" Children in South Texas.* M.Ed. 134 pp. (Education)

678   Riddle, Octavio Rodolfo. *The Coal and Steel Industries of Mexico.* M.A. 108 pp. (Economics)

679   West, Ruth Thoburn. *José Vasconcelos and His Contributions to Mexican Public Education.* M.Ed. 112 pp. (Education)

680   Barillas, María L. *Desenvolvimiento de la Economía doméstica y el Trabajo Manual en la República de Cuba.* M.Ed. 98 pp. (Education)

681   Benavides, Ilma Mariana. *General Adrian Woll's Invasion of San Antonio in 1842.* M.A. 130 pp. (Latin American Studies: History)

682   Bergmann, John Francis. *Resources and Development of the Pacific and Mountain Divisions of the K.C.M. & O. Railway Route, Mexico.* M.A. 183 pp. (Geography)

683   Blum, Owen Wilson. *Some Aspects of the Latin American Market of Austin, Texas, with Emphasis on the Radio as a Means of Reaching this Market.* M.B.A. 96 pp. (Business Administration)

684   Brewer, Sam Aaron, Jr. *Latin America in Texas High Schools.* M.A. 138 pp. (Latin American Studies: Education)

685   Broussard, Ray Francis. *Description of Atitlán and its Dependencies: A Translation with Introduction and Notes.* M.A. 148 pp. (Latin American Studies: History)

686   Carter, Robert Arthur, Jr. *Anthony Butler and His Mission to Mexico.* M.A. 131 pp. (History)

687   Cobb, Albert Folsome. *Comparative Study of the Athletic Ability of Latin American and Anglo American Boys on a Junior High School Level.* M.Ed. 59 pp. (Education)

688   Díaz-Risa, Ignacio. *A Speech Survey of Eighty Spanish-speaking Children in Four Elementary Schools of Austin, Texas.* M.Ed. 53 pp. (Education)

689   Dufner, Lucille Ashby. *The Teaching of Spanish in the Elementary Grades.* M.Ed. 117 pp. (Education)

690   Garza, Mrs. Consuelo M. *Woman in the Spanish Romance.* M.A. 117 pp. (English)

691   Gutiérrez, Emeterio, Jr. *A Study of School Attendance of Migrant Students in Grulla, Texas.* M.Ed. 102 pp. (Education)

692   Harrison, David Caldwell. *A Survey of the Administrative and Educational Policies of the Baptist, Methodist, and Presbyterian Churches Among Mexican-American People in Texas.* M.A. 153 pp. (Education)

693   Hayes, James Virgil. *An Analysis of Latin-American Partial Attendance and Drop-outs in the Elementary Schools of Eagle Pass, Texas, in Recent Years.* M.Ed. 180 pp. (Education)

694   Hnatek, Margaret. *A Survey of Population Factors Relating to the Education of Migrant Children in Victoria County, Texas.* M.Ed. 76 pp. (Education)

695   Howe, Anna Lynn. *Proposals for the Organization and Administration of a Special Education to Improve the English Speech of Certain Spanish-speaking Pupils, Eagle Pass, Texas.* M.Ed. 134 pp. (Education)

696   Jackson, Mrs. Doris Goforth. *Educational Status of Mexican Children in a Texas Elementary School.* M.Ed. 71 pp. (Education)

697   Kielman, Chester Valls. *The History and Culture of the Five Civilized Tribes of American Indians.* M.A. 323 pp. (History)

698   Kuhl, Jerome Miller. *Agricultural Land Utilization in Ecuador.* M.A. 152 pp. Economics)

699   Linares, Silvia Margarita. *La enseñanza del inglés en Cuba.* M.A. 91 pp. (Education)

700   Lowry, Sarah Jean. *A Comparison of Certain Physical Abilities of Anglo and Latin American Fifth and Sixth Grade Girls.* M.Ed. 76 pp. (Education)

701   Nichols, Paul Edward. *A Study of the Co-operative Inter-american Tests of Language Usage at the Junior High School Level.* M.Ed. 75 pp. (Education)

702   Olivard, Lois Claire. *Sixteenth-Century Methods of Sermon Preaching in New Spain.* M.A. 78 pp. (History)

703   Quintanilla Reyes, Mrs. Sara. *The Place of Moisés Sáenz in Mexican Education.* M.A. 90 pp. (Education)

704   Red, William Stuart, III. *National Banking Systems of Central America.* M.A. 261 pp. (Latin American Studies: Economics)

705   Rollman, Howard Edwin. *Developments in the Iron and Steel Industries of Colombia and Venezuela—Some Aspects of Steel in Economic Development.* M.A. 164 pp. (Economics)

706   Saunders, Mrs. Maxine Pleydell-Pearce. *Some Educational Problems of Spanish-speaking Children of the Intermediate Grade Level.* M.Ed. 102 pp. (Education)

707   Singletary, Coyle Edward. *Geography of the Municipios of La Huacana and Churumuco, State of Michoacán, Mexico.* M.A. 147 pp. (Geography)

708   Tubbs, Lowell Lester. *A Survey of the Problems of Migratory Mexicans.* M.Ed. 117 pp. (Education)

709   Tunnell, William Kerr. *The Career of Bernardo O'Higgins to 1818.* M.A. 108 pp. (Latin American Studies: History)

710   Vallve, Graciela. *Adult Education in the Evening Schools of Cuba and Texas.* M.Ed. 72 pp. (Education)

711   Walsh, Brother Albeus. *The Work of the Catholic Bishops' Commit-

*tee for the Spanish-speaking People in the United States.* M.A. 122 pp. (History)

712  Williamson, Robert Lee. *A History of Company E of the Texas Frontier Battalion, 1874–1879.* M.A. 165 pp. (History)

713  Willis, James Frederick. *The Industrialization of Chile.* M.A. 104 pp. (Economics)

1953

714  Atkinson, Rosa M. *The Educational Retardation of the Spanish-speaking Child and Recommendations for Remediation.* M.Ed. 86 pp. (Education)

715  Deveau, Augustine Francis. *Fray Antonio Margil de Jesús, Apostolic Missionary.* M.A. 105 pp. (Latin American Studies: History)

716  Fernández-López, María. *El viaje de don Ramón de la Sagra a los Estados Unidos. M.A.* 86 pp. (Romance Languages)

717  Flores, Consuelo. *English through Latin American Contest Materials for High School Pupils.* M.A. 113 pp. (Education)

718  Garnett, Mrs. Hattie Mae. *Boy-Girl Relationships of Latin American Children as Shown in Anecdotal Records by Teachers.* M.Ed. 164 pp. (Education)

719  Garza, Mrs. María Azcunia. *Teaching of English to Spanish-speaking Beginners.* M.Ed. 97 pp. (Education)

720  Hatter, Curtis R., Jr. *Anglo-Guatemalan Controversy over British Honduras.* M.A. 186 pp. (Latin American Studies: Government)

721  Hernández, Nivea M. *American Idioms and the Teaching of English in Puerto Rico.* M.A. 127 pp. (Education)

722  Janto, Stephen Anthony. *Contributing Factors in the Foundation of Spanish Indian Policy.* M.A. 213 pp. (Latin American Studies: History)

723  Kalmbach, Frank. *The Argentine State Merchant Marine since 1939.* M.A. 147 pp. (Latin American Studies: International Trade)

724  Long, Stanton C. *Early Nineteenth Century El Paso.* M.A. 124 pp. (Latin American Studies: History)

725  McCall, Cristina Vinolo. *A Proposed Plan of In-Service Education for Superintendents of Schools in Puerto Rico.* M.Ed. 204 pp. (Education)

726  McCrary, Mrs. Mallie Muncy. *These Minorities in our Midst: with Emphasis on Latin Americans in Texas.* M.A. 128 pp. (Education)

727  Magalhães, María Borges de. *Pronunciation Difficulties Encountered by Brazilian Students of English.* M.A. 40 pp. (English)

728  Marshall, John F., Jr. *An Index to the Literary Content of "El Uni-*

versal" and "El Universal Ilustrado," 1916–1931. M.A. 409 pp. (Romance Languages)

729 Massey, Leonard Ellis. *Migration of the Spanish-speaking People of Hidalgo County.* M.A. 67 pp. (Education)

730 Newcomer, Hale Alden. *Some Aspects of American Direct Private Investment in Venezuela.* M.B. 83 pp. (Business Administration)

731 Paredes, Américo. *Ballads of the Lower Border.* M.A. 228 pp. (English)

732 Rosbach, Mrs. Edith Virginia Hunter. *The History of the Mission Period of Pimería Alta to 1828.* M.A. 163 pp. (History)

733 Ruby, Mrs. Carrie Louise Lokey. *Attitudes toward Latin Americans as Revealed in Southwest Literature.* M.A. 95 pp. (English)

## 1954

734 Brogdon, Dewey Robert. *Beach Sands of the Gulf Coast, Northern Tamaulipas, Mexico.* M.A. 68 pp. (Geology)

735 Chutro, John Joseph. *The Dynamic Decade in the Industrial Growth of Mexico, 1939–1950.* M.A. 169 pp. (Latin American Studies: Economics)

736 Hernández, Elías Vega. *Reading Retardation of Children in Zavala School, Austin, Texas.* M.A. 65 pp. (Education)

737 Hiester, Mrs. Miriam Webb. *Los Paisanos, Folklore of the Texas-Mexicans of the Lower Río Grande Valley.* M.A. 137 pp. (English).

738 Hood, Anita Louise. *The Reorganization of Secondary Education in Mexico since 1926.* M.A. 93 pp. (Latin American Studies: Education)

739 Knabe, Robert George. *Geology of Totumo Anticline, Northeastern Venezuela.* M.A. 54 pp. (Geology)

740 Massey, Gloria Walker. *Spanish in Texas Junior High Schools.* M.A. 71 pp. (Education)

741 Mellenbruch, Julia Ida Klatenhoff. *Teaching Spanish to Spanish-speaking Students in Teaxs High Schools.* M.A. 91 pp. (Education)

742 Rea, George Harold. *A Study of Four Cooperative Inter-American Tests.* M.A. 56 pp. (Education)

743 Smith, Leonard Thomas. *A Survey of the Development of the United Fruit Company.* M.B.A. 95 pp. (Business Administration)

744 Stohl, Mrs. Darthula Davis. *A Study Treating the Teaching of Language Skills Through Music to Spanish-speaking Children.* M.A. 77 pp. (Music)

745 Stullken, Virginia Pauline. *Keystone of Mexican Government—the*

*Secretaría de Gobernación*. M.A. 105 pp. (Latin American Studies: Government)

746    Villareal, Albert. *The Cultural Missions of Mexico*. M.A. 71 pp. (Latin American Studies: Education)

747    Whipps, Jacqueline Jean. *The Story of UNESCO in Latin America*. M.A. 190 pp. (Latin American Studies: Government)

748    White, Byron. *The Economic and Policy Development of the Republic of Cuba*. M.A. 333 pp. (Latin American Studies: Economics)

## 1955

749    Akery, Nicholas. *An Exploratory Study of the Education of Spanish-speaking Children in the Primary Grades in Edinburg, Texas*. M.A. 103 pp. (Education)

750    Ball, Fred, Jr. *The Development of Milhaud's Polytonal Technique as Evidenced by the Orestes Trilogy and the "Saudades do Brasil."* M.A. 60 pp. (Music)

751    Chernosky, Adelma Shirley. *Educational Enrichment for Spanish-speaking Children in the Third Grade and Its Effect upon Intelligence and Achievement Test Scores*. M.A. 146 pp. (Education)

752    de Villa, Gregorio Carlos. *Some Aspects of the Industrialization of Mexico*. M.A. 127 pp. (Latin American Studies: Economics)

753    Emerson, Mrs. Barbara Lee Priest. *Latin American in the Secondary Schools of Bryan, Texas*. M.A. 122 pp. (Education)

754    Frierson, Edward Bernard. *"Excelsior" of Mexico City: Study of a Spanish-American Newspaper*. M.J. 119 pp. (Journalism)

755    Martínez, Rodolfo. *The Ideal of Central American Union and Confederation*. M.A. 157 pp. (Latin American Studies: Government)

756    Patterson, Jerry Eugene. *The Literary Criticism of Pedro Henríquez Ureña*. M.A. 93 pp. (Latin American Studies: Romance Languages)

757    Presley, James Wright. *Anglo-Spanish Rivalry in the Pacific Northwest, 1770–1800*. M. A. 146 pp. (History)

758    Rothwell, Jack C. *Exchange Control in Selected South American Countries*. M.A. 104 pp. (Business Administration)

759    Ruecking, Frederick Henry. *The Coahuiltecan Indians of Southern Texas and Northeastern Mexico*. M.A. 404 pp. (Anthropology)

760    Schumann, Melba Thekla. *An Outline for Eighth Grade Exploratory Spanish in the Junior High Level*. M.A. 122 pp. (Education)

761    Singh, Daljeet. *Diplomatic Asylum in Latin America*. M.A. 243 pp. (Latin American Studies: Government)

762 Solís-Flores, Roberto Hiram. *Production and Marketing of Cotton in the Matamoros Area of Mexico.* M.A. 97 pp. (Business Administration)

763 Taylor, Mrs. Virginia Rogers. *The Spanish Archives of the General Land Office of Texas.* M.A. 100 pp. (History)

764 White, Mrs. Jean Dempewolf. *Time Orientation as a Factor in the Acculturation of Southwestern Spanish-speaking Groups.* M.A. 118 pp. (Anthropology)

## 1956

765 Blaisdell, Darius Othniel. *Aspects of Life in Lima in the Sixteenth Century Based on "Los Libros de Cabildo de Lima."* M.A. 188 pp. (Latin American Studies: History)

766 Clark, George, *A Study of the Achievement of the Spanish-speaking Child.* M.A. 130 pp. (Education)

767 Cox, Albert Harrington. *Financial Policy and the Economic Development of Guatemala.* M.A. 102 pp. (Business Administration)

768 Dobson, John Alver. *The Banco de México: The Development of a Central Bank in an Under-developed Economy.* M.A. 116 pp. (Latin American Studies: Economics)

769 Garner, Mrs. Veldron R. *Development Tasks and Television Choices of Latin American and Anglo-American School Children.* M.A. 97 pp. (Education)

770 Harrington, Ann Kay. *Recent Borrowings from English Found in Mexican Spanish.* M.A. 72 pp. (English)

771 Lemus, George. *Partido Acción Nacional: A Mexican Opposition Party.* M.A. 142 pp. (Latin American Studies: Government)

772 Lipscomb, Patrick Cleburne. *The Church of England and the Negro Slaves in the West Indies, 1783–1883.* M.A. 106 pp. (History)

773 Powers, Jack Lee. *Some Aspects of the Economic Development of Argentina in Recent Decades.* M.A. 119 pp. (Latin American Studies: Economics)

774 Reuthinger, Hortense. *A Comparative Study of Two Methods of Theory Instruction for Seventh-Grade Latin American Girls.* M.A. 54 pp. (Music Education)

775 Taylor, Julia R. *Critical Review of the Literature of Teaching English to Foreign Home-Language Children.* M.A. 97 pp. (Education)

776 Treviño, Emma. *Concern with Concepts of the Life and Ideals in the United States as Presented in Portions of the Venezuelan Course of Study for Elementary Schools.* M.A. 171 pp. (Education)

777 Valerius, John Behner. *The Spanish-Speaking Population of Texas: 1954–1955, Estimates and a Study of Estimation Methods.* M.A. 110 pp. (Business Administration)

778 Walker, Donald Anthony. *The Role of the Government in the Development of Mexico's Water Resources for Agricultural and Health Purposes.* M.A. 216 pp. (Latin American Studies: Economics)

779 Westbrook, Helene. *An Analytical Index of the Complete Poetical Works of Rubén Darío.* M.A. 150 pp. (Romance Languages)

780 Williams, Charles Howard. *A Study of the Adjustment of Students from Latin America at The University of Texas.* M.A. 219 pp. (Sociology)


## 1957

781 Allen, Robert. *Structure of Sierra de los Fresnos, Chihuahua, Mexico.* M.A. 64 pp. (Geology)

782 Anglin, Mrs. Stella Campbell Glass. *A Study for the Improvement of Spanish-speaking Children's Problem-Solving Ability in Third-Grade Arithmetic.* M.A. 90 pp. (Education)

783 Chapman, Ruthven Hoyt. *Geology of the Lake Guija District, El Salvador, Central America.* M.A. 63 pp. (Geology)

784 Gardner, Mrs. Yvonne Clare Gebhard. *West Indies Federation: Development of a Progressive British West Indies.* M.A. 110 pp. (Government)

785 Garibay, Rubín Robert. *Spanish-Mexican Diplomacy Antecedent to the French Intervention in Mexico, 1836–1862.* M.A. 109 pp. (Latin American Studies: History)

786 Graham, Thomas Richard. *The Jesuit Antonio Vieira and His Plans for the Economic Rehabilitation of Seventeenth-Century Portugal.* M.A. 197 pp. (History)

787 Marshall, Mrs. Alice Swan. *Activities and Materials for Vocabulary Development of Spanish-speaking Children in the Primary Grades.* M.A. 114 pp. (Education)

788 Murphy, Patrick Joseph. *The Suspension of the Constitution of British Guiana.* M.A. 186 pp. (Government)

789 Ramírez, Sara Leonil. *The Educational Status and Socio-economic Backgrounds of Latin-American Children in Waco, Texas.* M.A. 102 pp. (Education)

790 Trillo-Garriga, Mrs. Ana Marie. *The Place of the English Language in the Public Educational System of Puerto Rico.* M.A. 104 pp. (Education)

791 Vásquez de Ruiz, Mrs. Celia E. Vega. *Vocabulary Overlap among*

*Primary Spanish Readers for Puerto Rican Schools.* M.A. 136 pp. (Education)

792    Yeager, Barbara Stone. *Meeting the Educational Needs of Migrant Children.* M.A. 92 pp. (Education)

## 1958

793    Clutterbuck, Donald Booth. *Structure of Northern Sierra Pilares, Chihuahua, Mexico.* M.A. 44 pp. (Geology)

794    Day, James Milton. *Jacob de Córdova: Land Merchant.* M.A. 145 pp. (History)

795    Díaz, Berta Ceballos. *A Descriptive Analysis of the Visiting Teacher Program in Selected Río Grande Valley School Districts.* M.A. 110 pp. (Education)

796    Eastlack, Charles Leonard. *Herbert Eugene Bolton (1870–1953): His Ideas and Practice as a Historian of the Americas.* M.A. 66 pp. (Latin American Studies: History)

797    Ferrell, Alton Durane. *Stratigraphy of Northern Sierra Pilares, Chihuahua, Mexico.* M.A. 77 pp. (Geology)

798    Goldwert, Marvin. *The Struggle for the Perpetuity of Encomiendas in Viceregal Peru, 1550–1600.* M.A. 156 pp. (History)

799    Hammond, Charles Wilbur. *Glossary of Aviation Terms, English-Spanish.* M.A. 116 pp. (Romance Languages)

800    Hauser, Ronald Joseph. *The Annual Reproductive Cycle of the Boat-tailed Grackle* (Cassadix mexicanus prosopidicola). M.A. 55 pp. (Zoology)

801    Nichols, John Conner. *Stratigraphy of Sierra de los Fresnos, Chihuahua, Mexico.* M.A. 64 pp. (Geology)

802    Salazar, Hermencia Corella. *Fourteen South American Folk Dances.* M.A. 135 pp. (Education)

803    Troike, Mrs. Nancy Patterson. *Mesoamerican and Pawnee Arrow Sacrifice Ceremonies: A Comparative Analysis.* M.A. 102 pp. (Anthropology)

## 1959

804    Baldwin, Edward Franklin. *Venezuelan Petroleum: A Case Study of the United States Participation in the Development of Foreign Resources.* M.B.A. 171 pp. (Business Administration)

805    Campbell, Richard A. *Stratigraphy of Borrachera Anticline, Municipio de Ojinaga, Chihuahua, Mexico.* M.A. 78 pp. (Geology)

806    Cohen, Pedro I. *An Introductory Comparative Study of Panamanian Spanish and American English.* M.A. 103 pp. (English)

807 Daugherty, Franklin Wallace. *Structure of Sierra Pilares, Municipio de Ojinaga, Chihuahua, Mexico.* M.A. 40 pp. (Geology)

808 Guerra, Irene J. *The Social Aspirations of a Selected Group of Spanish-Name People in Laredo, Texas.* M.A. 128 pp. (Sociology)

809 Harwell, George Mathis, Jr. *Stratigraphy of Sierra del Porvenir, Chihuahua, Mexico.* M.A. 65 pp. (Geology)

810 Hixon, Summer Best. *Facies and Petrography of the Cretaceous Buda Limestone of Texas and Northern Mexico.* M.A. 152 pp. (Geology)

811 Juarez, Joseph Robert. *Factors in the Withdrawal of the United States from Santo Domingo in 1924.* M.A. 134 pp. (Latin American Studies: History)

812 McCleskey, David Murray. *The Attitude of the Sixteenth-Century Spanish Missionaries toward the Religion of the Indians of New Spain.* M.A. 64 pp. (History)

813 Mounger, Mrs. María Julia Ferrán. *Mission Espíritu Santo of Coastal Texas: An Example of Historic Site Archeology.* M.A. 489 pp. (Anthropology)

814 Raab, Mrs. Patricia Verdi. *The Nutrition of the Maidu and the Maya Indians: A Comparison.* M.A. 229 pp. (Anthropology)

815 Smith, Mrs. Mary Jane. *Education Among the Pre-Colombian Aztecs, Maya, and Pueblos.* M.A. 69 pp. (Latin American Studies: Anthropology)

816 Spielberg, Joseph. *Social and Cultural Configurations and Medical Care: A Study of Mexican-Americans' Responses to Proposed Hospitalization for the Treatment of Tuberculosis.* M.A. 135 pp. (Sociology)

817 Vest, Harry Arthur. *Structure of Sierra del Porvenir, Chihuahua, Mexico.* M.A. 47 pp. (Geology)

818 Zakrzewski, Juan de. *Gregorio Funes, Dean de la Catedral de Córdoba, su actuación política, sus escritos, sus ideas.* M.A. 113 pp. (Latin American Studies: History)

819 Zorilla-Quintana, Gonzalo. *El impacto de la inflación en la industrialización de México.* M.A. 145 pp. (Economics)

## 1960

820 Anderson, William Woodrow. *The Development of Literacy in Mexico.* M.A. 132 pp. (Education)

821 Atwill, Edward Robert, IV. *Stratigraphic Nomenclature in Sierra Pilares, Chihuahua, Mexico.* M.A. 90 pp. (Geology)

822 Bradshaw, Benjamin Spencer. *Some Demographic Aspects of Mar-*

*riage: A Comparative Study of Three Ethnic Groups*. M.A. 89 pp. (Sociology)

823 Graves, Mrs. Ersilee Ruth Parker. *A History of the Interrelationships between Imported Mexican Labor, Domestic Migrants, and the Texas Agricultural Economy*. M.A. 155 pp. (History)

824 Key, Mrs. E. Mary Ritchie. *The Phonemic Pattern of Bolivian Chama*. M.A. 41 pp. (Linguistics)

825 Key, Harold Hayden. *Phonotactics of Cayuvava*. M.A. 49 pp. (Linguistics)

826 Kushinsky, Mrs. Karen Popp. *A Report of the Circulation of Books from the Lima Binational Center Library, March–April 1959*. M.L.S. 100 pp. (Library Science)

827 Law, Howard William. *Mecayapan, Veracruz: An Ethnographic Sketch*. M.A. 116 pp. (Anthropology)

828 Letbetter, Mrs. Mary Louise. *A Study of the Effectiveness of an Oral Language Program in Relation to Overcoming Speech Difficulties in a Second Grade Class of English-Speaking and Bilingual Children*. M.Ed. 98 pp. (Education)

829 Petesch, Donald Anthony. *Mexican Urban Ecology*. M.A. 219 pp. (Sociology)

830 Ratliff, Mrs. Yvonne Reppeto. *Spanish-speaking and English-speaking Children in Southwest Texas: A Comparative Study of Intelligence, Socio-Economic Status, and Achievement*. M.A. 94 pp. (Education)

831 Raynes, Mrs. María Guadalupe Leal. *An Annotated Study of José Joaquín Fernández de Lizardi's "La educación de las mujeres o la quijotita y prima."* M.A. 115 pp. (Latin American Studies: Romance Languages)

832 Williamson, Mrs. Helen Keith Chapman. *Latin American Interventionism in Central America*. M.A. 180 pp. (Government)

833 Yeager, John Conner. *Stratigraphy of Southern Sierra Pilares, Municipio de Ojinaga, Chihuahua, Mexico*. M.A. 116 pp. (Geology)

1961

834 Brenner, Henry. *The Auto de Fe of 1659 and Don Guillén Lombardo de Guzmán*. M.A. 148 pp. (Latin American Studies: History)

835 Danforth, Peter Davis. *Some Effects of Taxation on United States Direct Private Investment in Mexico*. M.B.A. 103 pp.

836 Dill, George Meyer. *Structure of Northern Sierra de Ventana Municipio de Ojinaga, Chihuahua, Mexico*. M.A. 58 pp. (Geology)

837 Hamilton, Samuel Clinton. *Structure of Southern Sierra Pilares, Municipio de Ojinaga, Chihuahua, Mexico.* M.A. 85 pp. (Geology)

838 Herring, Marcia Lou. *Mestizaje in Mexico, 1760 to 1810: A Survey of Opinion.* M.A. 79 pp. (Latin American Studies: History)

839 Jennings, C. A. *A Production and Production Book of "The Cradle Song" by Gregorio and María Martínez Sierra.* M.F.A. 246 pp. (Drama Education)

840 Meyer, Joachim Dietrich. *Geology of the Ahuachapan Area, Western El Salvador, Central America.* M.A. 107 pp. (Geology)

841 Mowery, Susan. *An Image of the Contemporary Mexican: A Study of His Personality.* M.A. 68 pp. (Romance Languages)

842 Spiegelberg, Frederick, III. *Stratigraphy of Northern Sierra de Ventana, Municipio de Ojinaga, Chihuahua, Mexico.* M.A. 90 pp. (Geology)

843 Stanislawski, Mrs. Doris Barr. *A Study of Leadership in a Spanish-Speaking Community.* M.A. 84 pp. (Anthropology)

844 Stouse, Pierre Adolphe Ducros, Jr. *Municipio of Huasca, Hidalgo, Mexico: A Study in Land Settlement Patterns.* M.A. 210 pp. (Geography)

845 Tandrón, Humberto. *The Commerce of New Spain and the Free Trade Controversy, 1796–1821.* M.A. 181 pp. (History)

1962

846 Baxter, Thomas Richard. *Caribbean Bishops: The Establishment of the Bishoprics of Jamaica and of Barbados and the Leeward Islands, 1824–1843.* M.A. 86 pp. (History)

847 Breedlove, James McShane. *Mexico and the Spanish-American War.* M.A. 83 pp. (History)

848 Fantini, Albino Edward, Jr. *Illness and Curing among the Mexican-Americans of Mission, Texas.* M.A. 100 pp. (Latin American Studies: Anthropology)

849 Grumbles, Mrs. Mineola Page. *The Problems of Mexican Children in Language Learning.* M.Ed. 169 pp. (Education)

850 Hagle, Paul Ivan. *Military Life on New Spain's Northern Frontier: The Presidio of Janos: 1787–1800.* M.A. 113 pp. (Latin American Studies: History)

851 Harris, Charles Houston, III. *The Sánchez Navarros: A Socioeconomic Study of a Coahuilan Latifundio, 1846–1853.* M.A. 163 pp. (History)

852 Jones, Benton McLain. *A Study of the Acculturation and Social As-*

*pirations of Sixty Junior High School Students from the Mexican Ethnic Group.* M.A. 102 pp. (Education)

853    Kostka, Mrs. Roberta Jo Nunn. *Contradictions in the Poetry of Alfonsina Storni.* M.A. 98 pp. (Romance Languages)

854    Lance, Donald Max. *A Comparison of* DOÑA PERFECTA *and* THE RETURN OF THE NATIVE. M.A. 87 pp. (English)

855    Lattimer, Robert Kehoe. *Two Measured Sections from the Mesozoic of Northwestern Guatemala.* M.A. 170 pp. (Geology)

856    Maurer, Gerhard. *Power Configuration in the Dominican Republic after the Assassination of Trujillo.* M.A. 186 pp. (Government)

857    Scarff, Mrs. Frances Beatriz González. *A Study of the Matachine Dance in Selected Areas of Mexico and Texas.* M.Ed. 147 pp. (Education)

858    Schoenhals. Alvin. *A Grammatical Classification of Totontepec Mixe Verbs.* M.A. 62 pp. (Linguistic)

859    Taylor, Clark Louis, Jr. *Medicinal Customs of the Zoque.* M.A. 120 pp. (Anthropology)

860    Waddell, Jack O'Brien. *Value Orientations of Young Mexican-American Males as Reflected in Their Work Patterns and Employment Preferences.* M.A. 100 pp. (Anthropology)

861    Wait, Eugene Meredith. *Development of a Revolution: Argentina 1806–1816.* M.A. 132 pp. (History)

862    Williams, Roy, Jr. *The Role of Education in the Industrialization of Mexico.* M.A. 86 pp. (Latin American Studies: Education)

1963

863    Arellano, Richard Gibbs. *Growth in the Mexican Financial Sector and Its Relation to Economic Development; 1940–1960.* M.A. 81 pp. (Latin American Studies: Economics)

864    Berry, Charles Redmon. *The Conquest of the Desert: A Study of the Argentine Indian Wars (1810–1885).* M.A. 174 pp. (Latin American Studies: History)

865    Díaz, Pedro Luis. *A Reservoir Engineering Study of the South Catatumbo Reservoir-West Tara Field.* M.S. (Venezuela) 137 pp. (Petroleum Engineering)

866    Guggolz, Bess. *Modern Trends in Mexican Historiography.* M. A. 101 pp. (Latin American Studies: History)

867    McKnight, John Forrest. *Igneous Rocks of Sombreretillo Area, Northern Sierra de Picachos, Nuevo Leon, Mexico.* M.A. 90 pp. (Geology)

868 Megee, Vernon Edgar. *United States Military Intervention in Nicaragua, 1909–1932.* M.A. 236 pp. (Latin American Studies: History)

869 Miller, Clint Le Mon, Jr. *Investment Opportunities in Mexico: An Analysis.* M.B.A. 71 pp. (Business Administration)

870 Parchman, Otis Lyman, Jr. *The Economic Development of the Mexican Sugar Industry.* M.B.A. 148 pp. (Business Administration)

871 Pfeiffer, David Graham. *The Mexican Farm Labor Supply Program —Its Friends and Foes.* M.A. 221 pp. (Government)

872 Ramírez-Olmos, José Ulises. *A Reservoir Engineering Sudy of the B6X-107 Reservoir, Bolivar Coastal Field, Venezuela.* M.S. 156 pp. (Petroleum Engineering)

873 Rodriguez, Raymond. *Brazil's Economic Evolution: A Changing Pattern.* M.A. 116 pp. (Latin American Studies: Economics)

874 Scaperlanda, Anthony Edward, Jr. *The European Economic Community's Impact on Latin America: A Preliminary Survey.* M.A. 152 pp. (Economics)

875 Schoenhals, Mrs. Louise Conety. *A Dictionary of Totontepec Mixe.* M.A. (Mexico) 433 pp. (Latin American Studies: Anthropology)

876 Tarquinio, Laura Teixeira. *Alguns aspectos de linguagem do nordeste de Brazil.* M.A. 49 pp. (Romance Languages)

## 1964

877 Armistead, Robert Thomas. *The History of "Novedades"* M.J. 230 pp. (Communication)

878 Córdoba, Diego Arturo. *Geology of the Apizolya Quadrangle (East Half), Northern Zacatecas, Mexico.* M.A. 111 pp. (Geology)

879 Fuentes, Ruderico Procopio. *Stratigraphy of Sierra Santa Clara and Sierra Gómez, Nuevo León, México.* M.A. 217 pp. (Geology)

880 Hann, John Henry. *Luso-Brazilian-Platine Relations and their Impact 1808–1852.* M.A. 178 pp. (Latin American Studies: History)

881 Hinojosa, Tomas Rodolfo, Jr. *The Ethnic Preferences of Anglo, Latin American, and Latin American Juvenile Delinquents as Determined by Choice of Proper Names.* M.A. 43 pp. (Education)

882 Howard, Ryan Abney. *The Symbolism of Mexican Retablos of the Eighteenth Century (1718–1780).* M.A. 141 pp. (Art History)

883 Jansen, Rudolf Karl. *Implications of the European Common Market for Mexican Exports.* M.A. 95 pp. (Latin American Studies: Economics)

884 MacLean, Alberto Mario. *Indice analítico de la revista CONTEMPORÁNEOS.* M.A. 172 pp. (Romance Languages)

885  Milton, Arnold Powell. *Geology of Cajoncito Area in Municipio de Guadalupe, Chihuahua, and Hudspeth County, Texas.* M.A. 78 pp. (Geology)

886  Miranda, José Pablo. *An Exploratory Study of Mexican Foreign Students in Laredo, Texas in Fall Semester 1962–63.* M.Ed. 125 pp. (Education)

887  Nelson, Craig Eugene. *A Partial Systematic Revision of Mexican Microhylid Frogs of the Genus Hypopachus.* M.A. 104 pp. (Zoology)

888  Pajares, Luis Eduardo. *Diccionario de modismos contemporáneos peruanos.* M.A. 49 pp. (Romance Languages)

889  Siedhoff, Eleanor Diana. *The São Francisco River in Brazilian Literature.* M.A. 64 pp. (Romance Languages)

890  Smith, Gaylord Ewing. *The Short Stories of Juan Rulfo.* M.A. 135 pp. (Romance Languages)

891  Stout, John Maxwell. *Religious Influence in the Writings of Alceu Amoroso Lima.* M.A. 89 pp. (Romance Languages)

892  Truett, Dale Brian. *The Development of the Transport Equipment Industry in Mexico.* M.A. 82 pp. (Latin American Studies: Economics)

893  Williams, Lyle Wayne. *The Northwest Frontier of New Spain, 1750–1800: A Social Study.* M.A. 126 pp. (Latin American Studies: History)


1965

894  Anderson, Mrs. Ada Collins. *Race and Ethnic Origin as a Determinant of Acceptibility for Employment in Austin, Texas.* M.Ed. 77 pp. (Education)

895  Burns, Tommye Helen. *Bartolomé de las Casas: A Review of His Writings and Their Repercussions.* M.A. 99 pp. (Latin American Studies: Education)

896  Cyr, Mrs. Joanne Jeffries. *Some Intonational Features of Brazilian Portuguese.* M.A. 108 pp. (Linguistics)

897  Findling, John Ellis. *Robert Lowther, Governor of Barbados 1710–1720.* M.A. 129 pp. (History)

898  Flesher, Mrs. Helen Little. *Lisandro de la Torre: Champion of Political Economic Reform in Argentina.* M.A. 116 pp. (Latin American Studies: History)

899  Garza, David Trippe. *Spanish Origins of Mexican Constitutionalism: An Analysis of Constitutional Development in New Spain, 1808 to Independence.* M.A. 162 pp. (Government)

900  Goss, Allen Miles. *A Developmental Study of Estimated Versus*

*Actual Physical Strength in Three Ethnic Groups.* M.A. 29 pp. (Psychology)

901 Hilburn, William Grant, Sr. *The Highway Without End: The Inter-American Highway.* M.A. 122 pp. (History)

902 Hudspeth, Marguerite Burnett. *The Griselda Story in Timoneda's Patrañuelo: An Essay.* M.A. 45 pp. (Romance Languages)

903 Jackson, Mrs. Gail Cathryn Craghead. *Implications for Teachers from a Study of the Culture of Mexican-Americans.* M.Ed. 119 pp. (Education)

904 Law, Mrs. Joan Alice. *An Ethnolinguistic Study of Nahua Consanguineal Kinship Terminology.* M.A. 154 pp. (Linguistics),

905 Moseley, Frank Nathaniel. *Biology of the Red Snapper* LUTJANUS AVA *Block of the Northwestern Gulf of Mexico.* M.A. 53 pp. (Zoology)

906 Nolan, Sidney David, Jr. *Relative Independence of Two Mexican Dailies: A Case Study of EL NORTE and EL PORVENIR of Monterrey.* M.J. 157 pp. (Journalism)

907 Pajares, Mrs. Jean Sullivan. *The Peruvian Literary Magazine, 1916–1960.* M.A. 97 pp. (Romance Languages)

908 Peterson, Edward James. *The Role of the United States in the De la Huerta Rebellion in Mexico, 1923–1924.* M.A. 99 pp. (Latin American Studies: History)

909 Rosson, Mary Ada. *Elements of Mexican Fatalism in Juan Rulfo's Works.* M.A. 89 pp. (Latin American Studies: Romance Languages)

910 Stearns, Joseph Edward. *Informal Relations between Mexico and the United States, 1854–1877.* M.A. 170 pp. (History)

911 Stenglein, Joseph Arthur. *The Development of Civil Aviation in Mexico and Central America.* M.A. 120 pp. (Geography)

912 Stout, Mrs. Mary Helen Jarnagin. *The Indian, the Negro, and the Jew in the Sermons of Antonio Vieira,* M.A. 149 pp. (Romance Languages)

913 Swietlicki, Alain. *Estructura novelística de Rómulo Gallegos y su relación con la problemática venezolana.* M.A. 62 pp. (Romance Languages)

914 Wares, Mrs. Iris Lueva Mills. *Linguistic and Related Problems in Mexican Indian Literacy.* M.A. 144 pp. (Linguistics)

1966

915 Anderson, Mrs. Martha Davis. *Latin-American Teenagers and the News in Ten Rio Grande Valley Districts.* M.A. 123 pp. (Communications)

916 Benavides-Hinojosa, Artemio. *Migración y fuerza de trabajo en*

*Nuevo León, 1960: descripción de una muestra censal.* M.A. 89 pp. (Sociology)

917   Boyd, Alston, III. *Geology of the Western Third of La Democracia Quadrangle, Guatemala.* M.A. 79 pp. (Geology)

918   Brooks, Sammy Kent. *Graham Greene and Mexico: A Critical Study of THE POWER AND THE GLORY and ANOTHER MEXICO,* M.A. 119 pp. (English)

919   Christoph, Sharon Lea. *The Fictional World of Eduardo Mallea.* M.A. 68 pp. (Romance Languages)

920   Davis, George Herbert. *Geology of the Eastern Third of La Democracia Quadrangle, Guatemala.* M.A. 78 pp. (Geology)

921   Denton, Charles Frederick. *Panama and the Central American Common Market.* M.A. 101 pp. (Latin American Studies: Government)

922   Durston, John W. *Power Structure in a Rural Region of Guatemala: The Department of Jutipa.* M.A. 145 pp. (Latin American Studies: Anthropology)

923   Flores Caballero, Romeo Ricardo. *La expulsión de los españoles: ensayo de historia de México (1808–1836).* M.A. 136 pp. (Latin American Studies: History)

924   Greer, Mrs. Margaret Helen Rich. *Indigenismo in Peru.* M.A. 129 pp. (Latin American Studies: History)

925   Heiken, Grant Harvey. *Geology of Cerros Prietos, Municipio de Ojinaga, Chihuahua, Mexico.* M.A. 101 pp. (Geology)

926   Hinds, Marjorie Sue. *The Politics of Economic Planning in Brazil.* M.A. 112 pp. (Latin American Studies: Government)

927   Hudspeth, John Robert. *Fragmentation in Argentine Radicalism.* M.A. 90 pp. (Government)

928   Kazen, Phyllis Marie. *Mexican-American Kinship Interaction: A Study of Twenty Families in Austin, Texas.* M.A. 94 pp. (Latin American Studies: Anthropology)

929   Kennard, Claude Louis. *Ornamentation of Title-Pages in New Spain: Examples from the University of Texas Latin American Collections.* M.A. 149 pp. (Art History)

930   Luna-Traill, Eduardo. *An International Airport for Mexico City: A Case Study.* M. of Architecture. 160 pp. (Architecture)

931   McClurkan, Burney Boyd. *The Archeology of La Cueva de la Zona de Derrumbes, A Rockshelter in Nuevo León, México.* M.A. 181 pp. (Anthropology)

932   Mir, Adolfo. *Movilidad social, educación y grupos de referencia en Monterrey, México: un estudios sociológico.* M.A. 141 pp. (Sociology)

933　Okel, Mrs. Eileen Frances Silver. *Occupational Name Repertoire as a Function of Sex, Grade Level, Ethnic Group, and Socio-Economic Class.* M.A. 53 pp. (Psychology)

934　Randel, Mrs. Marjorie MacEachin. *Quechua and Aymara: Control Cases and Application of Glottochronology for Two South American Indian Languages.* M.A. 144 pp. (Anthropology)

935　Randle, Mrs. Sarah Margaret Blair. *Measurement of Change Resulting from Small Group Activities with Latin American Culturally Deprived High School Students.* M.Ed. 144 pp. (Education)

936　Rodríguez-Risquez, Policarpo Antonio. *Development of United States Oil Policies and Its Effects on Venezuela.* M.A. 162 pp. (Economics)

937　Rodríguez-Sardiñas, Orlando. *Cuba: poesía de guerra y de destierro. (1760–1960).* M.A. 124 pp. (Romance Languages)

938　Ruemping, Gary Ronald. *Mexico and the Case of Regional Analysis for Economic Development.* M.A. 148 pp. (Economics)

939　Thompson, Richard Allen. *A Study of Yucatec Maya Curing Utilizing the Techniques of Formal Elicitation.* M.A. 255 pp. (Anthropology)

940　Vassberg, David Erland. *The Use of Mexicans and Mexican-Americans as an Agricultural Work Force in the Lower Rio Grande Valley in Texas.* M.A. 110 pp. (Latin American Studies: History)

1967

941　Acevedo, Mary Ann. *The Effect of Socio-Economic Level and Language Background on Vocabulary Ability.* M.A. 53 pp. (Communications)

942　Adams, Thomas M. *Reports: The Bolivian M.N.R., the Indian and the Agrarian Reform; The Growth of the Christian Democratic Party in Chile, 1935–1964; The Mapuche in Chilean Society.* M.A. (Latin American Studies: History; Educational Psychology)

943　Anderson, Thomas Howard. *Geology of the Middle Third of La Democracia Quadrangle, Guatemala.* M.A. 81 pp. (Geology)

944　Athon, William Craig. *Colonial Costa Rica and Colonial South Carolina, 1660–1760: A Contrast in Democratic Development.* M.A. 94 pp. (Latin American Studies: History)

945　Bittinger, Mrs. Vivian Irene Swihard. *The Novels of Julio Ardiles Gray.* M.A. 53 pp. (Latin American Studies: Romance Languages)

946　Bryant, Mavis Anne. *Agricultural Interest Groups in Guatemala.* M.A. 255 pp. (Latin American Studies: Anthropology)

947　Butler, Robert Wayne. *The Cabildo and the Intendant.* M.A. 40 pp. (History)

948 Carpenter, Carl L. *Reports: The New National Ideal of General Marcos Pérez Jiménez; The Role of the Military in Twentieth Century Colombian Politics.* M.A. (Latin American Studies: History; Government)

949 Castillo, Eunice Duarte. *Comparison of Knowledge of the Law and Attitude Toward the Law by Lower-Economic Negro, Lower-Economic Latins, and Lower-Economic Anglo Respondents.* M.S. 56 pp. (Social Work)

950 Chapman, John Gresham. *Yucatecan Secessionism, 1839–1843.* M.A. 79 pp. (Latin American Studies: History)

951 Clegg, Joseph Halvor. *Análisis espectrográfico en los renofas /a e o/ en un dialecto en Cuba.* M.A. 13 pp. (Romance Languages)

952 Dalton, Starrette Lee. *Mariátegui—Marxist Critic.* 58 pp. (Latin American Studies: Romance Languages)

953 Davis, Mrs. Leslie Eager. *Myth in* OFICIO DE TINIEBLAS. M.A. 66 pp. (Romance Languages)

954 Dorough, Catherine Elaine. EL CRISTO DE ESPALDAS: *A Comparison with* THE POWER AND THE GLORY. M.A. 66 pp. (Romance Languages)

955 Feil, Roberta Marie. *A Description of the Demographic Characteristics of the Three Hundred Respondents from Six Ethnic-Economic Groups, Residents of Travis County Who Were Interviewed in Relation to Their Knowledge of and Attitude Toward Texas Laws.* M.S. 46 pp. (Social Work)

956 Ferrusquía-Villafranca, Ismael. *Rancho Gaitan Local Fauna, Early Chadronian, Northeastern Chihuahua, Mexico.* M.A. 131 pp. (Geology)

957 Foster, Thomas P. *A Study to Determine Gaps in the Knowledge of Law between Six Ethnic-Economic Groups.* M.S. 46 pp. (Social Work)

958 Franklin, Judy Ellen. *The Rise and Decline of the Chilean Parliamentary Period, 1891–1925.* M.A. 93 pp. (Latin American Studies: Government)

959 Frankman, Mrs. Patricia Ottolenghi. *La realidad en la obra de Manuel Mijica Lainez.* M.A. 85 pp. (Latin American Studies: Romance Languages)

960 Frisz, Joseph Frederic. ACCIÓN DEMOCRÁTICA *in Venezuela: A Curious Mixture of Dogmatism and Pragmatism.* M.A. 104 pp. (Latin American Studies: Government)

961 Gibbs, Donald Lloyd. *The Mestizo in Alto Peru with Special Emphasis on Potosí.* M.A. 168 pp. (Latin American Studies: History)

962 Grimes, James Larry. *Cakchiquel-Tzutuhil: A Study in Linguistic Unity.* M.A. 36 pp. (Anthropology)

963 Gutiérrez, Nicanor Fernando. *400 años en la colonización del nor-Oriente peruano*. M.A. 212 pp. (Latin American Studies: Geography)

964 Jewell, Wilton Gray. *A Study of Dissatisfaction with Present Laws as Revealed Through Interviews with a Sample of Individuals in Six Economic-ethnic Groups in Austin, Texas During July, August, and September, 1966*. M.S. 58 pp. (Social Work)

965 Jiménez, Julio M. *A Critique of the Policies and Attitudes Affecting Cotton Agriculture in Guatemala Through a Study of its Development*. M.A. 136 pp. (Economics)

966 Jones, Herbert Harmon. *Reports*: Higher Education in Mexico; Cultural Assimilation in Nuevo Santander and in Successor States to 1910. M.A. 121 pp. (Latin American Studies: History; Education—History and Philosophy)

967 Keith, Alma Jean. *A Study of Six Ethnic and Economic Groups Consisting of 300 Residents of Travis County with Relation to Their Knowledge of Texas Laws Regarding Housing*. M.S. 56 pp. (Social Work)

968 Kurz, Hans Dieter. *Uruguay: A Case Study of Economic Stagnation*. M.A. 158 pp. (Economics)

969 Lillard, William Clair. *The Economics of Beef Production in El Salvador*. M.A. 99 pp. (Economics)

970 Nolan, Mrs. Mary Lee. *Aspects of Middle Class Family Organization in Monterrey, Mexico*. M.A. 186 pp. (Anthropology)

971 Noyola, Benito Xavier. *Housing of Social Interest in Latin America and Especially in Mexico*. M.S. 78 pp. (Community and Regional Planning)

972 Pearson, Donald Watson. *The Role of Foreign Investment in Brazil's Public Utility Sector*. M.A. 121 pp. (Economics)

973 Premo, Daniel Lawrence. *La teoría novelística de Ignacio Manuel Altamirano y su contribución al desarrollo de una literatura nacional*. M.A. 74 pp. (Latin American Studies: Romance Languages)

974 Ray, Mrs. Connie Claire Todd. *The Works of Carlos Fuentes—A General Analysis*. M.A. 72 pp. (Romance Languages)

975 Roberts, Guy Otha. *Knowledge and Attitudes Toward Welfare Laws in Texas of Low Income Negroes, Latins, and Anglos in Austin, Texas*. M.S. 44 pp. (Social Work)

976 Self, Michael Marvin. *A Survey of Automobile Manufacturing in Latin America*. M.A. 137 pp. (Latin American Studies: History)

977 Sipperly, David William. *Tectonic History of the Sierra del Alabre, Northern Chihuahua, Mexico*. M.A. 78 pp. (Geology)

978 Smith, Elliott Varner. *Reports*: Community Development: The Co-

lombian and Venezuelan Experience; Politics and Economic Change: A Study of the Colombian Agrarian Reform Act of 1961; The Role of Urban Labor in the Mexican Political System since Alemán. M.A. 142 pp. (Latin American Studies: Government; History; Economics)

979  Smith, Mrs. Gerda Hansen. *The Purpose of the Law as Seen by Economic and Ethnic Groups.* M.S. 55 pp. (Social Work)

980  Staples, Anne Folger. *Ecclesiastical Affairs in the First Mexican Federal Republic, 1823–1834.* M.A. 240 pp. (Latin American Studies: History)

981  Sweet, Richard William. *A Comparative Study of Six Ethnic-Economic Groups by Education, Age and Sex, with Reference to Their Knowledge and Opinion of Texas Law Regarding Police Activities.* M.S. 62 pp. (Social Work)

982  Toness, Odin Alf. *Power Relations of a Central American Slum.* M.A. 71 pp. (Latin American Studies: Anthropology)

983  Urbina, Manuel, Jr. *The Impact of the Texas Revolution on the Government and Politics of Mexico 1836–1838.* M.A. 118 pp. (Latin American Studies: History)

984  Varner, Dudley Meriwether. *An Archaeological Investigation of Hearths in Northeastern Mexico.* M.A. 149 pp. (Anthropology)

985  Villarreal, Victor Xavier. LA REGIÓN MÁS TRANSPARENTE: *An Analysis of the Feminine Characters in Carlos Fuentes' Novel.* M.A. 48 pp. (Romance Languages)

986  White, Robert Allan. *Brazilian Nationalism, Its History and Ideology.* M.A. 113 pp. (Latin American Studies: History)

987  Wilson, Wade Eugene. *Knowledge of the Law with Respect to Ethnic Economic Status.* M.S. 54 pp. (Social Work)


1968

988  Almeida, Mauro Lauria de. *A General View of the Development of the Mass Media and Advertising in Brazil.* M.A. 83 pp. (Communication—Journalism)

989  Alvermann, Mrs. Donna Elaine. *A Supplementary Social Studies Program for Mexican-American Children in the Third Grade at Govalle School, Austin, Texas.* M.A. 107 pp. (Education—Curriculum and Instruction)

990  Arnold, William Metcalf. *Central and South America: The Movement of Integration.* M.A. 113 pp. (Latin American Studies: Government)

991  Balboa, Arnulfo. *The Escala de Inteligencia Wechsler Para Niños—*

*An Experimental Adaptation for South Texas.* M.A. 120 pp. (Education—Educational Psychology)

992   Becerra, Alejandro. *Report:* The Economic Welfare of Mexicans: in Mexico, the United States and the United States-Mexico border area. M.A. 105 pp. (Latin American Studies: Economics)

993   Belton, Hugh. *Community Development in the Peruvian Sierra 1952–1966.* M.A. 140 pp. (Economics)

994   Calder, Bruce Johnson. *Growth and Change in the Guatemalan Catholic Church, 1944–1966.* M.A. 214 pp. (Latin American Studies: History)

995   Carrasco-Velázquez, Baldomero. *The Upper Austin Group in Jimenez, Coahuila (Mexico).* M.A. 53 pp. (Geology)

996   Dick, Philip James. *Reports:* Three studies on Latin America. M.A. 173 pp. (Latin American Studies: Romance Languages; Economics)

997   Eddy, Hilda Marie. *Reports:* The Role of Education in Revolutionary Cuba; Organized Labor in Argentina before Perón. M.A. 107 pp. (Latin American Studies: History; Government)

998   Godard, Donald Duane. *Reports:* The Role of Interstitial Industrialization in Economic Development; Interest Groups in the Brazilian Political System: A Consideration of Political Style before and after a Social Revolution. M.A. 86 pp. (Latin American Studies: Economics; Government)

999   Gonzalez, Gustavo. *A Linguistic Profile of the Spanish-Speaking First-Grader in Corpus Christi.* M.A. 83 pp. (Linguistics)

1000   Hannon, Donald Paul. *The Argentine Educational System: A Quantitative Analysis.* M.A. 100 pp. (Education—History and Philosophy)

1001   Hinton, Hugh Frank. *The National Action Party of Mexico: A Response to Political Modernization.* M.A. 172 pp. (Latin American Studies: Government)

1002   Jordan, Robert Edward. *Reports:* The Cultivation and Production of Maize in Venezuela; The Role of the Guatemalan Indians in a Central American Economy; An Examination of Contemporary Political Parties in Venezuela, 1957–1964. M.A. (Latin American Studies: Geography; Economics; Government)

1003   Melton, Mrs. Jo Anne Chamberlin. *A Comparison of Two Methods of Teaching Reading to Disadvantaged Mexican-American First Grade Children.* M.A. 74 pp. (Education—Curriculum and Instruction)

1004   O'Hagan, Maryann Joan. *The Distribution of Economically Active Women in Major Industrial and Occupational Sectors in Latin America.* M.A. 70 pp. (Latin American Studies: Economics)

1005  Osborne, Duncan Elliott. *The Assassination of Anastasio Somoza.* M.A. 132 pp. (Latin American Studies: History)

1006  Paek, Pong Hyon. *The Koreans in Mexico: 1905–1911.* M.A. 76 pp. (Latin American Studies: History)

1007  Parker, James Russell. *The Development of a Contemporary Latin American Problems Course.* M.A. (Education—Curriculum and Instruction)

1008  Plasker, Robert Leo. *Reports:* Three Reports: Folk Medicine; Migration; Marginality. M.A. 87 pp. (Latin American Studies: Anthropology)

1009  Ramón, Alberto Manuel. *An Exploratory Study of the Socio-Cultural Determinants of Discontinuation of Family Planning Services by Mexican-American and Negro in Austin and Travis County, Texas.* M.S. 100 pp. (Social Work)

1010  Solem, Richard Ray. *Reports:* Mexico's Conservative Revolution: Private Enterprise and the Mexican Government; Development Programs in Northeast Brazil. M.A. 106 pp. (Latin American Studies: History; Government)

1011  Termini, Mrs. Deanne May Lanoix. *Socio-Economic and Demographic Characteristics of the Population of Guatemala City with Special Reference to Migrant-Non-migrant Differences.* M.A. 161 pp. (Sociology)

1012  Toness, Mrs. Kay Sutherland. *Woman-Focality in a Central American Slum.* M.A. 88 pp. (Latin American Studies: Anthropology)

1013  Vallejo-Claros, Bernardo. *The Ayoré—Their Cultural and Linguistic Identity.* M.A. 120 pp. (Anthropology)

1014  Wistrand, Lila May. *Cashibo Relative Clause Constructions.* M.A. 81 pp. (Linguistics)

## 1969

1015  Brownell, Mary Elizabeth. *Reports:* Brazilian Foreign Policy Decisions, 1961 and post 1964; A Comparison of the Negro in Nineteenth Century Cuban and Brazilian Social Novels. M.A. 119 pp. (Latin American Studies: History; Romance Languages)

1016  Chapman, Mrs. Barbara Austin. *Uruguay: A Study in National Identity.* M.A. 76 pp. (Romance Languages)

1017  Collier, Vivian. *Reports:* The Role of Education in Planned Development: A Case Study of Puerto Rico; The Religion of Mankind: Poetry and Poetics of Octavio Paz. M.A. 125 pp. (Latin American Studies: Education; Romance Languages)

1018  Dieli, Robert M. *Reports:* Coffee Production in El Salvador: A Survey and a Constructive Suggestion; The Effects of the Social Stratification System of the Immediate Post-Revolutionary Era on the Formation of the Partido Nacional Revolucionario. M.A. 111 pp. (Latin American Studies: International Business; Government)

1019 Echeverría, Patricia. *Mexican Education in the Press and Spanish Cortes: 1810–1821.* M.A. 155 pp. (Latin American Studies: History)

1020 Ellis, Charles William. *Business Pressure Groups in Mexico and Their Strategies Since 1940.* M.A. 85 pp. (Latin American Studies: International Business)

1021 Escotet Alvarez, Miguel Angel. *Student Problems in Venezuelan High Schools and Universities.* M.A. 42 pp. (Educational Psychology)

1022 Espinosa, José Raul. *Reports:* An Economic Study of Costa Rica: Implications for Communication in Economic Development; United States Private Investment: Factors Associated within Latin America; How Public Relation Techniques Work. M.A. 319 pp. (Latin American Studies: International Business)

1023 Gittler, Jacob. *Reports:* Fidel Castro como lider mesianico; la dicotomía de la Pax Porfiriana. M.A. 164 pp. (Latin American Studies: Government; History)

1024 Grothey, Mina Jane. *Seventeenth Century Mexican News-Sheets, Precursors of the Newspaper: A Description of the García Icazbalceta Collection.* M.L.S. 102 pp. (Library Science)

1025 Hellums, Frances John. *A Study of Word-Attack Skills of Disadvantaged Mexican-American and Negro-American Seventh Grade Children.* M.A. 97 pp. (Education—Curriculum and Instruction)

1026 Huey, Raymond Burnson. *Ecological Relations of Sympatric Philodactylus in the Sechwa Desert of Peru.* M.A. 74 pp. (Zoology)

1027 Hupp, Bruce Foster. *The Urban Indians of Quezaltenango, Guatemala.* M.A. 190 pp. (Anthropology)

1028 Huser, Herbert C. *Reports:* The Role of the Military in Argentina, *1930–1968; Argentine Foreign Policy, 1955–1966.* M.A. 185 pp. (Latin American Studies: Government; Economics)

1029 Jones, Diane Louise Carlson. *The Military and Political Development: A Comparative Analysis of Argentina and Brazil.* M.A. 97 pp. (Government)

1030 Jones, Dixie Lee Franklin. *The Plight of the Migrant Child in the Lower Rio Grande Valley.* M.A. 84 pp (Education—Curriculum and Instruction)

1031 Kalmon, Winn Loraine. *Reports:* The Doctrine of Limpieza as Utilized in Spain and the Spanish Colonies; Juan Antonio Mon and His

Influence on the Development of Antioquía. M.A. 84 pp. (Latin American Studies: History)

1032   Kitaoji, Yuriko. *Japanese Immigrant Society in Brazil.* M.A. 66 pp. (Anthropology)

1033   Letonoff, Victor Theodore. *A Geographic Evaluation of San Blas, Nayarit, Mexico, as a Resort Area.* M.A. 181 pp. (Geography)

1034   Littlewood, David Scott. *Reports:* Cuban University Reform; The Armed Forces under Fidel Castro. M.A. 127 pp. (Latin American Studies: History; Government)

1035   Livas Cantú, Eduardo. *Mexico's Exports to the Latin American Free Trade Area, 1962–66.* M.A. 97 pp. (Economics)

1036   McCaslin, Carl George, Jr. *Preliminary Appraisal of the Operational Feasibility of a Fishing Fleet in Brazil.* M.B.A. 143 pp. (Business Administration)

1037   MacNeil, Anne Worthington Surget. *The Supreme Harmonizing Power (El Supremo Poder Conservador) 1837–1841.* M.A. 196 pp. (Latin American Studies: History)

1038   Mangum, Robin. *Reports:* Threats and the Continuous Response; Political Styles in Brazil, 1822–1960; Toward a Stronger Executive. M.A. 110 pp. (Latin American Studies: Government)

1039   Merritt, Martha Sue. *Reports:* Hispanismo and Right-Wing Nationalism in Colombia; The Sources of the Shifts in Brazilian Foreign Policy. M.A. 78 pp. (Latin American Studies: History, Government)

1040   Moss, Val, Jr. *Factionalism in Acción Democrática of Venezuela, 1958–1968.* M.A. 102 pp. (Latin American Studies: Government)

1041   Murphy, Brian Richard. *Campesino Organizations in Guatemala: A Study in Changing Power Relationships.* M.A. 66 pp. (Latin American Studies: Anthropology)

1042   Newcomb, Sidney Howard. *Reports:* The Alliance for Progress and United States Interests; The Adelantado in the Old World and the New. M.A. 87 pp. (Latin American Studies: Government; History)

1043   Palmer, Ernest Charles. *Reports:* The Mita de Potosí and The Depopulation of Highland Colonial Peru; Development of the Sugar Cane Industry in Cuba and Puerto Rico and the Social Effects of Centralization. M.A. 178 pp. (Latin American Studies: Geography; History)

1044   Paviani, Lea Lima Andrade. *Brazilian Portuguese Morphophonology —A Generative Approach.* M.A. 90 pp. (Linguistics)

1045   Pojman, John Joseph. *Real Property Taxation in Central America.* M.A. 148 pp. (Economics)

1046   Redmond, Walter Bernard. *Bibliography of the Philosophy of the*

*Colonial Period in Latin America.* M.A. 229 pp. (Latin American Studies: Philosophy)

1047    Samuels, George Edwin, III. *Capital Equipment Imports, Development, and Import Shares: Selected Latin American Countries, 1953–1963.* M.A. 64 pp. (Economics)

1048    Sanchez, Elizabeth Lyons Doremus. *The Motif of Descent into Inferno in "Los pasos perdidos" and "Pedro Páramo."* M.A. 95 pp. (Romance Languages)

1049    Schmidt, Henry Conrad. *Horacio Quiroga: His Creative Essence.* M.A. pp. (Latin American Studies: Romance Languages)

1050    Thompson, Don F. *The Spanish Theory of Empire as Revealed through Selected Golden Age Spanish Drama.* M.A. 103 pp. (Latin American Studies: Education)

1051    Treviño, Jesús, Jr. *Attempts at Organizing and Reforming the Mexican National Army, 1821–1824.* M.A. 73 pp. (History)

## GRADUATE DEGREES CONFERRED IN LATIN AMERICAN STUDIES

### 1944–1969

| Field | M.A. | Ph.D | Field of Reports† |
|---|---|---|---|
| Anthropology | 8 | | |
| Business Administration* | 3 | 1 | |
| Economics | 16 | 4 | 4 |
| Education | 8 | 4 | 2 |
| Educational Psychology | | | 1 |
| Geography | 1 | | 2 |
| Government | 14 | 3 | 10 |
| History | 34 | 24 | 14 |
| Philosophy | 1 | | |
| Romance Languages | 8 | 4 | 3 |
|     Linguistics | | | |
|     Literature | | 1 | |
| Persons doing 2 Reports<br>    in lieu of Thesis | 18 | | |
| | 111 | 41 | |

\* International Trade

† This does not represent number of graduates but only the fields of the reports of those students doing 2 reports in lieu of thesis.

## DEGREES IN THE LATIN AMERICAN FIELD NOT CONFERRED BY THE INSTITUTE, BY DEPARTMENT AND FIELD
### 1893–1969

| Field | M.A. | M.B.A. | M.Ed. | M.F.A. | M.J. | M.L.S. | M.Mus. | Ed.D. | Ph.D. |
|---|---|---|---|---|---|---|---|---|---|
| Anthropology | 22 | | | | | | | | |
| Architecture | 2 | | | | | | | | |
| Art History | 2 | | | | | | | | |
| Botany | 1 | | | | | | | | 1 |
| Business Adminis. | 9 | 14 | | | | | | | 6 |
| Communications | 3 | | | | 2 | | | | |
| Community and Regional Planning | 1 | | | | | | | | |
| Drama Education | | | | 1 | | | | | |
| Economics | 35 | | | | | | | | 24 |
| Education | 93 | | 67 | | | | | 3 | 29 |
| Education–Curriculum & Instruction | 5 | | | | | | | | 8 |
| Educ. Psychology | 3 | | | | | | | | 2 |
| Engineering | 5 | | | | | | | | |
| English | 15 | | | | | | | | 3 |
| Geography | 5 | | | | | | | | 2 |
| Geology | 31 | | | | | | | | 11 |
| Government | 27 | | | | | | | | 10 |
| History | 196 | | | | | | | | 76 |
| Home Economics | 7 | | | | | | | | |
| Journalism | | | | | 2 | | | | |
| Library Science | | | | | | 2 | | | |
| Music | 2 | | | | | | 3 | | |
| Music Education | 1 | | | | | | | | |
| Psychology | 3 | | | | | | | | 2 |
| Romance Languages | 98 | | | | | | | | 3 |
| Linguistics | 9 | | | | | | | | 12 |
| Literature | 1 | | | | | | | | 7 |
| Social Work | 10 | | | | | | | | |
| Sociology | 13 | | | | | | | | 7 |
| Special Education | | | | | | | | | 1 |
| Zoology | 5 | | | | | | | | 2 |

# PUBLICATIONS OF THE INSTITUTE OF LATIN AMERICAN STUDIES, THE UNIVERSITY OF TEXAS PRESS LATIN AMERICAN PUBLICATIONS, AND OTHER PUBLICATIONS AT THE UNIVERSITY OF TEXAS

(All numbers refer to entries and not to page numbers)

## Author Index

[ 150 ]

McGann, Thomas F., 58, 147
McKinlay, R. Michael, 152
McLemore, Samuel Dale, 292, 293
MacMillan, Robert W., 300
McNerney, Robert F., Jr., (trans.), 190
Mainland, G. B., 233
Mann, Graciela, 262
Manuel, Herschel T., 231, 263, 264
Marulanda R., Carlos Arturo, 174
Matluck, Joseph H., 50, 76
Mecham, J. Lloyd, 148
Magargee, Edwin I., 271
Miñano-García, Max H., 232
Monteiro, Palmyra V. M., 143
Morland, Harold (trans.), 207
Morse, Richard M., 162
Munro, Dana G., 222

Nance, Joseph Milton, 265
Natalicio, Luiz, 113
Nist, John, 217

O'Leary, Daniel Florencio, 190
O'Nell, Carl W., 97
Ordóñez, Ezequiel, 224
Orozco, José Clemente, 220
Oswald, J. Gregory, 163, 181
Ott, Elizabeth H., 301

Pack, Greta, 251
Paredes, Américo, 63, 71, 83, 95, 124, 185, 266, 275
Parker, Franklin, 155
Pascin, Jules, 267
Patterson, J. T., 233
Pauck, Frederick G., 302
Paz, Octavio, 158
Pearse, Andrew, 164

Peden, Margaret Sayers (trans.), 198, 199
Peña, Albar A., 303
Pennington, Campbell W., 270
Pereira, Antonio Olavo, 211
Phipps, Helen, 268
Pichardo, José Antonio, 269
Pontes, Joel, 80
Putnam, Howard L., 17

Queiroz, Rachel de, 212
Quirarte, Jacinto, 130

Ramos, Graciliano, 213
Ramos, Samuel, 191
Ramos Arizpe, Miguel, 11
Ramsdell, Charles (trans.), 194
Rands, Robert L., 270
Remmling, Gunter W. (comp.), 142
A Report on the Health and Nutrition of Mexicans Living in Texas, 237
*Revista Interamericana de Psicología*, 285
Riley, Carroll L., 270
Rioseco, Arturo Torres, 224
Rippy, Merrill, 248
Roberts, Bryan R., 110, 115, 167
Rodrigues, José Honorio, 192
Rosenquist, Carl M., 271
Ross, Stanley R., 132
Rout, Leslie R., Jr., 37
Rubel, Arthur J., 57, 69, 103, 272,
Rueda, Julio Jiménez, 224
Rulfo, Juan, 203

Sánchez, George Isidore, 17, 240
Sánchez, Luis Oscar, 156
Saunders, John (trans.), 211

Walker, Thomas F., 248
Wauchope, Robert, 277
Waugh, Julia Nott, 278
Weddle, Robert S., 279, 280
Weismann, Elizabeth Wilder (trans.), 221
Wheelock, Carter, 281
Wilson, Clotilde (trans.), 209

Wythe, George, 222

Yáñez, Agustín, 204, 205, 289
Ynsfran, Pablo Max, 8, 223

Zárate, Alván O., 94, 168
Zuidema, R. T., 72

# PUBLICATIONS OF THE INSTITUTE OF LATIN AMERICAN STUDIES, THE UNIVERSITY OF TEXAS PRESS LATIN AMERICAN PUBLICATIONS, AND OTHER PUBLICATIONS AT THE UNIVERSITY OF TEXAS

## Subject Index

Delinquency, 271

Demography: Mexico, 94; Peru, 135

Development: Guatemala, 120; Latin America, 26, 61

Díaz, Porfirio, 195

Directories: Latin American sociologists, 142

Diseases: Mexico City, 21

Drama: Brazil, 80; Caribbean, 123; Latin America, 160, 260

Ecology: Mexico, 238

Economic development: 222; Latin America, 146; Mexico, 25, 28, 34, 151; Panama, 86

Economic history: Latin America, 109

Economic integration: Brazil, 65; Latin America, 178

Economic problems: Latin America, 6

Education: 96; bilingual, 129; Brazil, 113; Inter-american, 240; Latin America, 5; Mexican-Americans, 17, 231, 263, 264, 294, 295, 296, 297, 298, 299, 300, 301, 302, 303; Peru, 232

Entrepreneurship: Brazil, 78; Latin America, 174

Explorations: Portuguese, 84; pre-colombian, 270; Spanish, 84

Fierro, Martin, 104

Folklore: British West Indies, 87, 116; Maya, 69; Mexico, 63, 71; Mexican-American, 57; see also Ballads

Folk medicine, 124

Folk practices: Mexico, 20, 97

Foreign policies: United States, 111, 245

Foreign relations: Argentina and United States, 58; see also Inter-American relations

Frontiers: Texas-Mexico, 265; see also Borders

Gas industry: Mexico, 175

Geography: Mexico, 145

Geology: Latin America, 226; Mexico, 227, 228, 235; Texas, 227, 228

Health and nutrition: Mexican American, 237

Herrera, José Joaquín de, 7

Highways: Peru, 128

History: Chile, 3; Gulf region, 255; Latin America, 179; Mexico, 136, 147, 184, 185, 247, 248; Peru, 186; Texas, 99, 243

History, Intellectual: Mexico, 32, 188; Peru, 189

History, Social: Argentina, 19

Immigration: Argentina, 36; Chile, 36

Imports: to United States, 171

Incas, 4, 186

Indians: American, 29; Mexico, 117, 169, 219, 244; Middle-American, 277

Industrialization: Brazil, 35; Latin America, 174

Industries: Mexico, 9; Texas, 9

Insects: Mexico, 233

Intellectual cooperation, 225

Intellectual trends: Latin America, 1

Political development: 222; Mexico, 194
Political instability, 125
Political problems: Latin America, 6
Politics: Brazil, 252; Guatemala, 115; Latin America, 48, 51; Mexico, 158, 253; Peru, 33; Puerto Rico, 38; *see also* Power
Positivism: Mexico, 73
Power: 74; Central America, 170; Guatemala, 241; Latin America, 90
Press: Honduras, 43; Inter-American, 24, 67
Protestantism: Guatemala, 110, 167
Psychology: 66, 79, 119; Mexico, 89

Quechua, 144

Revolutions: Costa Rica (1948), 40; Mexico (1910), 32, 132, 134, 195, 250, 253; *see also* Wars of Independence

Sabato, Ernesto R., 62
Salcedo, Manuel, 242
Sickness, 103
Slavery: Cuba, 27
Social anthropology: ethics, 88; Latin America, 48
Social mobility: Brazil, 81
Social order, 106
Social problems: 271; Latin America, 6

Social relations, 103
Social status: Brazil, 75
Social stratification: Latin America, 59, 161
Social structures: Brazil, 56; Guatemala, 241; Latin America, 90
Social systems: 72
Spanish Americans, *see* Mexican-Americans
Spanish Cortes: Mexico, 11, 23
Spanish language: 76; in Brazil, 77; Mexico, 50; Puerto Rico, 291; Texas, 246, 295
Students, *see* Universities

Taracena Flores, Arturo, 45
Tax reform, 22
Technology: 70; Latin America, 137
Theater, *see* Drama
Trade policies: Latin America, 173
Translators' handbook, 259

Universities: Argentina, 284; Latin America, 51, 157; Puerto Rico, 38
Urbanization: Latin America, 150, 162; Peru, 68, 82

Valdivia, Pedro de, 3
Vasconcelos, José, 188
Vargas, Getulio, 254
Villa, Pancho, 187

Wars of Independence: Bolivia, 190
Wheat: Argentina, 19

# MASTERS THESES AND DOCTORAL DISSERTATIONS OF LATIN AMERICAN INTEREST
## 1893–1969

(Entries #1–254: Ph.D.'s; entries #255–1051: M.A. theses and reports)

### *Author Index*

Abat, Mary Lee, 585

Abbott, Raymond Robert, 644

Acevedo, Mary Ann, 941

Adams, Thomas M., 942

Aikin, Mrs. Welma Morphew, 569

Akery, Nicholas, 749

Almeida, Mauro Lauria de, 988

Alisky, Marvin Howard, 73

Allemand, Paul, 377

Allen, Robert, 781

Allen, Winnie, 309

Alvermann, Mrs. Donna Elaine, 989

Ambía, Sister María de la Paz, 539

Anderson, Mrs. Ada Collins, 894

Anderson, Mrs. Martha Davis, 915

Anderson, Thomas Howard, 241, 943

Anderson, William Woodrow, 197, 820

Anglin, Mrs. Stella Campbell Glass, 782

Anthony, Samuel Cooper, 490

Anttila, Earl, 74

Aponte, Barbara Ann Bockus, 158

Aponte-Hernández, Rafael, 182

Aponte Rivera, Luz Loarina, 586

Apstein, Theodore, 40, 521

Arellano, Richard Gibbs, 863

Armas-Hernández, Salvador, 551

Armistead, Robert Thomas, 877

Arnold, Charles August, 349

Arnold, William Metcalf, 990

Arrington, Frank Wade, 600

Arrowood, Mrs. Flora Register, 440

Ashby, Joe Charles, 100, 645

Ashton, Price Richard, 616

Athon, William Craig, 944

Atkinson, Rosa M., 714

Atwill, Edward Robert, IV, 821

Avrett, William Robert, 350

Bacarisse, Charles Albert, 87

Baena-Zapata, Luis Angel, 198

Balán, Mrs. Elizabeth Jelin, 221

Balán, Jorge, 222

Balboa, Arnulfo, 991

Baldwin, Edward Franklin, 804

Ball, Fred, Jr., 750

Barbour, Lizzie Messick, 502

Barillas, María, 680

Barker, Bernice, 367

Barton, Mable Exa, 451

Bass, Thomas Edwin, 617

Baugh, Lila, 421

Baxter, Thomas Richard, 846

Becerra, Alejandro, 992

Belaunde, Rafael, Jr., 452

Bell, Holland Edwards, 265

Belton, Hugh, 993

Benavides, Ilma Mariana, 681

Benavides- Hinojosa, Artemio, 916

Benfer, Robert Alfred, Jr., 223

Bennett, Catherine, 503

Bennett, Hazel Marylyn, 587

Bennett, Peter Dunne, 169

Bennett, Robert Lee 149

Bennett, Rosemary, 646

Benson, Nettie Lee, 48, 466

Beresford, Martha, 618

Bergmann, John Francis, 682

Bernhardt, George Marcellus, 491

Bernstein, Marvin David, 57

Berry, Charles Redmon, 199, 864

Bills, Garland Dee, 242

Birge, Mamie, 271

Bishop, Bobby Arnold, 183

Bittinger, Mrs. Vivian Irene Swihard, 945

Blair, Calvin Patton, 109

Blair, Evelyn, 30

Blaisdell, Darius Othniel, 765

Blazek, Leda Frances, 492

Blocker, William Robert, 330

Blum, Owen Wilson, 683

Boren, James Harlan, 243

Bourgeois, Louis Clarence, 159

Boxley, Katie Clara, 467

Boyd, Alston, III, 917

Brack, Gene Martin, 200

Bradshaw, Benjamin Spencer, 822

Brandenberger, William Samuel, 272

Breedlove, James McShane, 847

Brenizer, Lester C., 320

Brenner, Henry, 834

Breswick, William Neale, 75

Brewer, Sam Aaron, Jr., 684

Bridges, Clarence Allan, 27, 310

Bridges, Luther Wadsworth, II, 139

Brien, Richard Herman, 184

Brinsmade, Robert Turgot, 441

Bristow, Robert B., 468

Brogdon, Dewey Robert, 734

Brooks, Richard Sinclair, 422

Brooks, Sammy Kent, 918

Brookshire, Mrs. Marjorie Shepherd, 81

Broom, Perry Morris, 32

Broussard, Ray Francis, 121, 685

Brown, Mrs. Alma Howell, 351

Brown, Elsie Denison, 267

Brown, Lyle Clarence, 160

Brown, Mary Sue, 453

Brown, Maury Bright, 300

Brown, Willie Leonzo, 442

Browne, Philip Dale, 311

Brownell, Mary Elizabeth, 1015

Browning, Horace Noel, 556

Browning, Vivian Alma, 454

Brownlee, Haskell, 443

Brown-Wrinkle, Mary Helen, 647

Brubaker, George Allen, 130

Bryant, Bill Bernice, 131

Bryant, Mavis Anne, 946

Buckner, Dellos Urban, 368

Bugbee, Lester Gladstone, 255

Burke, Linda Lou Waite, 224

Burmeister, Sarah Eva, 648

Burns, Tommye Helen, 895

Burrell, Dick Múzquiz, 444

Bushnell, Clyde Gilbert, 115

Butler, Mrs. Carolyn Jane Matthews, 649

Butler, May Angie, 312

Butler, Robert Wayne, 947

Cabaza, Berta, 650

Cabrera, María Guadalupe, 601

Calder, Bruce Johnson, 994

Caldwell, Edward Maurice, 13

Callahan, Sister M. Generosa, 41

Callicutt, Mrs. Dorothy Hinds, 561

Callicutt, Laurie Timmons, 33, 445

Campbell, Richard A., 805

Cárdenas, Leonardo, Jr., 161

Caro-Costas, Aída Raquel, 562

Carpenter, Carl L., 948

Carrasco-Velázquez, Baldomero, 995

Carroll, Edward Leroy, 504

Cartagena Colón, Demetrio, 588

Carter, Eula Lee, 313

Carter, James David, 82

Carter, Robert Arthur, Jr., 686

Carter, Thomas Pelham, 170

Casey, Clifford B., 4

Castañeda, Alberta Maxine Mondor, 201

Castañeda, Carlos Eduardo, 7, 294

Castillo, Eunice Duarte, 949

Castillo, Henrietta Amparo, 505

Catterton, Conn DeWitt, 455

Cavness, Raymond McCarey, 378

Cerda, Evangelina, 482

Cerda, Gilberto, 651

Cezeaux, Louise Catherine, 423

Chapman, Mrs. Barbara Austin, 1016

Chapman, John Gresham, 950

Chapman, Ruthven Hoyt, 783

Charlton, Agnes Adalyn, 331

Chavez, David Julian, 295

Cheavens, Sam Frank, 110

Chernosky, Adelma Shirley, 751

Christian, Chester Carsel, Jr., 202

Christie, Christina Cloe, 530

Christoph, Sharon Lea, 910

Chutro, John Joseph, 735

Clark, Daniel Hendricks, 493

Clark, George, 766

Clark, Madeline, 469

Clark, Robert Carlton, 257

Cleaves, Wilbur Shaw, 391

Clegg, Joseph Halvor, 244, 951

Clemons, Russell Edward, 185

Clinkscales, Orline, 111

Clutterbuck, Donald Booth, 793

Coan, Bartlett E., 470

Cobb, Albert Folsome, 687

Cockrell, Myrtle, 284

Cockrum, Amil Blake, 522

Cogdell, Ava Consuelo, 405

Cohen, Pedro I., 806

Cole, Ruth, 540

Cole, William Edward, 171

Collier, Vivian, 1017

Collins, James William, 531

Condron, Stuart Harkins, 273

Connell, Earl Monroe, 314

Connor, Mrs. Ruth Patton, 619

Coole, Mrs. Ruth Musgrave, 494

Coon, Ruby Irene, 379

Coons, Dix Scott, 162

Cooper, Donald Bolon, 150

Coor, Minnie, 369

Coplen, Mrs. Cora Elna Reese, 424

Córdoba, Diego Arturo, 878

Cornehls, James Vernon, 172

Cornejo, Ricardo Jesús, 245

Cotner, Thomas Ewing, 44, 506

Covington, Mrs. Carolyn Callaway, 541

Covington, Nina, 370

Cowart, Billy Frank, 151

Cowling, Annie, 321

Cox, Albert Harrington, 767

Coy, Edna, 507

Craddock, Vina Marie, 620

Crain, Forest Burr, 602

Cramer, Martin John, 76, 652

Crane, Olatia, 261

Crasilneck, Harold Bernard, 603

Cravens, Lucy Elizabeth, 332

Cravens, Mattie Ella, 296

Crawford, Helen Royse, 495

Crawford, Polly Pearl, 315

González de Gueits, Mrs. Francisca, 573
Goodstein, Barnett Morris, 543
Goss, Allen Miles, 900
Grace, Mrs. Delfina Gómez, 511
Graham, Nora Agnes, 471
Graham, Thomas Richard, 135, 786
Graves, Mrs. Ersilee Ruth Parker, 823
Greding, Edward James, Jr., 227
Greene, Lila Thrace, 456
Greer, James Kimmins, 287
Greer, Mrs. Margaret Helen Rich, 924
Greer, Viola Ann, 630
Gregory, Gladys Grace, 18
Griffith, Verona Theresa, 485
Grimes, James Larry, 962
Grothey, Mina Jane, 1024
Grumbles, Mrs. Mineola Page, 849
Guerra, Fermina, 533
Guerra, Irene J., 808
Guggolz, Bess, 866
Gunn, Ewing Leyton, 457
Gutiérrez, Emeterio, Jr., 691
Gutiérrez, Nicanor Fernando, 963

Hackett, Bess Greer, 428
Haddick, Jack Allen, 83, 661
Hadley, Bedford Keith, 90
Haenggi, Walter Tiffany, 187
Haggard, Juna Villasana, 36
Hagle, Paul Ivan, 850
Hamilton, Samuel Clinton, 837
Hammond, Charles Wilbur, 799
Hammond, John Hays, 458
Hancock, Walter Edgar, 10
Handy, Mary Olivia, 631
Hann, John Henry, 205, 880
Hannon, Donald Paul, 1000

Hardt, Annanelle, 228
Harrington, Ann Kay, 770
Harris, Charles Houston, III, 229, 851
Harris, Mrs. Helen Willits, 14
Harris, James Kilbourne, 335
Harris, Townes Malcolm, 288
Harrison, David Caldwell, 692
Harrison, Helene Westbrook, 206
Harrison, Horace Virgil, 62
Harwell, George Mathis, Jr., 809
Hatcher, Mrs. Mattie Alice, 262
Hatter, Curtis R., Jr., 720
Hauser, Ronald Joseph, 800
Havins, Mary Sue, 606
Hay, Mrs. Gray Southern, 662
Hayes, James Virgil, 693
Hedrick, Elinor May, 592
Heiken, Grant Harvey, 925
Hellums, Frances John, 1025
Helms, James Ervin, 91
Henderson, Mary Virginia, 324
Henderson, Seth Ward, 429
Hensey, Frederick Gerald, 207
Hernández, Arcadia, 497
Hernández, Elías Vega, 736
Hernández, Nivea M., 721
Herr, Selma Ernestine, 38
Herring, Marcia Lou, 838
Hestir, Bluford Bradford, 593
Hiester, Mrs. Miriam Webb, 737
Hilburn, William Grant, Sr., 901
Hill, Floyd William, 249
Hilton, Stanley Eon, 250
Hinds, Marjorie Sue, 926
Hines, Calvin Warner, 230
Hinojosa, Tomas Rodolfo, Jr., 881
Hinton, Hugh Frank, 1001
Hixon, Summer Best, 810
Hnatek, Margaret, 694

Hodges, Claudius Brashier, 459
Hoffmann, Fritz Leo, 15, 384
Hogan, William Ransom, 37, 409
Holden, Narcissa Jane, 669
Holden, William Curry, 2, 301
Holmes, Jack David Lazarus, 124
Hood, Anita Louise, 738
Hoskin, Charles Morris, 144
Householder, Fred Walter, 268
Howard, Ryan Abney, 882
Howe, Anna Lynn, 695
Hudspeth, John Robert, 927
Hudspeth, Marguerite Burnett, 902
Huey, Raymond Burnson, 1026
Hughes, Mrs. Lois Spears, 356
Hughes, Vernon, 336
Hunley, Josephine Keller, 486
Hunnicutt, Helen Margaret, 316
Hupp, Bruce Foster, 1027
Huser, Herbert C., 1028
Huston, Edgar, 394
Hutchinson, Cecil Alan, 46
Hutchison, Mrs. Cornelia, 563
Ingenhuett, Arthur Hilmer, 325

Ivey, Alfred Joe, 337

Jackson, Mrs. Doris Goforth, 696
Jackson, Dorothy Jean, 524
Jackson, Mrs. Gail Cathryn Crag-
  head, 903
Jackson, Mrs. Lillis Tisdale, 410
Jackson, Lola, 326
Jackson, Mrs. Lucile Prim, 498
Jaén, Diedier Tisdel, 173
James, George William, 632
Jameson, Gloria Ruth, 208
Jansen, Rudolf Karl, 883
Janto, Stephen Anthony, 722
Jáuregui Fernández, Beatriz, 534

Jeffrey, Sylvia Viera, 132
Jennings, C. A., 839
Jennings, Vivian, 448
Jewell, Wilton Gray, 964
Jiménez, Julio M., 965
Johnson, Cecil Earl, 84
Johnson, Mrs. Claudia Loris Parker,
  574
Johnson, Harvey Leroy, 357
Johnson, Richard Abraham, 20, 430
Johnson, Roberta Muriel, 411
Johnston, Edith Louise, 487
Johnston, Marjorie Cecil, 24, 395
Jones, Albert Pearson, 338
Jones, Benton McLain, 852
Jones, Diane Louise Carlson, 1029
Jones, Dixie Lee Franklin, 1030
Jones, Herbert Harmon, 966
Jones, Lamar Babbington, 174
Jordan, Robert Edward, 1002
Juarez, Joseph Robert, 209, 811

Kaderli, Albert Turner, 525
Kaderli, James Nicholas, 499
Kahle, Louis George, 63, 488
Kalmbach, Frank, 723
Kalmon, Winn Loraine, 1031
Kazen, Phyllis Marie, 928
Keefe, Edgar S., 431
Keen, Marvin Spruce, 535
Keith, Alma Jean, 967
Kellam, Frances Wade, 317
Kennard, Claude Louis, 929
Kerbow, Mrs. Blewett Barnes, 472
Kerbow, Frances Virginia, 412
Kerr, Homer Lee, 78
Key, E. Mary Ritchie, 153, 824
Key, Harold Hayden, 154, 825
Kielman, Chester Valls, 697
Kilgo, Reese Danley, 188

Saunders, Mrs. Maxine Pleydell-Pearce, 706
Saville, Thomas Keith, 236
Scaperlanda, Anthony Edward, Jr., 168, 874
Scarff, Mrs. Frances Beatriz González, 857
Schiller, Mae Dell, 612
Schmidt, Henry Conrad, 1049
Schoenhals, Alvin, 858
Schoenhals, Mrs. Louise Conety, 875
Schooler, Robert Dale, 179
Schumann, Melba Thekla, 760
Scott, Elizabeth, 580
Scott, Mrs. Florence Johnson, 462
Seay, Stiles Noel, 253
Self, Michael Marvin, 976
Shannon, Fain Gillock, 518
Shearer, Ernest Charles, 28
Shelby, Charmion Clair, 17, 344
Shelton, Edgar Greer, Jr., 581
Siedhoff, Eleanor Diana, 889
Singh, Daljeet, 761
Singletary, Coyle Edward, 707
Sipperly, David William, 977
Skelton, Byron G., 364
Slaughter, Mrs. Grace McClain, 438
Sloan, John William, 237
Smith, Mrs. Avis Dowis, 529
Smith, Cecil Bernard, 365
Smith, Mrs. Elizabeth Parkes, 345
Smith, Elliott Varner, 978
Smith, Gaylord Ewing, 890
Smith, Mrs. Gerda Hansen, 979
Smith, Helen Perrin, 388
Smith, Leonard Thomas, 743
Smith, Margaret Harrison, 137
Smith, Mrs. Mary Jane, 815
Smith, Ola Lee, 547
Smith, Rosaileen May, 463

Smith, Ruby Cumby, 278
Smither, Harriet, 291
Sobrino, Josephine, 582
Solem, Richard Ray, 1010
Solís-Flores, Roberto Hiram, 762
Sparks, Dade, 403
Sparks, Earle Sylvester, 281
Spell, Jefferson Rea, 282
Spell, Mrs. Lota May Harrigan, 1
Spiegelberg, Frederick, III, 842
Spielberg, Joseph, 816
Splawn, Mary Ruth, 376
Sprague, William Forrest, 11, 439
Stambaugh, Jacob Lee, 303
Standefer, Harmon Bishop, 641
Stanislawski, Mrs. Doris Barr, 843
Staples, Anne Folger, 980
Stasieluk, Laura Ann, 613
Stauffer, David Hall, 108
Stekley, Dan Lewis, 480
Stearns, Joseph Edward, 910
Stenberg, Richard Rollin, 8
Stenglein, Joseph Arthur, 911
Stenning, Walter Francis, 219
Stephens, Andrew Jackson, 346
Stohl, Mrs. Darthula Davis, 744
Stolz, Alberta Louise, 404
Story, Anna B., 501
Stouse, Pierre Adolphe Ducros, Jr., 844
Stout, John Maxwell, 891
Stout, Mrs. Mary Helen Jarnagin, 912
Streeter, Vivian, 366
Strickland, Rex Wallace, 19
Strieber, Mrs. Mary Esther, 489
Studhalter, Margaret Ruth, 538
Stullken, Virginia Pauline, 745
Sullivan, Ben Dell, 568
Svec, William Rudolph, 193

Sweet, Richard William, 981
Swietlicki, Alain, 913

Tandrón, Humberto, 845
Tarquinio, Laura Teixeira, 876
Taylor, Clark Louis, Jr., 859
Taylor, Julia R., 775
Taylor, Thomasine Hughes, 254
Taylor, Mrs. Virginia Rogers, 763
Teichert, Pedro Carlos Máximo, 96
Termini, Mrs. Deanne May Lanoix, 1010
Terry, Hubert Hendrix, 554
Terry, Zula, 418
Thompson, Don F., 1050
Thompson, Richard Allen, 939
Thurston, Raymond LeRoy, 464
Timm, Charles August, 304
Timmons, Wilbert Helde, 51
Toness, Mrs. Kay Sutherland, 1012
Toness, Odin Alf, 982
Toward, Agnes Elizabeth, 194
Travis, David Edward, 138
Treviño, Mrs. Bertha Alicia Gámez, 238
Treviño, Emma, 776
Treviño, Jesús, Jr., 1051
Trillo-Garriga, Mrs. Ana Marie, 790
Troike, Mrs. Nancy Patterson, 803
Troike, Rudolph Charles, Jr., 128
Truett, Dale Brian, 892
Tubbs, Lowell Lester, 708
Tunnell, William Kerr, 97, 709

Urbina, Manuel, Jr., 983

Valdés, Pérez, Carlos Manuel, 548
Valerius, John Behner, 777
Vallejo-Claros, Bernardo, 1013
Vallve, Graciela, 710

Van Patton, James Jeffers, 147
Varner, Dudley Meriwether, 984
Vassberg, David Erland, 940
Vaughan, Ernest Heath, Jr., 98, 642
Vásquez, Antonio C., 266
Vázquez, Diamantina Minerva, 583
Vázquez, Elfida, 643
Vázquez de Ruiz, Mrs. Celia E. Vega, 791
Velasco Terres, Raoul, 555
Vernon, Mrs. Ida Stevenson Weldon, 43
Vest, Henry Arthur, 817
Vetters, Mrs. Anna Hill, 549
Vigness, David Martell, 70, 614
Villareal, Albert, 746
Villarreal, Victor Xavier, 985
Von Bertrab Erdmann, Hermann Raimund, 239

Wackerbarth, Allie Mae, 419
Waddell, Jack O'Brien, 860
Wait, Eugene Meredith, 861
Waits, Caron Richard, 156
Walker, Donald Anthony, 778
Walker, Elna LaVerne, 157, 598
Walker, Thomas Fonso, 71
Walper, Jack Louis, 120
Walsh, Brother Albeus, 711
Walsh, Sister Natalie, 465
Walters, Paul Hugh, 559
Ward, Berta Elena, 420
Wares, Mrs. Iris Lueva Mills, 914
Warren, Bonnie Davis, 615
Watkins, Mrs. Willye Ward, 292
Weaver, A. J. S., 305
Weaver, Charles Norris, 220
Webb, Jesse Owen, 306
Webb, Walter Prescott, 9, 283
Weir, Avis, 599

# MASTERS THESES AND DOCTORAL DISSERTATIONS OF LATIN AMERICAN INTEREST
## 1893–1969

(Entries #1–254: Ph.D.'s; entries # 255–1051: M.A. theses and reports)

### Subject Index

Delgado, Rafael: 377; *La Calandria*, 601
*Despoblado*: 88, 604
DeWitt's Colony: 260
d'Halmar, Augusto: 159
*Diario de México*: 107
*Diario Histórico*: 45
Díaz, Porfirio: 365, 427, 562
Díaz Rodríguez, Manuel: *Sangre Patricia*, 570
Diet: Cuba, 595; Indians, 814; Mexicans in the U.S., 388, 550; Mexico, 372, 526; Puerto Rico, 586
Diplomatic Asylum: Latin America, 761
Doblado, Manuel: 217
Dollar Diplomacy: Latin America, 192
Dominican Republic: Politics and Government, 856; U.S. withdrawal (1924), 811

Ecology: Mexico (Chih.), 21
Economic Development: 998; Argentina, 773; Brazil, 214, 668, 873, 926, 1010; Costa Rica, 1022; Cuba (pre 1959), 129, 748; Guatemala, 212, 218, 767; Mexico, 89, 149, 165, 166, 212, 239, 863, 938, 1010; Panama, 42; Peru, 622; Puerto Rico, 129, 133, Venezuela, 156
    *see also* Industrialization
Economic Integration: Central America, 990; Latin America, 168, 874; South America, 990
Economic Stagnation: Uruguay, 968
Ecuador: Land Utilization, 698
    *see also* Education, Literature

Education: Argentina, 1000; Brazil, 194, 418, 453; Caribbean, 74; Colombia, 399; Cuba (pre 1959), 710; Cuba (post 1959), 997; Ecuador, 195; El Salvador, 188; Latin America, 701; Mexico, 30, 58, 147, 151, 313, 375, 495, 502, 633, 670, 679, 703, 738, 820, 862, 966, 1019; New Spain, 53; Peru, 170, 191; Philippine Islands, 29; Puerto Rico, 131, 182, 307, 573, 579, 586, 588, 673, 725, 790, 791, 1017; Republic of Texas, 35; Texas, 238, 284, 503; Venezuela, 1021
    *see also* Mexicans in Texas, Mexicans in the U.S.
Education and Vernacular Languages: 110
*El Chamizal*: 18
El Paso: 724; Anglo-American Occupation, 397
El Salvador: *see* Cattle, Coffee, Education, Geology
Elections: Guatemala, 237; Mexico, 364; Texas, 290
Empresario Grants: Texas, 324
*Encomiendas*: Peru, 798
English Language: Brazil, 727; Cuba, 699; Puerto Rico, 721
English Language, Teaching of: 624, 717, 775
Enriqueta, María: 505
Epidemics: Mexico City, 150
Erauso, Catalina de: 396
Escuela Nacional Preparatoria de México: 646
*Estancias* (Argentina): 193
Ethnography: Veracruz, Mexico: 827

[ 176 ]

European Influence on Spanish American Novels: 571
*Excélsior*: 754
Exchange Controls: Latin America, 642, 758
Expansion in North America: French, 258; Spanish, 258; United States, 8, 27
Expeditions: Alarcón, 15; Gutierres-Magee, 261; St. Denis, 344; Texas-Rio Grande, 367
Explorations: North American Shoreline (16th c.), 489
Exports: Mexico, 883, 1035; Peru, 226
Expropriations: Latin America, 613

Fannin, James W. Jr.: 278
Fauna: Mexico (Chih.), 956
Federalism: Mexico, 48, 62
Fernández de Lizardi, José Joaquín: *Don Catrín de la Fachenda*, 553; *La educación de las mujeres*, 831
Filibustering: Lower California and Sonora, 560
Financial Policy: Guatemala, 767
Fishing: Brazil, 1036
Flora: Mexico (Chih.), 475
Florida as Spanish Colony: 26
Folkdancing: Mexico, 544, 857; South America, 802
Folklore: Texas, 666, Texas (Austin), 636
Folk medicine: 1009
Foreign Trade: Texas, 75
Fort Concho: 474
Fort St. Louis: 257
Fort Sam Houston: 631
Franquis de Lugo, Carlos: 359
Freemasonry: Texas, 82

Freestone County, Texas: 311
Free Trade: New Spain, 845
Free Trade Zone: Mexican Border, 641
French Language: Colombia, 576
Frías, Heriberto: 511
Frogs: Central America, 227; Mexico, 887
Frontier: New Spain, 850, 893; Texas, 2, 94
Fuentes, Carlos: 974, 985
Funes, Gregorio: 818

*Gaceta de México*: 625
Gallegos, Rómulo: 540, 913
Galveston: 306
Gálvez, Manuel: 424, 587
Gamboa, Federico: 390
Gamboa, José Joaquín: 521
García, Genaro: 326
García Icazbalceta Collection: 1024
Gaucho (Argentina): 357, 545
Gayoso de Lemos, Manuel: 124
Generación Romántica (Argentina and Chile): 173
Geography: Mexico (Mich.), 707; Mexico (Nayarit), 1033; Mexico (Tam.), 137
Geology: El Salvador, 783, 840; Guatemala, 120, 185, 241, 855, 917, 920, 943; Mexico (Chih), 136, 139, 187, 196, 781, 793, 797, 801, 805, 807, 809, 817, 821, 833, 836, 837, 842, 885, 925, 977; Mexico (Coah.), 140, 995; Mexico (N.León), 183, 867, 879; Mexico (S.L.P.), 178; Mexico (Tam.), 734; Mexico (Yuc.), 144; Mexico (Zac.),

878; South America, 567; Texas, 810; Venezuela, 739
Gómez Farías, Valentín: 46, 316
González-Martínez, Enrique: 350
González-Peña, Carlos: 138
*The Great Plains*: 9
Green, Graham: *Another Mexico*, 918; *The Power and the Glory*, 918, 954
Guano: Peru, 622
Guatemala: Demography, 213, 1010; Foreign Relations with Gt. Britain, 720; Industrial Wages, 233; Rural Politics, 922
    *see also* Agriculture, Church History, Cotton, Economic Development, Elections, Financial Policy, Geology, Indians, Peasant Organizations
Guerrero, Vincente: 11, 439
Guerrilla Warfare: Nicaragua: 177
Güiraldes, Ricardo: *Don Segundo Sombra*, 545
Gutierres-Magee Expedition: 261
Gutiérrez de Luna, Cristóval: *Life of Pedro Moya de Contreras*, 385
Gutiérrez Nájera, Manuel: 412, 612
Guzmán, Don Guillén Lombardo de: 834

Haiti: Diplomatic Relations with the U.S., 330; U.S. Occupation (1915–22), 407
Hardy, Thomas: *Return of the Native*, 854
Hearths: Mexico, 984
Hemisphere Defense System: 656
Henríquez Ureña, Pedro: 756

Hernández, José: *Martín Fierro*, 545
Hernández Catá, A.: 548
Herrera, José Joaquín de: 44
Hidalgo y Costilla, Miguel: 532
Historiography: Mexico, 326, 866; Peru, 181
Home Economics: Cuba, 680
Houston, Sam: 61, 346, 410, 448
Highways: Inter-American, 901; Venezuela, 551
Huerta, Victoriano: 454
Imperialism, U.S.: Cuba, 16; Southwest, 8

Imports: Latin America, 1047; U.S., 109, 659
Independence: Mexico (1810), 11, 51, 54, 60, 362, 386, 439, 532, 618; Texas, 271, 278, 410, 541, 983
Indians: Argentina, 864; Brazil, 108; Chile, 942; Guatemala, 1002, 1027; Mesoamerica, 803; Mexico, 914, 939; Mexico (pre-Colombian), 815; Mexico and Texas, 759; New Mexico, 345; New Spain, 812; U.S., 580, 697
    *see also* Diet; Tribal names
*Indigenismo*: Peru, 924
Industrialization: Chile, 713; Mexico, 735, 752, 819, 862; Uruguay, 96
    *see also* Economic Development
Inflation: Brazil, 240; Mexico, 819
Inquisition: Mexico, 834
Inter-American Highway: 901
Interest Groups: Brazil, 998

International Law: Mexico and
U.S., 23
Investment Opportunities in Mex-
ico: 869
Investments, European: Latin
America, 239
Investments, Foreign: Brazil, 214,
972
Investments, U.S.: Latin America,
1022; Mexico, 491, 617, 835;
Venezuela, 730
Iron and Steel: Colombia, 705;
Venezuela, 705
Iturrigaray, José de: 83, 661

Jesuits: Brazil (16th c.), 530;
Chile (16-17th c.), 101
Juárez, Benito: 495, 630
Junco, Alfonso: 539
*La Junta de los Ríos*: 604

Knox, Philander C.: 192
Koreans in Mexico: 1006

Labor: Argentina (pre Perón), 997;
Argentina (1950), 645; Mexico,
31, 100, 978; Texas, 288; Texas
(Mexicans), 176, 671, 871; Texas
(Migrants), 823
Labor, Women: Latin America,
1004
*see also* Trade Unions
Lamar, Mirabeau B.: 528
Lancasterian Education Movement
in Mexico: 670
Land Settlement: Mexico, 844
Land Tenure: Mexico, 143
Laredo, Texas: 465
Lares, Teodosio: 64
Las Casas, Bartolomé de: 895

Latin America: Attitude Towards
World War I, 634; Civic Education, 295; Colonial Administration, 105; Commerce, 674; Philosophy of the Colonial Period,
1046; Politics, 761
*see also* South America, Central America, Names of Countries, Agriculture, Automobile
Manufacturing, Aviation, Dollar Diplomacy, Economic Stagnation, Eduction, Exchange
Controls, Expropriations, Imports, Investments, Labor, Literature, Municipal Government, Protestantism, Steel,
Women
Latin America in Texas Schools:
253, 648, 684,753, 1007
Latin American Free Trade Association (LAFTA): 168, 1035
Latin American Students in Texas:
780
Lead: Mexico, 266
Lerdo de Tejada, Sebastián: 55, 437
Lima Binational Center Library: 826
*Limpieza*: 1031
Literarcy: Mexico (Indians), 914
Literary Journals: *see* Names of
Journals
Literature: Argentina, 173, 514;
Brazil, 889, 1015; Chile, 173,
358; Cuba, 361, 937, 1015; Ecua-
dor, 649; Latin America, 202,
589; Mexico, 204, 342, 482, 485;
New Spain, 107; Peru, 907;
South America, 515; Southwest,
500, 512, 733; Texas, 593
Literature, Juvenile, on Latin Amer-
ica: 598

[ 179 ]

López de Ayala, Abelardo: 394
Loveira, Carlos: 534
Lower Rio Grande Valley: 368, 614
Lowther, Robert: 897
Lynch, Eliza Alicia (Madama): 585

Madero, Francisco I.: 49, 438
Maize: Venezuela, 1002
Mallea, Eduardo: 919
Mann, Horace: 325
Margil de Jesús, Fray Antonio: 715
Mariátegui, José Carlos: 952
Marketing: Chile, 169; Texas, 303, 683
Martínez de la Rosa, Francisco: *Doña Isabel de Solís,* 467
Martínez Sierra, Gregorio and María: *The Cradle Song,* 839
Mass Media: Brazil, 988; Mexico: 754, 877
Mateos, Juan Antonio: 592
Maya: 939
Mexican-American Culture: Influence on Teachers, 903
Mexican-Americans: *see* Mexicans in Texas, Mexicans in the U.S.
Mexican Bandit in Literature: 204
Mexican Cession: 347
Mexican Folkdancing in Texas Schools: 487
Mexican Foreign Students: Laredo, Texas: 886
Mexican Free Zone: 299
Mexican Revolution: *see* Independence, Mexico (1810), Revolution, Mexico (1910)
Mexican Revolution in Literature: 482
Mexican War: 283
Mexicans in Texas: 176, 726, 470,

381, 1030; Acculturation, 525; Community-Home-School Problems, 619; Community Psychology, 473; Economic Welfare, 339, 992; Education, 126, 164, 335, 411, 513, 558, 577, 591, 611, 616, 621, 663, 677, 694, 789, 795; Education, Elementary, 461, 499, 696, 749, 989; Education, Higher, 113, 605; Education, Secondary, 32, 517, 741; Employment, 81, 363, 469, 602, 671, 894, 940; Family, 355, 1009; Folklore, 349, 737; Housing, 343; Illness and Curing, 848; Juvenile Delinquency, 603; Kinship Relationships, 928; Knowledge of the Law, 955, 964, 967, 975, 981; Labor Problems, 174; Language Education, 245, 498, 572, 688, 695, 999; Living Conditions, 492; Migration, 729; Political Conditions, 581; Population, 777; Population (Austin), 314; Reading Problems, 736; Religion, 692; School Achievement, 189, 830; School Attendance, 80, 655, 691, 693; Social Aspirations, 808; Testing, 991; Unionization, 167; Voluntary Associations, 231; Work Relief, 460
Mexicans in Texas and the Mass Media: 915
    *see also* Education, Labor, Migrants, Wetbacks
Mexicans in the United States*:
———
* Unless "Texas" is specifically included in title, the entry is under Mexicans in the United States.

Towns, Coal and Steel, Conquest, Constitutions, Consumer Goods, Industry, Cotton, Diet, Ecology, Economic Development, Education, Elections, Epidemics, Exports, Fauna, Federalism, Flora, Folkdancing, Frogs, Geography, Geology, Hearths, Historiography, Independence, Indians, Inflation, Inquisition, International Law, Investments, Koreans, Labor, Land Settlements, Land Tenure, Literacy, Literature, Mass Media, Migration, Mining, National Character, Nationalism, Pamphlettering, Petroleum, Positivism, Protestantism, Radio Broadcasting, Railroads, Revolutions, Silver, Silversmithing, Social Mobility, Social Planning, Social Stratification, Spanish Language, Steel, Subsoil Resources, Sugar, Theatre, Transport Industry, Women, Zoology

Mier Noriega y Guerra, José: 444
Mier y Terán, General Don Manuel de: 25
Migrants: Texas, 691, 694, 1030; United States, 708, 792
Migration: Mexico (N. León), 916
Mijica Lainez, Manuel: 959
Milhaud, Darius: 750
Military: Argentina, 142, 1028; Colombia, 948; Cuba (post 1959), 1034
Mina, Francisco Xavier: 477
Mining: Mexico, 57

Missions: 256; Candelaria, 478; Espíritu Santo, 813; Espíritu Santo de Zúñiga, 398; Primería Alta, 732; San Francisco de los Tejas, 257; San Joseph de San Miguel de Aguayo, 389; San Lorenzo, 478
Mita de Potosí: 1043
Mixed Claims Commission: 296
Mon, Juan Antonio: 1031
Mora, José María Luis: 54, 429
Morazán, Francisco: 566
Morelos, José María: 51, 362
Morfi, Fray Juan Agustín: 7
Movimiento Nacional Revolucionario (MNR): 942
Municipal Government: Latin America, 675
Music, Teaching of (16–17th c.), 1

Nahua: 904
Nariño, Antonio: 235
National Character: Mexico, 841
Nationalism: Argentina, 142; Brazil, 986; Colombia, 1039; Mexico, 72; Nicaragua, 116
Nacogdoches, Texas: 309
The Negro in Literature (Brazil and Cuba): 1015
Neighbors, Robert S.: 94
Nervo, Amado: 319
New Spain: *see* Art History, Church History, Commerce, Constitutionalism, Education, Free Trade, Frontier, Indians, Literature, Trade Guilds
Newspaper, Spanish: Texas, 337
*see also* Mass Media; Names of Newspapers

Nicaragua: Foreign Relations with the U.S. (20th c.), 3; U.S. Intervention, 868
see also Guerrilla Warfare, Nationalism
Nueces County, Texas: 425
Nuevo Santander: 966

Oaxaca: 199
Ocantos, Carlos María: 420
O'Higgins, Bernardo: 97, 709
Oil: see Petroleum

Pamphleteering: Mexico: 71
Pan American Conferences (1889–1928): 4
Pan American Union: 597
Panama: Diplomatic Relations with the U.S. (20th c.), 459
see also Economic Development, Spanish Language
Panama Canal: 297
Paredes y Arrillaga, Mariano: 95
Parrott, William Stuart: 557
Partido Acción Nacional (PAN): 771, 1001
Partido Nacional Revolucionario (PNR): 1018
Payno, Manuel: 488
Payró, Roberto Jorge: 569
Pax Porfiriana: 1023
Paz, Octavio: 1017
Peasant Organizations: Guatemala, 1041
Pérez Galdós, Benito: Doña Perfecta, 854
Pérez Jiménez, General Marcos: 948
Pershing, John J.: 524
Peru: Colonization, 963; Mestizos,

961; Social History (Lima), 765; Spanish Administartion
see also Community Development, Economic Development, Education, Encomiendas, Exports, Guano, Historiography, Indigenismo, Literature, Railroads, Zoology
Peru-Bolivian Confederation (1936-39): 452
Petroleum: Costa Rica, 184; Mexico, 56, 125, 166; Mexico and the U.S., 12, 327; Venezuela, 600, 804, 865, 872; Venezuela and the U.S., 148, 936
Philippine Islands: Spanish Culture, 607
see also Education
Pious Funds of the Californias: 84
Political Parties: Venezuela (20th c.), 1002
see also Name of Party (in Spanish)
Portuguese Language: Brazil, 876, 232, 896, 1044
Portuguese Language, Grammars: 180
Positivism: Mexico, 646
Presidios: 22, 79; Janos, 850; Nuestra Señora de Loreto, 398
Prieto, Guillermo: 66
Protestantism: Latin America, 123; Mexico, 91
Provincias Internas de México: 334
Public Works: Texas (19th c.): 468
Puerto Rican Students: Socioeconomic status, 561
Puerto Rico: Government Development Banking, 133

Sierra, Justo: 58, 510
Silver: Mexico, 555
Silversmithing: Mexico, 67
Slavery: Louisiana, 287; Texas, 286, 578; West Indies, 772
Smith, Ashbel: 291
Social Class in Literature: 202
Social Mobility: Mexico (Monterrey), 932
Social Planning: Mexico, 102
Social Stratification: Mexico (Monterrey), 970
Somoza, Anastasio: 1005
South America: Cultural Relations with Europe, 507; Foreign Relations with the U.S., 531
    See also Latin America: Economic Integration, Folkdancing, Geology, Literature
Spain: Colonial Administration, 665; Foreign Relations with Gt. Britain (16th c.), 660; (18th c.), 757; Foreign Relations with the U.S., 369; Intellectual History (16th c.), 422
Spaniards in Mexico (19th c.): 247; Expulsion of, 923
Spanish American War: 369, 847
Spanish Archives in Texas: 294
Spanish Clubs: 479
Spanish Colonies in North America (18th c.): 17
Spanish Cortes: 1019
Spanish Indian Policy: 722
Spanish Land Grants: Texas, 462
Spanish Language: 39, 33, 252, 348, 542, 626; Colombia, 163, 198; Cuba, 951, Mexico, 770; Panama, 806; Puerto Rico, 146; Texas, 244, 627, 650, 651, 667

Spanish Language, Aviation Terms in: 799
Spanish Language, Dictionaries: 888
Spanish Language, Grammars: 371, 446
Spanish Language, Publications in U.S.: 623
Spanish Language, Relationship to English: 24
Spanish Language, Teaching of: 132, 282, 312, 318, 366, 379, 419, 537, 568, 658, 664, 689, 740, 760
Spanish Language, Translation into English: 426
Spanish Missions: see Missions
Spanish Settlements: Lower Rio Grande Valley, 315; Orcoquisac, 267
Spanish Theory of Empire: 1050
Steel: Latin America, 98, 632; Mexico, 171; see also Iron and Steel
Storni, Alfonsina: 853
Subsoil Resources: Mexico, 583
Sugar: 657; Cuba, 1043; Cuba (1920), 328; Mexico, 870; Puerto Rico, 1043
Sugar, International Trade of: 543

The Supreme Harmonizing Power: 1037
Tacanán: 153
Taxation: Central America, 1045
Teachers: Texas, 518
Teaching Materials: Mexico and Texas: 563
Tehuantepec Transit Route: 506
Telegraph and Texas Register: 401

WITHDRAWAL